Lecture Notes in Computer Science          1700
Edited by G. Goos, J. Hartmanis and J. van Leeuwen

# Springer

*Berlin*
*Heidelberg*
*New York*
*Barcelona*
*Hong Kong*
*London*
*Milan*
*Paris*
*Singapore*
*Tokyo*

Rolf Stadler   Burkhard Stiller (Eds.)

# Active Technologies for Network and Service Management

10th IFIP/IEEE International Workshop
on Distributed Systems:
Operations and Management, DSOM'99
Zurich, Switzerland, October 11-13, 1999
Proceedings

 Springer

Series Editors

Gerhard Goos, Karlsruhe University, Germany
Juris Hartmanis, Cornell University, NY, USA
Jan van Leeuwen, Utrecht University, The Netherlands

Volume Editors

Rolf Stadler
Columbia University, New York
Center for Telecommunications Research and
Department of Electrical Engineering
500W 120th Street, New York, NY 10027-6699, USA
E-mail: stadler@ctr.columbia.edu

Burkhard Stiller
Swiss Federal Institute of Technology, Zürich, ETH Zürich
Computer Engineering and Networks Laboratory, TIK
Gloriastr. 35, CH-8092 Zürich, Switzerland
E-mail: stiller@tik.ee.ethz.ch

Cataloging-in-Publication data applied for

Die Deutsche Bibliothek - CIP-Einheitsaufnahme

**Active technologies for network and service management** : proceedings / 10th
IFIP/IEEE International Workshop on Distributed Systems: Operations and
Management, DSOM '99, Zurich, Switzerland, October 11 - 13, 1999. Rolf Stadler
; Burkhard Stiller (ed.). - Berlin ; Heidelberg ; New York ; Barcelona ; Hong
Kong ; London ; Milan ; Paris ; Singapore ; Tokyo : Springer, 1999
(Lecture notes in computer science ; Vol. 1700)
ISBN 3-540-66598-6

CR Subject Classification (1998): C.2, K.6, D.1.3, D.4.4

ISSN 0302-9743
ISBN 3-540-66598-6 Springer-Verlag Berlin Heidelberg New York

© Springer-Verlag Berlin Heidelberg 1999
Printed in Germany

Typesetting: Camera-ready by author
SPIN: 10704868    06/3142 – 5 4 3 2 1 0    Printed on acid-free paper

# Preface

This volume of the Lecture Notes in Computer Science series contains all papers accepted for presentation at the 10th IFIP/IEEE International Workshop on Distributed Systems: Operations and Management (DSOM'99), which took place at the ETH Zürich in Switzerland and was hosted by the Computer Engineering and Networking Laboratory, TIK.

DSOM'99 is the tenth workshop in a series of annual workshops, and Zürich is proud to host this 10th anniversary of the IEEE/IFIP workshop. DSOM'99 follows highly successful meetings, the most recent of which took place in Delaware, U.S.A. (DSOM'98), Sydney, Australia (DSOM'97), and L'Aquila, Italy (DSOM'96). DSOM workshops attempt to bring together researchers from the area of network and service management in both industry and academia to discuss recent advancements and to foster further growth in this field. In contrast to the larger management symposia IM (Integrated Network Management) and NOMS (Network Operations and Management Symposium), DSOM workshops follow a single-track program, in order to stimulate interaction and active participation.

The specific focus of DSOM'99 is "Active Technologies for Network and Service Management," reflecting the current developments in the field of active and programmable networks, and about half of the papers in this workshop fall within this category. Other papers report on advances in SNMP-based management, distributed monitoring, multi-domain management, enterprise management, and management tools. All technical sessions contain 20 papers, which have been selected out of more than 50 submissions via a thorough refereeing process. Showing a truly international scope, the final program includes 10 European, 8 North and South American, and 2 Asian papers, almost half of which evolved from industry. To round up the technical program, panels have been added. They focus on "Providing Managed Services to End-Users," "Are Programmable Networks Unmanageable?" and "Challenges for Management Research."

DSOM'99 has been supported by a number of different organizations and persons. Therefore, we would like to acknowledge the support of our DSOM'99 sponsors. Following the tradition established during the last nine years, the IEEE Communications Society and the IFIP WG 6.6 were technical co-sponsors of this workshop. Especially we would like to thank our DSOM'99 patrons: Ascom, BT, GTE, IBM, the IEEE Swiss Chapter on Broadband Communications, Lucent Technologies, and Swisscom for their contributions. With their support, these companies and organizations demonstrate their interest in the forum that DSOM provides and the results it disseminates.

This workshop owes its success to all members of the technical program committee, who devoted their expertise and much of their time to provide this year's DSOM with an outstanding technical program. Furthermore, we would like to express many thanks to

Marcus Brunner, who performed a great job in maintaining the DSOM'99 Web server and managing the system for paper submission and review. In addition, Marcus assisted us unceasingly during all phases of the DSOM'99 preparation with technical and administrative help. Thanks go also to Annette Schicker, who ran the DSOM'99 registration and on-site offices and provided our DSOM'99 participants a first-rate service. Finally, we would like to thank the ETH Zürich as well as the TIK for hosting the DSOM'99 workshop in this convenient and stimulating environment.

August 1999                                              Rolf Stadler

Burkhard Stiller

Zürich, Switzerland

# Organization

## General Chair
Rolf Stadler *Columbia University, New York, U.S.A.*

## Technical Program Co-chairs
Burkhard Stiller *ETH Zürich, Switzerland*
Rolf Stadler *Columbia University, New York, U.S.A.*

## Program Committee

| | |
|---|---|
| Sebastian Abeck | *University of Karlsruhe, Germany* |
| Nikos Anerousis | *ATT Research, U.S.A.* |
| Raouf Boutaba | *University of Toronto, Canada* |
| Seraphin B. Calo | *IBM Research, U.S.A.* |
| Rob Davison | *British Telecom, U.K.* |
| Metin Feridun | *IBM Research, Switzerland* |
| Kurt Geihs | *University of Frankfurt, Germany* |
| German Goldszmidt | *IBM Research, U.S.A.* |
| Sigmund Handelman | *IBM Research, U.S.A.* |
| Heinz-Gerd Hegering | *University of Munich, Germany* |
| Joseph Hellerstein | *IBM Research, U.S.A.* |
| Jean-Pierre Hubaux | *EPFL, Switzerland* |
| Gabriel Jakobson | *GTE Laboratories, U.S.A.* |
| Pramod Kalyanasundaram | *Lucent Technologies, U.S.A.* |
| Ryutaro Kawamura | *NTT, Japan* |
| Yoshiaki Kiriha | *NEC, Japan* |
| Emil Lupu | *Imperial College, U.K.* |
| Kenneth Lutz | *Telcordia Technologies, U.S.A.* |
| Thomas Magedanz | *IKV++, Germany* |
| Subrata Mazumdar | *Bell Laboratories, U.S.A.* |
| Branislav Meandzija | *General Instrument Corporation, U.S.A.* |
| George Pavlou | *University of Surrey, U.K.* |
| Pradeep Ray | *University of New South Wales, Sydney, Australia* |
| Morris Sloman | *Imperial College, U.K.* |
| Jürgen Schönwälder | *Technical University Braunschweig, Germany* |
| Roberto Saracco | *CSELT, Italy* |
| Adarshpal Sethi | *University of Delaware, U.S.A.* |
| Carlos B. Westphall | *Federal University of Santa Catarina, Brazil* |
| Wolfgang Zimmer | *GMD FIRST, Germany* |
| Simon Znaty | *ENST-Bretagne, France* |
| Douglas Zuckerman | *Telcordia Technologies, U.S.A.* |

## Local Organization

| | |
|---|---|
| Burkhard Stiller | *ETH Zürich, Switzerland* |
| Marcus Brunner | *ETH Zürich, Switzerland* |
| Annette Schicker | *Registration Office, Ringwil-Hinwil, Switzerland* |

## Liaisons

IFIP TC6 WG6.6: Wolfgang Zimmer, GMD FIRST, Germany
IEEE ComSoc: Douglas Zuckerman, Telcordia Technologies, U.S.A.

## Reviewers

The tasks of a reviewer requires serious and detailed commenting on papers submitted to DSOM'99. Therefore, it is of great pleasure to the Technical Program Committee Co-chairs to thank all reviewers listed below for their important work.

| | |
|---|---|
| Sebastian Abeck | Emil Lupu |
| Nikos Anerousis | Thomas Magedanz |
| Raouf Boutaba | Jean-Philippe Martin-Flatin |
| Marcus Brunner | Subrata Mazumdar |
| Monique Calisti | Branislav Meandzija |
| Seraphin B. Calo | Michael Nerb |
| Rob Davison | George Pavlou |
| Metin Feridun | Pradeep Ray |
| Kurt Geihs | Roberto Saracco |
| Roberto Gemello | Jürgen Schönwälder |
| Silvia Giordano Cremonese | Gora Sengupta |
| German Goldszmidt | Adarshpal Sethi |
| Sergio Gugliermetti | Morris Sloman |
| Sigmund Handelman | Graziella Spinelli |
| Heinz-Gerd Hegering | Rolf Stadler |
| Joseph Hellerstein | Burkhard Stiller |
| Gabriel Jakobson | Carlos B. Westphall |
| Pramod Kalyanasundaram | Kouji Yata |
| Ryutaro Kawamura | Ikuo Yoda |
| Yoshiaki Kiriha | Wolfgang Zimmer |
| Michael Langer | Simon Znaty |
| Xavier Logean | Douglas Zuckerman |

## DSOM'99 Supporters and Patrons

Ascom Systec AG, Mägenwil, Switzerland

British Telecommunications, London, U.K.

Center for Telecommunications Research, Columbia University, New York, U.S.A.

Computer Engineering and Networks Laboratory TIK, ETH Zürich, Switzerland

GTE Laboratories, Waltham, Massachusetts, U.S.A.

IBM Research, Zurich Research Laboratory, Switzerland

IEEE, Institute of Electrical and Electronics Engineers
IEEE Switzerland Chapter on Digital Communication Systems

IFIP, International Federation for Information Processing

Lucent Technologies, Bell Labs, Homdel, U.S.A.

Swisscom AG, Bern, Switzerland

# Table of Contents

# Session 1

# Decentralized Monitoring and Anomaly Detection

*Chair: Nikos Anerousis*
*AT&T Research, Florham Park, U.S.A.*

# On the Performance and Scalability of Decentralised Monitoring Using Mobile Agents

Antonio Liotta[1], Graham Knight[1], George Pavlou[2]

[1]Department of Computer Science, University College London, Gower Street,
London WC1E 6BT, United Kingdom
{A.Liotta, G.Knight}@cs.ucl.ac.uk
[2]Centre for Communication Systems Research, University of Surrey, Guildford
Surrey GU2 5XH, United Kingdom
G.Pavlou@ee.surrey.ac.uk

**Abstract.** The problem of improving the *performance* and *scalability* of current monitoring systems, which generally follow a centralised and static management model is considered herein. Several alternative solutions based on Mobile Agents (MAs), specifically tailored to network monitoring are described. In particular, the key problem of computing efficiently the initial *number* and *location* of MAs is addressed, and techniques for rapid MA deployment are described. Mathematical models for the proposed MA solutions and for the common technique of centralised polling are built and a comparative analysis of their performance is carried out. Performance is expressed in terms of *monitoring traffic* and *delay*. Results on traffic show that MAs typically offer improved performance, although they do not always scale better than polling. However, results on delay demonstrate that MA solutions improve both scalability and performance under most circumstances. **Keywords:** Monitoring, Polling, Mobile Agents, Agents Cloning, Scalability.

## 1 Introduction

Current management systems follow a centralised and static management model although several researchers have reported the limitations of this approach [6-10]. Systems that follow this model often involve the transmission of large quantities of raw data from remote systems to a central management station before the data can be further processed, disseminated and presented. Consequently, these systems are subject to network congestion causing delays, drops in performance, and inability to react promptly to faults. Therefore, in view of the exponential growth in size, distribution, and complexity of communication networks, current management systems present severe limitations as far as performance, scalability, and flexibility are concerned.

In practice, network monitoring relies largely on *centralised polling*, which inherits most of these limitations. Polling is a process whereby an issuing node or *polling station* in a communication network broadcasts a query to every node and waits to receive a unique response from each of them [1]. Polling finds wide application in the control of distributed systems and in the management of distributed databases (see references quoted in [1]). More generally, polling is used for a large class of applications that need to detect a variety of changing conditions and react to them, often subject to time constraints.

A potential approach to more decentralised, efficient, and flexible management solutions is to equip the management system with Mobile Agent (MA) capabilities [2, 7]. If management tasks are implemented using MAs, raw data can be pre-processed —e.g. filtered and aggregated— near the remote network devices. In fact, MAs can be located optimally in order to minimise network *traffic* (incurred by management) and monitoring *delay*. MAs can be organised in either a *hierarchical* or a *non-hierarchical* fashion. The former case tends to be particularly suitable for hierarchical networks — e.g. networks consisting of sub-networks. For example, monitoring tasks requiring first the *collection* and then the *aggregation* of raw data from each of the network levels —e.g. from each sub-network— can be implemented by distributing agents at each intermediate level. Each agent will be in charge of producing the required level of data aggregation for a specific sub-network and providing high-level information to the other agents in the hierarchy. Alternatively, a non-hierarchical MA organisation can be used, which is particularly suited to non-hierarchical networks and non-hierarchical monitoring tasks.

Another feature that can have a significant impact on the efficiency of monitoring systems is MA *cloning*, the ability of agents to create and dispatch copies, or 'clones', of themselves. Cloning can significantly reduce MA *deployment time* and *traffic*, which are critical factors in large-scale systems, and is particularly beneficial in the case of hierarchical networks. However, despite its benefits, cloning adds an extra degree of complexity to the MA system and is applicable only to a sub-class of monitoring tasks - e.g., tasks that can be decomposed into a finite number of identical sub-tasks.

Therefore, agent mobility and cloning can play a key role in the improvement of the efficiency of monitoring systems. In addition, the ability of agents to be re-programmed and re-configured dynamically introduces an attractive perspective of adding flexibility to the monitoring system. However, despite the great interest arisen in the application of MA technologies to Network and System Management [2-11], MAs have not yet found wide application for a number of reasons. For instance, MA systems are more complex than their centralised counterparts, particularly with respect to their design, implementation, and maintenance. Moreover, without reliable metrics by which to assess the benefits that such systems offer, it has been impossible to compare the overall value of different approaches.

Herein the problem of improving the performance and scalability of monitoring systems and quantifying the potential benefits introduced by MAs is addressed. Such evaluation requires the classification of potential MA solutions specifically tailored to network monitoring and the introduction of a suitable assessment methodology. Several alternative MA approaches are described in Sec.2. The method used to assess the performance and scalability of each technique and to compare them with centralised polling is described in Sec.3. Performance models for the specific solutions under study are presented in Sec.4 and, then, used in Sec.5 to carry out a comparative analysis of their performance and scalability. Modelling and analysis are restricted to the case of hierarchical networks.

The results of the present study are relevant to a wide range of applications since the problem of finding and assessing efficient, scalable, and flexible techniques to monitor distributed systems is not bound to the field of network monitoring. Monitoring is a fundamental function used for performance, fault and security management and therefore it is of paramount importance for their efficiency. Similarly, system management, as well as generic distributed systems relying on communication networks, can benefit from MA technologies.

## 2 Mobile Agent Approaches for Network Monitoring

MAs can support each of the four main monitoring activities performed in a loosely-coupled, object based distributed system —*generation, processing, dissemination* and *presentation* of information [17] (pp.303-347). They can generate monitoring data in the form of *status* and *event reports*, according to different modalities. For example, status reporting can be either periodic or on request; events can be detected by MAs acting as *probes* and reported in a variety of different *formats*. MAs are able to monitor a set of MOs through polling, then process and deliver (directly or otherwise) the acquired data to a management station. Data processing techniques include operations such as *merging* of monitoring traces; *combination* of monitoring information, thus increasing the level of abstraction of data; *filtering* of monitoring data, reducing the volume of data; and *analysis* of monitoring information, producing data statistics.

In the following sub-sections we present a classification of potential MA approaches to network monitoring. Our classification is based on the adopted monitoring model, MA organisation, MA deployment pattern, and MA configuration algorithm. Specific MA solutions based on this classification are described in Sec.4 and analysed in Sec.5.

### 2.1 MA Monitoring Models (MA Types)

We assume that monitoring tasks are specified by giving a set of MOs and of monitoring parameters. When tasks are implemented with MAs the set of MOs is partitioned into disjoint subsets and each subset is monitored by a different MA.

We consider three possible monitoring models and their respective MA types. In the first model, based on *polling*, each MA periodically polls the subset of MOs associated to it and periodically analyses the results. Each MA is periodically polled by either other MAs or the monitoring station. The second model is based on *periodic notification*. Each MA periodically polls its MOs, analyses the results, and *notifies* either other MAs or the monitoring station. Finally, the third model is based on *event-driven alarm generation*. As in the previous cases, an MA periodically polls its MOs and analyses the results. However, MAs generate data (alarms) only if specific events are detected. Therefore, in each of these three models MAs first collect data through polling and then pre-processed this data. The models only differ in the inter-agent communication mechanism. In the remaining part of this paper MA Types associated to the first, the second, and the third monitoring model are referred to as MA Type A, B, and C, respectively.

## 2.2  MA Organisation

MAs can be organised in either a *hierarchical* or a *non-hierarchical* (or *flat*) fashion, depending on the way monitoring tasks are implemented. In hierarchical MA organisations, MOs are monitored by MAs belonging to the last hierarchical level. MAs at each level can communicate only with the MAs at one level above and one level below, according to one of the monitoring models specified in Sec.2.1. Thus, only MAs at the first level communicate with the monitoring station. On the contrary, in the flat MA organisation there is no inter-agent communication and each MA monitors its MOs, analyses data, and communicates directly with the monitoring station.

Flat MAs can be of type A, B and C. In hierarchical MAs we distinguish between the MAs belonging to the last level and the ones belonging to the other levels. The MA types admitted in this case are AA, AB, AC, BB, BC, CC, where the first letter refers to the type of MAs belonging to the last level and the second letter refers to the remaining MAs.

## 2.3  MA Deployment Patterns

Another factor that can be crucial to performance and scalability is the technique, or *pattern*, used to deploy MAs. The way MAs travel does not depend only on their characteristics and on their communication paradigms and protocols. MAs can also implement migration rules and strategies according to predefined migration patterns. Existing patterns, which can find effective application to network monitoring and can be used as MA deployment patterns, are described in [4].

However, within the scope of our analysis we consider only four different deployment patterns that are based on MA organisation and on MA *cloning* capabilities —where cloning is ability of agents to create and dispatch copies or 'clones' of themselves. In the case of MA incapable of cloning, MAs can only be created at the monitoring station.

The first deployment pattern is the 'flat broadcast with no cloning' pattern (Fig.1a). In this case MAs are organised in a non-hierarchical fashion. Each of them is created by the manager at the monitoring station by using one or more MA *templates*. A template is a model used to create an MA which implement a specific task or part of a task. Each MA is, then, associated to a subset of the MOs, and is dispatched to a target location. The target location can be either pre-defined by the MA's creator or decided by the MA itself, depending on its degree of autonomy.

The second deployment pattern is the 'flat broadcast with cloning' one (Fig.1b). In this case, the manager dispatches a single MA (the MA template) which, in turn, clones the actual MAs. Each MA is then configured - e.g., its target MOs and monitoring parameters are set - and dispatched to an appropriate location. The third pattern is the 'hierarchical broadcast with no cloning' one (Fig.1c). All MAs are created by the manager at the monitoring station, like in the 'flat broadcast with no cloning' pattern. However, MAs are organised in a hierarchical fashion. Finally, the 'hierarchical broadcast with cloning' pattern is similar to the 'flat broadcast with cloning', but differs from it in the way MAs are organised.

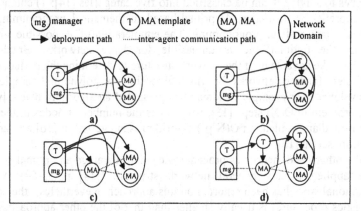

**Fig. 1.** MA deployment patterns: **a)** 'flat broadcast with no cloning' capabilities; **b)** 'flat broadcast with cloning' capabilities; **c)** 'hierarchical broadcast with no cloning'; **d)** 'hierarchical broadcast with cloning' capabilities.

The patterns admitting cloning (Fig.1b and Fig.1d) are generally preferable since they can result in a significant reduction of MA deployment traffic and time. This is a consequence of the fact that in most situations a single MA template is transmitted between intermediate MA locations instead of a set of MAs. An example showing a typical application of cloning is a case in which the network links involved in the MA deployment process are not uniform in bandwidth and latency. In fact, in this case the transmission of several MAs through congested links might be impractical. However, cloning cannot be used in all circumstances: it is applicable only to a sub-class of monitoring tasks - e.g., tasks that can be decomposed into a finite number of identical sub-tasks. Moreover, cloning requires a relatively complicated management of MAs, which in turn results in additional overheads.

The patterns involving hierarchical deployment (Fig.1c and Fig.1d) are particularly useful not only in the case of hierarchical networks, but also more generally when the monitoring task can be organised in a hierarchical fashion. On the other hand, flat patterns (Fig.1a and Fig.1b) represent a simpler alternative for non-hierarchical networks or monitoring tasks.

## 2.4 MA Configuration

The configuration of MAs involves two main problems: 1) the determination of the *number* of MAs suitable to a given monitoring task; 2) the determination of the *location* of each MA.

The MA configuration problem is analogous to the problem of locating multiple emergency facilities in a transport network and, more specifically, is equivalent to trying to minimise the total distance between these facilities and the nodes in the network. This problem has been studied extensively and is usually referred to as the *p-median problem* or the *minisum location problem* (see [14-16] and references quoted therein).

Unfortunately, the p-median problem on a general network is NP-hard [15]. The approaches to solving it can be classified into five categories [14]: 1) enumeration, 2) graph theoretic, 3) heuristics, 4) primal-based mathematical programming, and 5) dual-based mathematical programming. The enumeration of all possible solutions to determine the optimal one is unfeasible for large networks. Graph-theoretic approaches take advantage of the network structure to determine the p-median and are very efficient for tree networks for which algorithms of polynomial complexity have been developed. For example Goldman has presented an algorithm that solves the 1-median problem in $O(N)$ steps [13], where $N$ is the number of nodes in the network. For the p-median problem an $O(N^3p^2)$ algorithm is suggested in [16] and an $O(N^2p^2)$ one is proposed in [15].

On the other hand, heuristics procedures cannot guarantee an optimal solution but can be applied to any general network structure ([14] pp.55-58). Very little computational work has been reported on this approach. Nevertheless, the complexity of heuristics procedures is usually smaller than that of the other approaches. Finally, the mathematical programming approaches have attracted wide attention and have proved rather successful for general networks ([14] pp.58-68).

Despite the similarities between the p-median problem and the MA configuration problem, they have different algorithmic constraints and priorities. For instance, the former problem aims at finding solutions as close to optimality as possible, trying to minimise the computational time. Instead, in the latter case it is of paramount importance to minimise the traffic incurred into the network by the configuration algorithm as well as to solve the problem in a relatively shorter time.

In the remaining part of this section we sketch the description of two possible solutions, for the case of MAs capable of cloning and incapable of cloning, respectively. Both solutions make use of the routing information obtainable from network routers and are based on the assumption that such information is available to managers and MAs. We also assume that MOs belong to an Intranet and that MA hosts - i.e., locations in which MAs are entitled to run - are evenly distributed in the network. This, in other terms, means that for each router there is always an MA host that is located relatively close to it and, for each LAN, the number of MA hosts is proportional to the number of MOs belonging to the LAN. Under these assumptions, the MA distribution tree —i.e., the set of routes used for MA deployment— does not differ significantly from the routing tree rooted in the monitoring station. Without loos of generality, we envisage a scenario in which routers can act as MA hosts during MA deployment. In such case, the MA distribution tree would actually coincide with the routing tree.

**Configuration of MAs Capable of Cloning.** Initially a monitoring task is given by defining a set of monitoring parameters, such as a set of MOs, the required monitoring accuracy, a set of functions applied to process the monitored data, and so on. The monitored parameters are then analysed in order to determine the next-hop or hops that need to be followed in order to reach the objects. If $n_h$ is the number of alternative routes, *MO* is partitioned into $n_h$ disjoint sets, $MO_1, MO_2, ..., MO_h$, $n_h$ MAs are cloned and each one is associated to a different $MO_i$ and deployed through $next\_hop_i$. Then, each MA decides whether to keep cloning other MAs or start monitoring its subset of $MO$. This decision is based on the analysis of the local routing tables. In particular, an MA is cloned for each next-hop, which is also an MA host. Then, this process continues recursively until the last hierarchy of MA host has been reached and, thus, MA deployment has been completed. Therefore, in this case the number of MAs, $m$ is the result of this recursive mechanism; it is not pre-determined at start up time. Note that there are several possible variations to this algorithm. We have described a deployment scheme for hierarchical MA organisations. If they reflect a flat organisation no MAs remain in a switching device if a next-hop MA host if found. Thus, MAs are cloned only if more than one next-hop is found. Otherwise the MA simply migrates to the next-hop. Other variations can reflect different conditions for the interruption of the recursive cloning mechanism. For example, an MA may base its decision on whether on not to keep cloning upon additional conditions such as estimates on the number of MOs in its monitoring domain.

**Configuration of MAs Incapable of Cloning.** The number of MAs, $m$ is determined at start up time and is based on information which we assume is available to the manager, such as the number of MO domains - e.g., internet domains - and the number of MOs per domain. $m$ MAs are generated at the monitoring station and a subset of the given MOs is associated to each of them, according to a procedure which is analogous the one adopted for cloning-enabled MAs. Finally, each MA follows the distribution tree according to its target MOs and to the routing information extracted at each router. Each MA stops migrating towards its target MOs when it fails to find a unique next-hop destination. Then it starts monitoring its target MOs.

# 3 Method of Evaluation

The methodology used to assess monitoring systems is based on a mathematical, comparative analysis of the performance and scalability of various MA solutions against the common technique of centralised polling. Performance models of typical MA solutions based on the classification described in Sec.2 are included in Sec.4. In the following subsections we describe the basic assumptions on the network model, and the metrics and method used to assess performance and scalability.

**Network Model.** We have adopted the *network model* described in [1]. The network is modelled by a connected graph $G=(V,E)$ with the vertices corresponding to nodes (processors) and the edges corresponding to communication links, which are modelled by the *All Ports-Full Duplex* communication model. This network model has been widely used because it generally reflects the hardware characteristics of networks (see references quoted in [1]).

**Metrics.** The *traffic* incurred by the monitoring system and the monitoring *delay* are modelled using an approach similar to the one described in [18]. *Traffic* is modelled as the sum of packet hops incurred by monitoring —i.e., the number of edges traversed by monitoring packets— multiplied by their respective packet size, $b$ and packet rate, $P_r$. The traffic $T(v_1,v_2)$ between any two points $v_1, v_2 \in V$ subject to a bit rate $B_r$ is $T(v_1, v_2) = B_r{}^* d(v_1, v_2)$, where $B_r = b{}^*P_r$, $b$ is the size of a poll request or response, and $d(v_1,v_2)$ is the distance between $v_1$ and $v_2$. The *distance* in the network is measured using the "hop" metric, in which each edge has unit weight. Finally, the *delay*, $D(v_1,v_2)$ between any two points, $v_1$ and $v_2$ is measured as the distance $d(v_1,v_2)$. The *monitoring delay* is expressed as $max\{D(v_1,v_2)\}$ - i.e. the maximum number of time units required to perform a complete 'request-response' operation - where $v_1,v_2 \in S \subseteq V$ and $S$ includes the set of monitored nodes.

The *performance* of monitoring systems is expressed in terms of the above traffic and delay functions. In particular, the *relative monitoring traffic* and the *relative monitoring delay* are calculated for each of the proposed MA solutions. Thus, for a given monitoring solution, both he former and the latter are expressed as a percentage of their 'naive-polling' counterparts.

*Scalability* is defined in [12] as the ability to increase the size of the problem domain with a small or negligible increase in the solution's time and space complexity. For the purposes of our investigation, scalability is specifically defined as the ability to increase the number of monitored entities $N$, the polling rate $P_r$ or the network diameter $D(u)$ - i.e., the maximum distance between any two nodes in the network - with a small or negligible decrease in performance. The *scale* of a given monitoring problem is measured in terms of $N$, $P_r$, and $D(u)$.

**Analytical Evaluation.** The analysis includes the definition of typical MA solutions and the evaluation of the lower bounds on traffic and delay for each of them. Lower bounds on traffic and delay are also calculated for two solutions based on centralised polling: the naive approach used in practical system, and the optimal one described in [1]. *Optimal polling* differs from *naive polling* in the broadcasting of poll requests, which in the former case is very similar to the 'hierarchical broadcast with cloning' pattern depicted in Fig.1d.

These lower bounds on traffic and delay are first used to calculate the above defined relative traffic and delay and, then, to assess scalability. We consider that the factors limiting the scale of a monitoring system are the traffic incurred by it and the delay in gathering data. Consequently, scalability is assessed by studying the order of the above traffic and delay functions for $N$, $P_r$ or $D(u)$ tending to infinity.

## 4 Performance Models for Network Monitoring

In this section we describe mathematical models for two different solutions based on centralised polling and for several typical solutions based on MAs. These models are used in Sec.5 to carry out a comparative analysis of their performance and scalability. Since the main focus of this paper is to identify potential MA solutions rather than providing a detailed description of the mathematical models, most mathematical details have been omitted. The interested reader may refer to [19] for further details. Moreover, in order to simplify the complexity of the mathematical analysis, the models provided below assume that the network admits at least one *n-ary* routing tree rooted at the monitoring station, *u*. This simplifying assumption is in accordance with the properties of the routing trees of typical network topologies reported in [1]. In particular, the following models assume routing trees having *d(u)* binary sub-trees, where *d(u)* is the order of the node which hosts the monitoring station.

## 4.1 Naïve Centralised Polling

A polling operation can be modelled as a two-step process. First, a polling station *u* broadcasts a query to every node in the network that is being monitored. Then, each node sends a unique response back to *u* [1]. Thus, we can express traffic, *T* as the sum of two terms, the broadcast traffic $T_b$ and the gathering traffic $T_g$,

$$T = T_b + T_g = 2 * \sum_{j=0}^{D(u)-1} \sum_{i=j}^{D(u)-1} d(u) * P_r * b * 2^i \tag{1}$$

Where *d(u)* is the *degree* (or valence) of *u* in *G* —i.e. the number of edge ends at *u*— $P_r$ is *the Polling Rate* —i.e. the number of polling operations per unit of time— *b* is the size in bits of a poll request and response (assumed equal for simplicity), and *D(u)* is the network diameter. After some calculations we obtain the following expression:

$$T = 2 * d(u) * P_r * b * \left(1 + (D(u) - 1) * 2^{D(u)}\right) \tag{2}$$

This approach is the most widely used in current systems and is termed '*naive centralised polling*' within the scope of this paper.

The delay can be expressed again as the sum of two terms, the broadcast time and the gathering time. The lower bound on delay for general network topologies, as reported in [1] is:

$$D = P_r * \left\{ D(u) + \max\left\{ \left\lceil \frac{N-1}{d(u)} \right\rceil, D(u) \right\} \right\} \tag{3}$$

For the binary case $N = d(u) * (2^{D(u)} - 1)$ and, a lower bound on delay is

$$D = P_r * \left\{ D(u) + 2^{D(u)} - 1 \right\} \tag{4}$$

However, in this case the exact delay can be expressed as

$$D = 2 * P_r * \left\{ 2^{D(u)+1} - D(u) - 2 \right\} \tag{5}$$

## 4.2 Optimal Centralised Polling

A more efficient polling algorithm has been presented and proved optimal in [1]. In this case the polling station *u* sends a request only to its neighbours *N(u)* which, in turn, duplicate the request and forward it to their respective neighbours. The process continues until all nodes have been reached by a request. Therefore, the broadcast traffic will be smaller than its naive-polling counterpart, and the resulting incurred traffic can be expressed as

$$T = d(u) * P_r * b * \left( D(u) * 2^{D(u)} \right) \tag{6}$$

The lower bound on delay for general network topologies is reported in [1]. For the binary case and assuming that $D(u)$ is relatively large, delays can be expressed as:

$$D = P_r * \left\{ 2^{D(u)} + 1 \right\} \tag{7}$$

## 4.3 Mobile Agent Solutions: Traffic Models

The total traffic, $T$ incurred in the network by MAs is modelled as the sum of three terms, the *deployment traffic*, the *collection traffic*, and the *delivery traffic*. The first term accounts for the traffic incurred during MA deployment. The second term represents the traffic incurred when MAs gather information from MOs. The third term includes the traffic involved in the communication among MAs and between MAs and the monitoring station. Each of these terms may vary, depending on the MA type, organisation, deployment pattern, and configuration algorithm. In particular, the MAs' ability to reduce traffic is modelled by the MA *selectivity*, $\sigma$, defined as the ratio between the amount of data collected and delivered by an MA respectively. The selectivity is larger than one for MAs implementing tasks which perform data filtering or aggregation and is typically significantly larger than one. Lower bounds on the traffic incurred by three different MA solutions are expressed below. Finally, expressions for the selectivity of Type A, B, and C MAs are given. Further mathematical details of the following models are reported in [19].

**Flat MA, Type A, B or C, Incapable of Cloning.**

$$T = \frac{B * d(u)}{2 * O_p} * L * 2^L + P_r * b * d(u) * \left[ \left( \frac{D(u) - L - 1}{4} + \frac{L}{4 * \sigma} \right) * 2^{D(u)} + 2^L \right] \tag{8}$$

Where $B$ is the size in bits of MAs, $O_p$ is the duration of the monitoring task, $L$ is the network hierarchical level of MAs, and the remaining variables are as specified above.

**Hierarchical MA, Type A, B or C, Incapable of Cloning.**

$$T = \frac{B * d(u)}{O_p} * \left\{ (L - 1) * 2^L + 1 \right\} + P_r * b * d(u) * \tag{9}$$

$$* \left\{ \left( \frac{D(u) - L - 1}{4} + \frac{1}{4 * \sigma_p} \right) * 2^{D(u)} + \frac{\sigma_q + 1}{\sigma_q} * 2^L + \frac{2}{\sigma_q} \right\}$$

Where $\sigma_q$ and $\sigma_p$ are the selectivity of MAs at the intermediate and at the last hierarchical level, respectively.

**Hierarchical MA, Type A, B or C, Capable of Cloning.**

$$T = \frac{B * d(u)}{O_p} * \left(2^L - 1\right) + P_r * b * d(u) * \tag{10}$$

$$* \left\{ \left( \frac{D(u) - L - 1}{4} + \frac{1}{4 * \sigma_p} \right) * 2^{D(u)} + \frac{\sigma_q + 1}{\sigma_q} * 2^L + \frac{2}{\sigma_q} \right\}$$

**MA Selectivity.** The delivery traffic can be dramatically affected by the way MAs perform monitoring operations. The choice of MA monitoring model significantly affects their *selectivity* $\sigma$. If we distinguish between Flat configurations (*pMAs*, $\sigma = \sigma_{p,x}$) and hierarchical configurations (*qMAs*, $\sigma = \sigma_{p,x}$), the selectivity for *Type A, B,* and *C* MAs, in the case of binary sub-rooting trees, can be expressed as follows:

$$\sigma_{p,A} = \frac{2 * P_r * b * \left(|N_x| + 1\right)}{2 * P_r * b} = 2^{D(u) - L - 1}; \quad \sigma_{q,A} = \frac{2 * P_r * b * 2}{2 * P_r * b * 1} = 2; \tag{11}$$

$$\sigma_{p,B} = \frac{2 * P_r * b * \left(|N_x| + 1\right)}{N_r * b} = \frac{2 * P_r}{N_r} * 2^{D(u) - L - 1}; \quad \sigma_{q,B} = \frac{N_r * b * 2}{N_r * b} = 2;$$

$$\sigma_{p,C} = \frac{2 * P_r * b * \left(|N_x| + 1\right)}{\wp_p * O_p * b} = \frac{2}{\wp_p * O_p} * P_r * 2^{D(u) - L - 1}; \quad \sigma_{q,C} = \frac{\wp_p * O_p * b}{\wp_q * O_p * b} = \frac{\wp_p}{\wp_q}$$

where $|N_x|$ is the maximum number of nodes monitored by one MA, $\wp_p$ and $\wp_q$ represent the probability of an alarm being raised within any unit of time by *pMAs* and *qMAs* respectively, and $O_p$ is the duration, in units of time, of the monitoring task. Note that $\sigma_{p,B} = (2 * P_r / N_r) * \sigma_{p,A}$, $\sigma_{q,B} = \sigma_{q,A}$ and, since $N_r < P_r$, $\sigma_{p,B} > 2 * \sigma_{p,A}$. In addition, $\sigma_{p,C} = [2/(\wp_p * O_p)] * P_r * \sigma_{p,A}$ and $\sigma_{p,C}$ is a very large constant if we assume that the system does not generate relatively frequent alarms ($\wp_q << \wp_p$). Thus, assuming that $P_r \propto N_r$, the order of both $\sigma_{p,A}$ and $\sigma_{p,B}$ is $O(2^{D(u)}, N)$ whereas $\sigma_{p,C}$ is $O(P_r * 2^{D(u)}, P_r * N)$. Therefore, we can expect a comparable traffic behaviour for *Type A* and *B* MAs and a better traffic behaviour for *Type C* MAs.

### 4.4 Mobile Agent Solutions: Delay Models

The total monitoring delay, $D$ is modelled as the sum of three terms, the MA *deployment delay*, the data *collection delay*, and the data *delivery delay*. Lower bounds on the monitoring delay for five different MA solutions are expressed below. We assume that the transmission of 'polls' and 'responses' takes one unit of time, the transmissions of MAs takes 10 units of time, and an MA cloning operation takes 10 units of time, for each traversed link. The number of MAs is $m = d(u) * 2^{L-1}$ in the case of Flat MA solutions and $m = d(u) * (2^L - 1)$ in the case of hierarchical solutions, where $L \in \{1 \dots D(u)\}$.

**Flat MA, Type A, Incapable of Cloning.**

$$D = 10 * \left(2^L - 1\right) + P_r * \left(2^{D(u) - L} - 2\right) + P_r * 2^{L-1} \tag{12}$$

**Flat MA, Type A, Capable of Cloning.**

$$D = 20*L + P_r*\left(2^{D(u)-L} - 2\right) + P_r*2^{L-1} \tag{13}$$

**Hierarchical MA, Type A-A, Incapable of Cloning.**

$$D = 10*\left(2^{L+1} - L - 2\right) + P_r*\left(2^{D(u)-L} - 2\right) + P_r*L \tag{14}$$

**Hierarchical MA, Type A-A, Capable of Cloning.**

$$D = 20*L + P_r*\left(2^{D(u)-L} - 2\right) + P_r*L \tag{15}$$

**Hierarchical MA, Type C-C, Capable of Cloning.**

$$D = 20*L + P_r*\left(2^{D(u)-L} - 2\right) + \wp*L \tag{16}$$

where $\wp$ is the probability that MAs generate alarms.

# 5   Comparative Analysis

In this section we discuss the performance and scalability of the monitoring solutions modelled in Sec.4: MA solutions, centralised naïve polling, and centralised optimal polling. The analysis is carried out in two parts: the former is based on traffic functions; the latter is based on delay functions.

## 5.1   Analysis Based on Traffic

**Performance.** The *relative traffic*, $R_T$, incurred by a given monitoring solution can be expressed as the percentage of the traffic that would be incurred by its 'naive polling' counterpart solution. That is, $R_T=(T/T_{poll})*100$, where $T_{poll}$ is the 'naive polling' traffic and $T$ is the traffic incurred by the solution under comparison. The relative traffic of the 'optimal polling' solution and of four different solutions based on MAs is depicted in Fig.2. An important result is that for each of the considered solutions $R_T$ diminishes very rapidly with scale and settles at 10-20% or even lower, depending on the MA pattern and configuration.

The behaviour of $R_T$, determined using the *polling rate*, $P_r$, as scale indicator is shown in Fig.2a. Analogous trends are obtained adopting the *network diameter*, $D(u)$, or the *number of monitored entities*, $N$, as scale indicators. The theoretical minimal value of $R_T$ can be calculated by substituting the traffic expressions from equations 2, 6, 8, 9, and 10 into the expression of $R_T$. Notice that for all the MA solutions under study this value depends on a function of $Log(m/N)$ and is independent of the selectivity. This shows the importance of MA configuration in terms of number and location of agents. For example, a relatively large number of MAs may be required to reduce data collection traffic; however, MA deployment traffic may lead to significant performance degradation when $m \approx N$ (Fig.2b).

The effects of cloning and of the monitoring model can be observed from Fig.2. Cloning can lead to a significant reduction in MA deployment traffic, whereas the event-based model (*Type C* MAs) tends to reduce delivery traffic. Another interesting result is that MAs do not always represent the best solution. For instance, the first two sets of data in Fig. 2a show a specific monitoring problem for which none of the proposed MA solutions perform better than centralised polling. More generally, the analysis of equations 2, 6, 8, 9 and 10 highlights the conditions under which polling tends to be preferable, typically for relatively small values of $P_r$ and $O_p$.

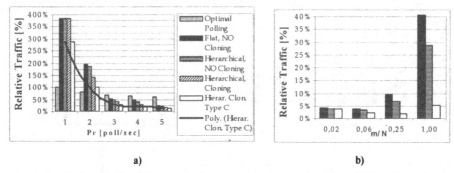

a)                                       b)

**Fig. 2.** Traffic incurred by different solutions, expressed as a percentage of the traffic generated by a 'Naïve Centralised Polling' solution. D(u)=15; P$_r$=10; d(u)=3; N=49149. All MA solutions are of Type A unless otherwise indicated. **a)** Traffic versus Polling Rate; **b)** Traffic versus the ratio between the number of MAs ($m$) and the number of monitored nodes ($N$).

**Scalability.** The analysis of equations 2 and 6 reveals that over increasing scales of the monitoring problem —i.e., for increasing values of $N$, $P_r$, and $D(u)$— both naïve polling and optimal polling traffic functions operate at $O[N, P_r, D(u)]$. If the expressions of $\sigma_{p,x}$ and $\sigma_{q,x}$ of equation 11 are substituted into equations 8, 9, and 10, we can conclude that type A, B, and C MAs operate at $O[N, P_r, D(u)]$ too, regardless of the difference in their selectivity. This is due to the fact that selectivity only affects delivery traffic, whereas the predominant term is collection traffic. Therefore, MAs do not generally scale better than polling, as shown by the behaviour of the polynomial approximation of a 'hierarchical with cloning Type C-C' solution, which does not tend to zero for $P_r$ tending to infinity. However, under some specific circumstances MA hierarchical solutions can scale better. For instance, when $[L=D(u)-1]$ traffic functions operate at most at $O[N, P_r]$ for type A and B MAs and at $O[N]$ for type C MAs.

### 5.2 Analysis Based on Delay

**Performance.** The *relative monitoring delay*, $R_D$, of a given monitoring solution can be expressed as a percentage of the delay of its 'naive polling' counterpart solution. That is, $R_D=(D/D_{poll})*100$, where $D_{poll}$ is the 'naive polling' monitoring delay and $D$ is the delay of the solution under comparison. The relative delay of the 'optimal polling' solution and of five different solutions based on MAs is depicted in Fig.3. A notably important result is that, for the chosen MA configuration parameters, the relative delay is always smaller than the 'naive polling' delay for all the proposed MA solutions, and decreases very rapidly with scale.

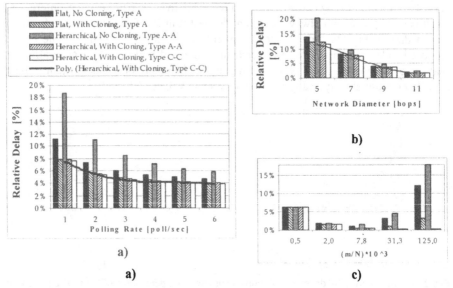

a)

a)

c)

**Fig. 3.** Monitoring Delay, expressed as a percentage of the delay obtained with a 'Naïve Centralised Polling' solution. All MA solutions are of Type A unless otherwise specified. **a)** Relative delay versus polling rate. The relative delay obtained with a 'centralised optimal polling' solution (not shown) is 25.6%. $D(u)=8$; $d(u)=3$; $N=765$; $L=FLOOR(D(u)/2.5, 1)$; $m=12$ for flat solutions; $m=21$ for hierarchical solutions. Probability of event generation, for type C MAs is $FLOOR(P_r/4, 1)$. **b)** Relative delay versus network diameter. The relative delay obtained with a 'centralised optimal polling' solution (not shown) is in the range [25-29%]. $P_r=5$; $d(u)=3$; $N=[45-6141]$; $L=FLOOR(D(u)/2.5, 1)$; $m=[3-24]$ for flat solutions; $m=[3-45]$ for hierarchical solutions. Probability of event generation, for type C MAs is $FLOOR(P_r/4, 1)=1$. **c)** Relative delay against the ratio between the number of MAs ($m$) and the number of monitored nodes ($N$). The relative delay obtained with a 'centralised optimal polling' solution (not shown) is 25%. $D(u)=12$; $P_r=7$; $d(u)=3$; $N=12285$; $L=FLOOR(D(u)/2.5, 1)$; $m=[3-1536]$ for flat solutions; $m=[3-3069]$ for hierarchical solutions. Probability of event generation, for type C MAs is $FLOOR(P_r/4, 1)=1$.

Cloning can lead to a significant reduction in MA deployment time, as well as deployment traffic, at the expenses of a more complicated deployment technique. The benefits of cloning are particularly evident for relatively small values of $P_r$ and $O_p$, that is when the monitoring system is more sensitive to the MA delivery overheads (traffic and delay). Examples of this effect are shown in Fig.3a and Fig.3b, in which significant differences among MA solutions are obtained only for small values of $P_r$. Hierarchical solutions are particularly sensitive to cloning since they typically involve deploying a relatively large number of MAs.

The impact of the number of MAs on performance can be observed in Fig.3c. Solutions having a relatively large number of MAs tend to be characterised by high performance gains. However, increasing the number of MAs results in large deployment times, which often require the use of cloning.

Finally, the 'hierarchical with cloning solution' (type C-C) has been shown to represents the most efficient solution in general (Fig.3). However, 'flat with cloning' solutions have comparable efficiency in several cases and present the advantage of smaller deployment overheads.

**Scalability**. The analysis of equations 5 and 7 reveals that, over increasing scales of the monitoring problem, both 'naïve polling' and 'optimal polling' delay functions operate at $O[P_r, 2^{D(u)}]$. On the other hand, the analysis of equations 11-15 reveals that MA solutions scale at most as $O[P_r, 2^{[(k-1)/k]*D(u)}]$ for L<D(u) and as $O[P_r, 2^{L-1}]$ for L~D(u), where $k=L/D(u)\geq1$; hierarchical MA solutions scale as $O[P_r, D(u)]$ for L~D(u). Two main conclusions can be drawn from this analysis. Firstly, if $P_r$ is used as scale indicator MA solutions do not represent a more scalable solution than 'naive polling', although they result into smaller monitoring delays in typical cases. Secondly, if either $N$ or $D(u)$ are used as scale indicators, MA solution always scale better than their 'naive polling' counterpart solution.

Similar conclusions can be drawn from Fig.3a and Fig.3b, which show the behaviour of $R_D$ versus $P_r$ and $D(u)$ respectively. The behaviour of $R_D$ versus $N$ (not shown) is analogous to the one in Fig.3b. In Fig.3a the polynomial approximation of a 'hierarchical with cloning Type C-C' solution tends to a positive constant, in accordance with the finding that in this case there is no improvement in scalability. In contrast Fig.3b the polynomial approximation tends to zero, showing the improvement in scalability.

# 6   Conclusions

In this paper we have addressed the problem of improving the performance and scalability of network monitoring systems and quantifying the benefits obtainable with Mobile Agents against the more common technique of centralised polling. Results on traffic show that MAs typically offer improved performance, although they do not always scale better than polling. Nevertheless, in very-small scale monitoring problems, particularly for relatively small values of $P_r$, and for relatively short monitoring tasks, centralised polling tends to be preferable. Moreover, results on delay demonstrate that MA solutions improve both scalability and performance in most circumstances. Therefore, we believe that the results of this analysis provide quantitative evidence to support the application of MA technologies to network monitoring, provided that other issues related to their feasibility are addressed.

The modelling and analysis reported in this paper are restricted to the case of hierarchical networks such as telecommunications networks. This choice is motivated by two main reasons. Firstly, hierarchical networks are very common. Secondly, this case can be treated analytically, in contrast with arbitrary network topologies. It is conceivable that MAs may be beneficial also in the case of general networks such as the Internet. For this reason our future work is to extend the investigation to this case through simulations. This approach will allow the refinement of the network model, the introduction of new metrics for the assessment of performance, and the study of further aspects of code mobility.

# Acknowledgements

We are grateful to Hewlett-Packard for their sponsorship. We thank Keith Harrison and other researchers at HP Laboratories Bristol (HPLB), for providing interesting and stimulating ideas.

# References

1. Rescigno, A.: Optimal Polling in Communication Networks. In IEEE Transactions on Parallel and Distributed Systems, Vol.8, N.5 (1997)
2. Baldi, M., Picco, G.P.: Evaluating the Tradeoffs of Mobile Code Design Paradigms in Network Management Applications. In Proc. of ICSE'98, Kyoto, Japan, April 19-25 (1998).
3. Chiariglione, L.: Foundations for Intelligent Physical Agents. FIPA 98 Draft Specification, part 11, August 17 (1998). (http://drogo.cselt.it/fipa/spec/fipa98/ fipa98.html)
4. Aridor, Y., Lange, D.B.: Agent Design Patterns: Elements of Agent Applications Design. In Proc. of Second International Conference on Autonomous Agents (Agents '98), May (1998)
5. Liotta, A., Knight, G., Pavlou, G.: Modelling Network and System Monitoring Over the Internet Using Mobile Agents. In Proc. of IEEE/IFIP NOMS'98, Vol.2, Feb.(1998) 300-312
6. Kahani, M., Beadle, H.W.P.: Decentralised Approaches for Network Management. Computer Communications Review, ACM SIGCOMM, Vol. 27 N.3 July (1997)
7. Baldi, M., Gai, S., Picco, G.P.: Exploiting Code mobility in Decentralised and Flexible Network Management. In Proc. of Workshop on Mobile Agents, Berlin, April (1997)
8. Goldszmidt, G.: Distributed Management by Delegation. PhD Thesis, Columbia University, NY, (1996)
9. Yemini, Y., Goldszmidt, G. G., Yemini, S.: Network Management by Delegation. In Proc. of Integrated Network Management II, Amsterdam (1991)
10. Goldszmidt, G., Yemini, Y.: Delegated Agents for Network Management. In IEEE Communications Magazine, Vol.36 No.3, March (1998).
11. Liotta, A., Knight, G.: Decomposition Patterns for MobileCode-based Management. In Proc. of HP-OVUA 1998. ENST de Bretagne, Rennes, France, April 19-21 (1998)
12. Casavant, T.L., Singhal, M., Readings in Distributed Computing Systems. In IEEE Computer Society Press, ISBN 0-8186-3032-9 (1994)
13. Goldman, A.J.: Optimal Center Location in Simple Networks. In Transportation Science, Vol.5 (1971) 212-221.
14. Handler, G.Y., Mirchandani, P.B.: Location on Networks Theory and Algorithms. The MIT Press (1979)
15. Kariv, O., Hakimi, S.L.: An Algorithmic Approach to Network Location Problems - Part 2: The P-medians. SIAM J. Appl. Math., Vol.37 (1979) 539-560
16. Matula, D.W., Kolde, R.: Efficient Multi-Median Location in Acyclic Networks. ORSA/TIMS Bullettin, No.2 (1976)
17. Sloman, M.: Network and Distributed Systems Management. Addison-Wesley (1994)
18. Zegura, E.W, Calvert, K.L, Donahoo, M.J.: A Quantitative Comparison of Graph-based Models for Internet Topology. IEEE/ACM Transactions on Networking. In press.
19. Liotta, A., Knight, G.: Efficient Network Monitoring Using Mobile Agents. Research Notes RN/99/6, Computer Science Department, University College London, January (1999).

# Programmable Agents for Active Distributed Monitoring

Ehab S. Al-Shaer

Multimedia Networking Research Laboratory,
School of Computer Science, Telecommunications and Information Systems,
DePaul University,
Chicago, IL 60604
Ehab@cs.depaul.edu
http://www.cs.depaul.edu/Ehab

**Abstract.** The successful deployment of next-generation distributed systems is significantly dependent on the efficient management support that improves the performance and reliability of these applications at run-time. This paper motivates and describes a programmable agents approach for active monitoring as an important attribute for supporting scalable, highly-responsive and non-intrusive management architecture. Active monitoring enables defining re-configurable and self-directed management tasks that can be modified automatically at run-time in order to track the system behavior. Based on observed events and users' monitoring demands, monitoring agents can dynamically customize their assigned tasks and initiate the appropriate monitoring actions. This avoids activating unnecessary monitoring tasks and provides a dynamic monitoring operations. The presented system, which is referred to as HiFi, supports a comprehensive environment including code instrumentation, user subscription, event filtering and action service. The paper also shows monitoring examples that illustrates the application and the effectiveness of active monitoring in managing large-scale distributed systems.

## 1 Introduction

The next-generation distributed systems are large-scale, resource intensive and more complex. With the increasing demands of deploying large-scale distributed (LSD) systems, an efficient on-line monitoring has become an essential service for improving the performance and reliability of such complex applications. Examples of LSD systems include large-scale collaborative distance learning, video teleconferencing,distributed interactive simulation, and reliable multi-point applications. In an LSD environment, large numbers of events are generated by system components during their execution and interaction with external objects (e.g. users or processes). These events must be monitored to accurately determine the run-time behavior of an LSD system and to obtain status information that is required for management operations such as steering applications or performing a corrective action. However, the manner in which events are generated in an LSD system is complex and represents a number of challenges for an on-line monitoring system. Correlated events are generated concurrently and can occur from multiple locations distributed throughout the environment. This makes monitoring an intricate task and complicates the management decision process. Furthermore, the large number of entities and the geographical distribution inherent with LSD systems increases the challenge of addressing important issues, such as performance bottlenecks, scalability, and application perturbation.

HiFi is an attempt to deliver an active monitoring architecture that explicitly addresses the challenges and requirements associated with managing large-scale distributed systems. HiFi active monitoring approach supports dynamic and automatic customization for management operations as a response to changes in LSD systems behavior [16, 12]. This is achieved through programmable monitoring agents that re-direct their monitoring activities on-the-fly upon users' requests or based on the information (events) collected during the monitoring operations. For instance, instead of monitoring all events and processes in the system, the agents monitor a subset of events/processes and the monitoring activities expand based on the information of the generated events. Therefore, active monitoring reduces the monitoring space significantly and offers a scalable management architecture. The monitoring intrusiveness is also minimized because this architecture enables initiating few monitoring tasks (targets) at the proper time. In addition, HiFi active monitoring enables the agents react spontaneously (e.g., corrective actions) which improves the management operations response time compared with human-in-the-loop model [13].

A number of monitoring approaches and systems for monitoring distributed systems have been proposed (e.g., [5, 9–11, 13–15]). Although some of these systems provide mechanisms for modifying the monitoring requests dynamically, these mechanisms are manual and insufficient to support a programmable or self-directed monitoring tasks (actions) as described in this paper. In addition, they do not support a scalable and fine grain event filtering mechanism which is significant for monitoring "large-scale" distributed systems such as Internet-based applications. This paper is organized as follows: Section 2 explains the monitoring model and language specifications; Section 3 gives an overview of HiFi monitoring architecture and process; Section 4 describes our active monitoring approach and its impact on the management process; Section 5 presents an application example of using HiFi monitoring system for steering distributed reliable multicast protocols; and Section 6 presents the summary and concluding remarks.

## 2 Monitoring Model

In order to present a complete abstraction of the active monitoring architecture, our work must include modeling the *application behavior*, the *monitoring demands*, and the *monitoring mechanism* with considering the design objectives presented in Section 1. The program behavior can be expressed in a set of events revealed by the application during execution. In our monitoring model,

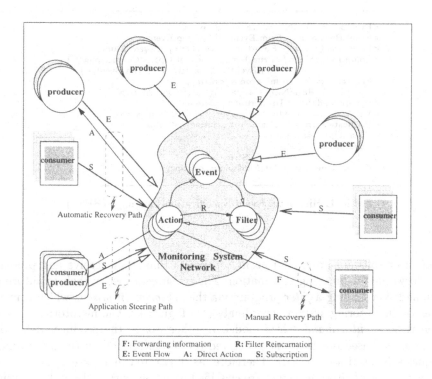

| F: Forwarding information | R: Filter Reincarnation |
| E: Event Flow    A: Direct Action | S: Subscription |

**Fig. 1.** Monitoring Model

we call the monitored programs *event producers* which continuously emit *events* that express the execution status. An *event* is a significant occurrence in a system that is represented by a *notification message* which typically contains event characteristics such as event type and event source. We classify two types of events used in our model: *primitive events* which are based on a single notification message, and *composite events* which depend on more than one notification message. In the monitoring language, the event format (notification) is a variable sequence of *event attributes* determined by the user but it has a fixed header used in the monitoring process. An event attribute is a predicate that contains the *attribute name* which typically represents a variable in the producer (i.e, program) and a value. The event format also determines the type of event signaling: *Immediate* to forward the generated event immediately, or *Delayed* to allow buffering or batching events in the producer before sending them. Table 1 shows the High-level Event Specification Language (HESL) in BNF. This event abstraction enables consumers (1) to specify any arbitrary event format in a declarative way, and (2) to construct a complex (multi-level) abstraction of a program behavior using composite events. In addition, the event abstraction enables the consumers/users to assign values to the event attributes and does not require specifying attribute type (e.g., int, float or string). This provides a simpler interface than CORBA IDL [9]. We call the monitoring objects (e.g.,

```
<Event> ::= EVENT = <Event_Body>.
<Event_Body> ::= <Prim_Event> | <Comp_Event>
<Prim_Event> ::= {<Fix_Att> ; <Var_Att>} <Event_Name>
<Comp_Event> ::= (<Prim_Event> <Event_Op> <Comp_Event> ) |
                 (<Prim_Event> <Event_Op> <Prim_Event> )
<Fix_Att> ::= ModuleName = <String>,
              FuncName = <String>, <Report_Mode>
<Report_Mode> ::= Immediate | Delayed
<Var_Att> ::= <Predicate> , <Var_Att> | <Predicate>
<Predicate> ::= <Att_Name> <Relation> <Value>
<Event_Op> ::= ∧ | ∨ | ~
<Relation> ::= < | > | = | ≠ | ≤ | ≥
<Value> ::= <Number> | <String>
<Event_Name> ::= <Att_Name> ::= <String>
```

**Table 1.** High-level Event Specification Language (HESL)

human or software programs) *event consumers* since they receive and present
the forwarded monitoring information. The consumers specify their monitoring
demands via sending a *filter* program via the *subscription process* which configures the monitoring system accordingly (see Figure 1). The monitoring operation is an *event-demand-driven* model. In other words, the producer behavior
is observed based on the event generated (event-based) and on the monitoring
requests (subscription-based). Therefore, as illustrated in Figure 1, events received in the monitoring system are classified based on exiting filters. If an event
is detected, the action specified in the filter is performed such as forwarding the
monitoring information to the corresponding consumers. The filter and action
specification is described in Section 4.

## 3    Overview of HiFi Monitoring Architecture

HiFi employs a hierarchical event filtering-based monitoring architecture to distribute the monitoring load in application environment. Based on a user's monitoring requests, the monitoring system determines the appropriate agent or set
of agents within the hierarchy to be tasked with inspection and evaluation of
application events. The monitoring system uses fine grain decomposition and
allocation mechanisms to ensure that filtering tasks are efficiently distributed
among the monitoring agents and prevent events propagation in the network.
Since our focus in this paper is on the programmable monitoring environment
in HiFi, we give a brief overview of the HiFi system and refer to [2–4] for more
details.

**Hierarchical Monitoring Agents:** In HiFi monitoring system, the task of
detecting primitive and composite events is distributed among dedicated monitoring programs called *monitoring agents* (MA). MA is an application-level monitoring program that runs independently of other applications in the system and

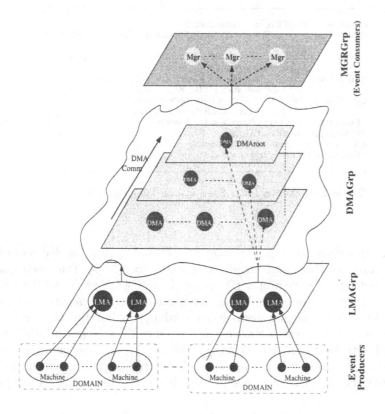

**Fig. 2.** Hierarchical Filtering-based Monitoring Architecture

that communicates with the outside world (including producers and consumers) via message-passing. HiFi has two types of MAs: *local monitoring agents (LMA)*, and *domain monitoring agents (DMA)* (see Figure 2). The former is responsible of detecting primitive events generated by local applications in the same machine while the latter is responsible of detecting composite events which are beyond the LMA scope of knowledge. One or more producer entities (i.e., processes) are connected to a local LMA in the same machine. Every group of LMAs related to one domain (geographical or logical domain) is attached to one DMA. These DMAs are also connected to higher DMAs to form a hierarchical structure for exchanging the monitoring information. Because of the different roles of LMA and DMA, LMAs use Direct Acyclic Graph (DAG) [6], however, DMAs use Petri Nets (PN) in order to record and track the event history [7].

**Subscription Process:** The monitoring process starts by a consumer sending a *filter program* that describes the monitoring request to the local MA. The filter is validated and decomposed into subfilters (e.g. F1,..,Fn) using the *decomposition algorithms* in such a manner that each one represents a primitive event [3]. Then, each decomposed subfilter is assigned to one or more LMAs using the

```
<Filter> ::= FILTER = <Filter_Body>
<Filter_Body> ::= [<Event_Expr>]; [<Filter_Expr>]; [<Actions>];
                  <Filter_Name>.
<Event_Expr> ::= ( <Event_Name> <Event_Op> <Event_Expr> )
               | <Event_Name>
<Filter_Expr> ::= ( <Predicate> <Filter_Op> <Filter_Expr> )
                | <Predicate> | TRUE
<Predicate> ::= ( <Pred_Att> <Relation> <Pred_Att> )
              | ( <Pred_Att> <Relation> <Value> )
<Pred_Att> ::= <Event_Name>.<Att_Name>
<Filter_Op> ::= <Event_Op>
<Actions> ::= <Action> ; <Actions>
<Filter_Name> ::= <Program_Name> ::= <String>
```

**Table 2.** High-level Filter Specification Language (HFSL)

*allocation algorithms* based on the event sources and application distribution. Decomposition and Allocation algorithms are described in [3]. The monitoring system also determines the proper DMAs for evaluating the event and the filter expression of the filter program. When MAs receive delegated monitoring tasks (subfilters) [8], they configure themselves accordingly by inserting this subfilter in the filtering internal representation which is a direct acyclic graph (DAG) for LMAs and Petri Nets (PN) for DMAs [4]. This architecture alleviates any performance bottlenecks or scalability problems by distributing the monitoring load among MAs and limiting the events' propagation to the originating sources [3].

## 4   Techniques for Active Monitoring

The main goal of active monitoring is to offer dynamically customizable monitoring tasks. This provides a flexible management infrastructure that scales very well with number of producers and causes a minimal overhead in the application environment. In addition, active monitoring, in HiFi, reduces the monitoring latency by supporting an automatic monitoring customization performed by MAs without the users involvement. In this section, we present several techniques developed in HiFi in order to support a programmable agents environment for active monitoring. We also describe the impact of these techniques on improving scalability and performance of HiFi.

### 4.1   Filter-Based Programmable Monitoring Agents

Users (or event consumers) describe their monitoring demands via programs called *filters* submitted to the monitoring system at run-time. A filter is a set of *predicates* where each predicate is defined as a boolean-valued expression that returns *true* or *false*. Predicates may be joined by *logical operators* (such as AND and OR) to form an expression. In our model, the filter consists of three major components: the *event expression* which specifies the relation between the interesting event, *filter expression* which specifies the attributes value or the relation between the attributes of different events, and the *action* to be performed if both event and filters expressions are *true*. Table 2 shows the High-level Filter Specification Language (HFSL) in BNF.

Consumers may add, modify or delete filters on-the-fly through the subscription service component [3]. When a consumer performs filter subscription, the monitoring agents re-configure itself accordingly by updating their internal filtering representation [4]. HiFi uses the *subscription protocol*, described in [2], to maintain state consistency and synchronize the monitoring agents. The filter-based programming abstraction enables the consumers to describe the expression relation not only between the events but also between the attributes of different events as well. This improves the expressive power of the monitoring language, and permits fine-grain filtering based on regular expressions.

**Example (1):** Assume agents have been configured through filter to detect any AudioWarning or VidWarning events generated from Audio and Video processes, respectively. Consumers can re-program or re-configure the MAs at run-time to detect only the *event correlation* between these two events such that they are both generated by the same machines via sending the following filter.

**FILTER=** [(*AudioWarning* ∧ *VidWarning*)];
[(*AudioWarning.Machine=VidWarning.Machine*)];
[FORWARD]; Warnings_Correlation_Filter.

After decomposing and allocating this filter, the DMA will only forward *Audio* and *Video* warning events that are generated by the same machine. Consumers can also delete (deactivate) or modify (re-activate) existing filters using *DEL* and *MOD* in the action part (see Table 3). In addition, the programming environment permits consumers to overload the attributes values in the events in order to create a different event instance in the filter program.

## 4.2 Event Incarnation

Actions in the monitoring model can be simply *executing a program* (local or remote) or *forwarding* the detected event to the corresponding consumers which are both necessary for automatic fault recovery and application steering, respectively. In order to improve the dynamism and the expressive power of the monitoring system, the model provides more complex actions: a *new event* or a *new filter*. In HiFi, generating new events as an action is called event incarnation. This feature improves the expressive power, performance and usability of the active monitoring system as follows:

- The event-filter-action programming model (see Figure 1) enables the consumer to activate a sequence of monitoring operations (filters and actions) automatically and without the human involvement. In addition, generating new events (as an action) may trigger other filters that are necessary to track

---

&lt;Action&gt; ::= &lt;Exec&gt; | &lt;Event_Name&gt; | &lt;Filter_Rinc&gt; | &lt;Filter_Registers&gt; | **FORWARD**
&lt;Exec&gt; ::= &lt;Path Name&gt; &lt;Program Name&gt;
&lt;Path Name&gt; ::= &lt;String&gt; / &lt;Path Name&gt; | &lt;String&gt; /
&lt;Filter_Register&gt; ::= &lt;Identifier&gt; = &lt;Event_Name&gt;.&lt;Att_Name&gt;
&lt;Filter_Registers&gt; ::= &lt;Filter_Register&gt; | &lt;Filter_Register&gt;;&lt;Filter_Registers&gt;;
&lt;Filter_Reinc&gt; ::= **ADD** &lt;Filter_Name&gt;; &lt;Filter_Reinc&gt; | **ADD** &lt;Filter_Name&gt; |
        **DEL** &lt;Filter_Name&gt;; &lt;Filter_Reinc&gt; | **DEL** &lt;Filter_Name&gt; |
        **MOD** &lt;New Filter&gt;; &lt;Filter_Reinc&gt; | **MOD** &lt;New Filter&gt; ;
&lt;New Filter&gt; ::= &lt;Filter_Name&gt;.**EX**= &lt;Event_Expr&gt; | &lt;Filter_Name&gt;.**FX**= &lt;Filter_Expr&gt; |
        &lt;Filter_Name&gt;.**EX**= &lt;Event_Expr&gt;; &lt;Filter_Name&gt;.**FX**= &lt;Filter_Expr&gt;

---

**Table 3.** High-level Action Specification Language (HASL)

the observed problem. For example, a failure that occurs in a producer (process) as a result of abnormal close of a communication connection (primitive event) may involve two actions: *failure recovery* and *sending* a new event in order to diagnose this failure further (e.g., checking memory usage). Based on this event, new actions (e.g., recovery procedures) could be performed.

- A new event could be an "aggregate" event that summarizes the information of multiple (composite). This reduces event traffic and avoid event report implosion in the monitoring environment. For example, an aggregate event may convey the *average drop rate* of a set of receivers. Section 5 shows how this aggregate event is useful for monitoring reliable multicasting.
- Performing an action such as executing a program may change the state of a running program. Therefore, sending an event that reveals the state change to the monitoring system is important to allow re-observing the behavior, and attaining stability in automatic application steering.

### 4.3 Filter Incarnation

In addition to the user (manual) re-configuration via dynamic users subscription (described in Section 3), HiFi active monitoring also supports programmable agents that re-configure themselves automatically based on events occurrences. An action can be a filter manipulation (typically, adding a filter, deleting a filter, and modifying a filter). For example, another new filter can be activated in the monitoring environment as a result of detecting an event. We call this *filter incarnation* (see Figure 1) because a filter may add, delete or modify a new filter in the system. Filter incarnation is defined in Table 3 of the monitoring language. Adding a new filter means activating a pre-defined filter that has not been submitted to the system. This is specified in the monitoring language using a special reserved word (ADD) with the pre-defined filter name. On the other hand, deletion or modification must be performed on an existing filter for which consumers subscribed. This is specified using the reserved words, MOD and DEL, with an active filter name. When modifying an active filter, consumers must specify which parts to modify: event expression (EX), filter expression (FX), or both. This can be designated by appending the filter name as a prefix to EX and/or FX. The resulting EX and/or FX are the effective filter parts after the subscription is completed.

Filter incarnation enables users to define "general" monitoring tasks that can be automatically customized by agents at run-time to diagnose specific system behavior such as failures or performance bottlenecks. This also avoids overwhelming the system by a large number of "static" (hardwired) monitoring tasks to observe a large number of system activities. Therefore, consumers can monitor subset of events and request modifying (changing or expanding) the monitoring scope to include other events and processes whenever certain event patterns are detected. In the following, we describe various applications of filter incarnation in active monitoring.

**Adding/Deleting Filters for controlling monitor timing:** Consumers can specify start and end times for any given monitoring activity based on events. In other words, consumers can specify to start/stop a trace activity when a certain event (primitive or composite) is detected. This minimizes the monitoring overhead and produces concise traces.

**Example (2):** Assume a consumer wants to monitor the *drop rate* in the "receiving" events (*RecvEvent*) of *bar* program only when the *transmission rate* in the "transmission" event (*TransEvent*) of *foo* program drops below a certain threshold (*STHRESHOLD*). In this case, the consumer can specify a filter (*MonitorSender*) that monitors the "transmission" events of *foo* and triggers another filter (*MonitorReceiver*) that monitors *bar* "receiving" events, if the transmission rate drops below the threshold. The filters example is shown below.

**FILTER**= [(*TransEvent*)];
[(*TransEvent.ModuleName* = "foo" $\wedge$ *TransEvent.transrate* < *STHRESHOLD*)];
[*ADD MonitorReceiver*]; `MonintorSender`.

**FILTER**= [(*RecvEvent*)];
[(*RecvEvent.ModuleName* = "bar" $\wedge$ *RecvEvent.droprate* > *RTHRESHOLD*)];
[*FORWARD*]; `MonintorReceiver`.

The *MonitorReceiver* filter monitors "receiving" events (*RecvEvent*) from *foo* and forwards events to consumers if the *drop rate* exceeds the threshold. Similarly, the *MonitorReceiver* filter can be deactivated (Deleted) based on changes in the *drop rate* in TransEvent. This permits activating/deactivating *MonitorReceiver* filter automatically and at the proper time which minimizes the monitoring perturbation in the application environment.

**Modifying Filters Specifications:** Usually, monitoring tasks are static and defined prior to any monitoring operation. However, using filter incarnation, the filter specifications can be determined during the monitoring process itself based on event patterns and information. For this purpose, the HASL provides a set of virtual registers called *filter registers* that consumers can use for loading/restoring variables in/from the monitoring agents. These registers are used by MAs to store attribute values of received events. Consumers can simply assign the attribute value of an event used in EX or FX to a filter register and vice versa for this purpose.

**Example (3):** For example, consumers may want to generate an event trace (or history) for processes that have produced at least one security warning event (WarningEvent). In this case, the module name is not known to the monitoring system at trace specification time. Therefore, the monitoring system must determine the module name during the monitoring operations. This is achieved by using filer registers to save and restore the event information. In the following, the DynamicErrorTrace is the filter specification for this example. Notice that *ThisMod* is a filter register that restores the module name, *ModuleName*, after the occurrence of WarningEvent of type *SECURITY*. Then, the filer incarnation is used to modify the expression of *TraceProcess* filter so that the modified filter executes the new trace specifications.

**FILTER**= [*WarningEvent*];
[(*WarningEvent.ModuleName* = "ANY" ∧ *WarningEvent.Type* = "SECURITY")];
[*ThisMod* = *WarningEvent.ModuleName*;
*MOD TraceProcess.FX* = (*AnyEvent.ModuleName* = *ThisMod*)]; DynamicErrorTrace.

**FILTER**= [*AnyEvent*];
[(*AnyEvent.ModuleName* = "ANY")];
[FORWARD]; TraceProcess.

The *TraceProcess* is a "generic" filter that monitors and forwards all events from any module to the corresponding consumers[1]. However, this general filter/task is modified by *DynamicErrorTrace* filter to perform a special customized monitoring operation. Therefore, this technique enables activating/deactivating the appropriate monitoring operations (or filters) at the right time (event), and thereby relieving the system environment from the overhead of launching multiple filters or monitoring requests simultaneously. It also reduces the monitoring latency since the monitoring agent can react spontaneously without the consumers intervention. Moreover, the filter incarnation feature provides an extendible programming environment utilizing the power of the recursive event-filter-action model as shown in Section 5.

## 5 Active Monitoring of Distributed Multi-point Applications

The HiFi monitoring system is used in a number of applications such as application steering, fault recovery and debugging of distributed multimedia systems.

---

[1] "ANY" is a language keyword that means any string value.

In this section, we present an example of using HiFi for monitoring and steering Reliable Multicast Server (RMS) [1]. One of the known problems in reliable multicasting, is the effect of slow members (e.g., machines) in group communication. A machine is described as a slow machine if its receiving rate is "much" less than the other members in the group. In this case, a slow machine could typically slow down the communication of the entire group because the sender transmission rate, in RMS, eventually adapts to the rate of the slowest receiver. Developing a solution for slow members in multicast groups is beyond the focus of this paper. However, the effective use of HiFi active monitoring is presented in the *dynamic discovery* of slow members (machines) during a multicast session and the *automatic feedback* to the RMS senders which make the proper steering management decision accordingly. The criteria of slow members is defined based on the user specifications. For example, the user (or manager) may define a slow member whose performance is below a certain threshold. In our example below, the RMS sender acts as a manager and sends the threshold information. Figure 3 shows the event (HESL) and the filter (HFSL) specifications used to discover slow members in multicast groups. Each RMS receiver is instrumented (using HiFi) to send *McastRec* event that contains the machine name, the domain name, the group name, total bytes received (KBrec), and number of NACKs scheduled (NackSch) [2]. Because of NACK suppression mechanism [1], the number of *NackSch* gives more accurate estimation of the *drop rate* than number of Nacks sent. The McastRec event is sent periodically based on time limit or maximum number of bytes received. And the RMS senders send McastSend to indicate two things: the transmission rate (*TransRate*), and the drop rate threshold (*threshold*) for receivers in the group. The *TransRate* is first checked by MonMcastSender filters to determine if the "slow members" monitoring activity should be started. If *TransRate* is below the STHRESHOLD, then the Slow_Memebers filter is modified to use the *GrpName* stored in the filter register as described in Section 4. This also activates the Slow_Memebers filter that compares the NackSch in McastRec and threshold in McastSend to identify slow members. However, because the threshold value is dynamic and may be determined from the overall performance of the participants, another filter (Update_Threshold) is used to provide a feedback on the overall drop rate average to senders which consequently re-adjust the threshold value accordingly. Each LMA forwards McastSend and McastRec primitive events to its DMA that evaluates the filter expression upon receiving both events. The second filter, Slow_Members, waits to receive one McastSend and McastRec events from all LMAs in the domain. Then, the filter expression is evaluated. The _ctr and _LMAs are HiFi reserved key words and used to denote the number of the event occurrences and the number of LMAs in the domain, respectively. The filter expression evaluates to *true* if all RMS receivers in the domain send McastRec event from the indicated group name (*GrpName*) and the NackSch of one receiver or more is higher than the threshold. If the filter expression becomes true, then three actions are performed: (1) the average scheduled Nacks for receivers

---

[2] $NackSch = Number\ of\ NacksSent + Number\ of\ NacksCancelled$

**EVENT**= { ModuleName=RMS,FuncName=McastSend,Immediate; Machine="ANY", Domain="ANY", GrpName="ANY", TransRate=ANY, threshold= ANY } McastSend.

**EVENT**= { ModuleName=RMS,FuncName=McastRecv,Immediate; Machine="ANY", Domain="ANY", GrpName="ANY", KBrec= ANY, NackSch=ANY } McastRec.

**EVENT**= { ModuleName=DMA,FuncName=ANY,Immediate; Machine="ANY", Domain="ANY", KBrec= ANY, NackSch=ANY } DomAVG.

**FILTER**= [McastSend];
[McastSend.TransRate < STHRESHOLD];
[ThisGrp=GrpName; MOD $Slow\_Memebrs.FX$=(McastRec.GrpName=ThisGrp);
ADD $Update\_Threhold$]]; MonMcastSender.

**FILTER**= $[(McastSend \wedge McastRec)]$;
$[(McastRec.\_ctr = \_LMAs \wedge McastRec.GrpName = ``*") \wedge$
$McastRec.NackSch > McastSend.threshold)]$;
$[CalcAvg; DomAVG; $FORWARD$]$; Slow_Memebrs.

**FILTER**= $[DomAVG]$;
$[DomAVG.\_ctr = \_DMAs]$;
$[UpdateThrehold; McastSend]$; Update_Threhold.

**Fig. 3.** Active Monitoring Example of Reliable Multicasting.

in same domain is calculated (CalcAVG), (2) the DomAVG, which represents an aggregate (summary) event, is sent to the containing DMA to reveal the domain average, (3) the McastRec event that matches the slow member criteria represented in the filter expression (i.e., NackSch < threshold) is forwarded to the manager (RMS sender). The third filter, Update_Threshold, receives the DomAVG events from the DMAs and then calculate the total NackSch average, update the threshold and send the McastSend with new threshold to the LMAs/DMAs again. This filter can be a DMA task, instead of RMS senders. However, users must provide the action *UpdateThreashold* to this DMA which then can take care of updating the threshold dynamically while the RMS senders can take care of managing slow members problem. Since senders or receivers could be members in various multicast groups, the group name (GrpName) is used to limit the slow members monitoring activities (filters) on the multicast groups that suffers from this problem. Similarly, another filter can be used to deactivate Slow_Memebers filter when the *TransRate* becomes less then STHRESHOLD. In other words, the slow members filter can activated and deactivated dynamically based on the condition of the multicast group.

The slow members and NackSch average information are collected from each receiver via LMAs and then combined and propagated in hierarchical fashion via DMAs to the RMS of the sender. In addition to the dynamic feedback service offered in this example, this mechanism is scalable because it avoids the notifications implosion that may occur when McastRec are forwarded to one RMS sender

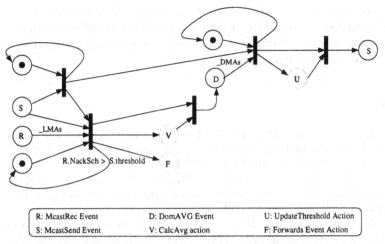

| R: McastRec Event | D: DomAVG Event | U: UpdateThreshold Action |
| S: McastSend Event | V: CalcAvg action | F: Forwards Event Action |

**Fig. 4.** The PN Filter Representation in HiFi Monitoring Agents.

from group of receivers. Furthermore, distributing the processing load such as calculating the average drop rate contributes to the monitoring performance.

# 6 Conclusion and Future Work

This paper describes a novel architecture for supporting active distributed monitoring. The monitoring system, called HiFi, uses a hierarchical monitoring agents architecture that distributes the monitoring load and limits the event propagation. The monitoring agents are programmable and can be reconfigured manually through users' interactions at run-time or automatically by the agents themselves based on the information of the detected events. Users utilize a simple language interface, called filter, to define their monitoring demands and associated actions. Users can also specify "general" monitoring tasks that can be customized automatically by the monitoring agents to perform specialized monitoring operations. We developed several techniques to support an efficient programmable agents environment for active monitoring. This includes *event incarnation* to enable event-filter-action programming model, *filter incarnation* and *filter registers* to enable automatic modifications and self-directed monitoring operations, and *dynamic subscription* that enables users to add, delete or modify their requests at run-time. We demonstrate an example of using HiFi for monitoring and steering a reliable distributed multicast server (RMS). This active monitoring architecture offers significant advantages in the scalability and performance of the monitoring systems. It also enables consumers to control the monitoring granularity, and thereby minimizing its intrusiveness.

Although HiFi is developed and used in real-life applications, it remains a prototype monitoring system. Many open issues remain to be addressed in the HiFi research plan. These include improving the filter incarnation mechanism to provide higher abstraction such that users can specify the ultimate monitoring target without having to specify intermediate monitoring tasks, integrating system and network management, and extending the monitoring language to support temporal event relations.

# References

1. Al-Shaer, E., Abdel-Wahab, H., Maly, K.: Application-Layer Group Communication Server for Extending Reliable Multicast Protocols Services. IEEE Int. Conference on Network Protocols. **10** (1997) 267–274
2. Al-Shaer, E., Abdel-Wahab, H., Maly, K.: Dynamic Monitoring Approach for Multi-point Multimedia Systems. International Journal of Networking and Information Systems, Vol. 2. **6** (1999) 75–88
3. Al-Shaer, E., Abdel-Wahab, H., Maly, K.: HiFi: A New Monitoring Architecture for Distributed System Management. Proceedings of International Conference on Distributed Computing Systems (ICDCS'99). **5** (1999) 171–178
4. Al-Shaer, E., Fayad, M., Abdel-Wahab, H., Maly, K.: Adaptive Object-Oriented Filtering Framework for Event Management Applications. To appear in ACM Computing Surveys.
5. Alexander, S., Kliger, S., Mozes, E., Yemini, Y., Ohsie, D.: High Speed and Robust Event Correlation. IEEE Communication Magazine. **5** (1996) 433–450
6. Bailey, M.L., Gopal, B., Pagels, M.A., Peterson, L., Sarkar, P.: PathFinder: A Pattern-Based Packet Classifier. USENIX Symposium on Operating System Design and Implementation. **11** (1994) 24–42
7. Gatziu, S., Dittrich, K.R.: Detecting Composite Events in Active Database Systems Using Petri Nets. Int. Workshop on Research Issues in Data Engineering: Active Database Systems. **2** (1994) 2–9
8. Goldszmidt, G., Yemini, S., Yachiam, Y.: Network Management by Delegation - the MAD approach. CAS Conference. (1991) 347–359
9. Object Management Group. The Common Object Request Broker: Event Service Specification, Tech. Rep. CCITT X.734/ISO 10164-5. (1993)
10. Joyce, J., Lomow, G., Slind, K., Unger, B.: Monitoring Distributed Systems. ACM Transactions on Computer Systems, Vol. 5. (1987) 121–50
11. Marzullo, K., Cooper, R., Wood, M.D., Birman, K.P.: Tools for distributed Application Management. IEEE Computer, Vol. 24. **8** (1991) 42–51
12. Merwe, J.V.D., Rooney, S., Leslie, I., Crosby, S.: The tempest: A practical framework for network programmability. IEEE Network Magazine. **6** (1998)
13. Parulkar, G., Schmidt, D.C., Kraemer, E., Turner, J., Kantawala, A.: An architecture for monitoring, visualization, and control and gigabit networks,. IEEE Network Magazine, Vol. 11, **10** (1997) 32–38
14. Schroeder, B.: On-line Monitoring: A Tutorial. IEEE Computer, Vol. 28. **6** (1995) 72–78
15. Sloman, M. editor. Network and Distributed System Management. Addison-Wesley, Reading, Massachusetts (1994)
16. Tennenhouse, D.L., Smith, J.M., Sincoskie, W.D., Wetherall, D.J., Minden, G.J.: A Survey of Active Network Research. IEEE Communications Magazine, Vol. 35. **1** (1997) 80–86

# A Distributed and Reliable Platform for Adaptive Anomaly Detection in IP Networks

L. Lawrence Ho, Christopher J. Macey, and Ronald Hiller

Communications Sciences Research Laboratory
Bell Laboratories, Lucent Technologies
101 Crawfords Corners Road
Holmdel, NJ 07733, USA
{llho, macey, ronbo}@bell-labs.com

**Abstract.** Algorithms for anomaly detection in IP networks have been developed and a real-time distributed platform for anomaly detection has been implemented. These algorithms automatically and adaptively detect "soft" network faults (performance degradations) in IP networks. These algorithms are implemented as a reliable and fully distributed real-time software platform called NSAD (Network/Service Anomaly Detector). IP NSAD has the following novel features. First, it provides a flexible platform upon which pre-constructed components can be mixed/matched and distributed (to different machines) to form a wide range of application specific and fully distributed anomaly detectors. Second, anomaly detection is performed on raw network observables (e.g., performance data such as MIB2 and RMON1/2 variables) *and* algebraic functions of the observables (objective functions), making NSAD an objective driven anomaly detection system of wide detection range and high detection sensitivity. Third, controlled testing demonstrates that NSAD is capable of detecting network anomalies reliably in IP networks.

## 1   Introduction and Algorithmic/System Design

Anomaly detection is concerned with detecting "soft" network faults (e.g., performance degradation) in network and their services, which in turn enables "proactive" containment and correction of network/service faults for reliable networking [1,2]. Since anomalies are signatures of network/service exceptions and are preludes to service level failures, being able to detect them reliably and quickly enables network failures to be anticipated (hence "proactive") [1–5]. This implies that fault correction and containment can be applied in a timely manner to manage the performance and optimize the reliability of networks and their services.

With the explosive growth of heterogeneous data networks (the Internet and intranets) in the past decade, there has been a corresponding leap in the types, frequencies, and severity of network/service faults and outages [6]. Some examples of these network faults include network mis-configuration, hardware problems (e.g., line card failure), networking software exceptions (e.g., "bugs" in routing software, exceptions in routing table updates), "bugs" in network-enabled applications (e.g., video streaming software), traffic anomalies (e.g., packet storms), and so on [7–10]. These anomalies and faults, if not contained and corrected in time, will degrade network quality-of-service (QoS) parameters such as delay, jitter, and packet drop/error rate, which in turn lead to network/service degradations and ultimately failures. As modern data networks and their support software become more complex (in physical/logical topologies and software complexity), the number of potential network/service points of failures are increasing exponentially, their faults correspondingly less predictable, and detecting them increasingly difficult.

Recently, there has been another trend in networking—increasing demand on network QoS and reliability [11]. As electronic commerce (E-commerce) and real-time applications (e.g., video and audio based applications) become more prevalent, guaranteeing QoS and reliability is becoming increasingly important [12,13]. This in turn demands that network/service faults be detected and identified reliably and quickly for rapid fault alert, containment, and correction [1–5].

Together, these two trends have fueled the recent surge in research concerning network fault detection and performance management [14–17]. These challenges motivated our previous research in anomaly detection in non-IP based networking environment [1,2], and our current work in IP based anomaly detection.

To detect network/service anomalies and faults reliably and in real-time, two set of design factors are relevant, one set is algorithmic, the other system-related [1,2]. For network/service anomaly detection, algorithms should be:

- *Adaptive to the performance fluctuation and the evolution of networks and their services*
- *Performing detection in real-time*
- *A reliable (self-recovering) real-time system*
- *A flexible and distributed system*

It will be explained in detail that most fault detection systems to date do not achieve all of the above design goals, including algorithms and systems developed by other researchers and us [1–5,24–27]. The current IP network and service anomaly detection (IP NSAD) system reported in this paper fulfills these design requirements.

Traditionally, research and development in network fault management emphasize the detection and processing of network and element failures in the form of alarms [18]. For example, most network elements such as routers and switches are equipped with software agents (e.g., SNMP agents) that can emit traps/alarms upon detecting exceptional states such as a router interface being "down," or the utilization of a network segment exceeding a predefined threshold (e.g., a constant 80% threshold). Event correlation deals with inferring the root cause(s) of network faults from an avalanche of network alarms. Recent research and deployment testify to its usefulness in monitoring and controlling networks [19]. In network fault management, the past few years have also witnessed much progress in path failure detection (including break faults) [20–22], billing fraud detection in telecommunication voice networks

[23], anomaly detection in Ethernet [24,25], anomaly and performance change detection in small networks [26,27], and network alarm correlation [28–30]. With the advent and the explosive growth of the global Internet and the electronic commerce environments, adaptive/automatic network and service anomaly detection in IP wide area data networks and IP based E-commerce infrastructures (e.g., web based transaction infrastructures) is fast gaining critical research and practical importance [5]. In these cases, being able to proactively detect performance degradations (termed "soft" faults [1–5] as opposed to the "hard" alarms/failures of networks and their elements [18,19,28–30]) in networks and their services is becoming crucial for speedy fault recovery, and for preventing the onset of network/service failures.

Most of the developed algorithms and their implementations do not fully conform to the above algorithmic and system-related design requirements. For example, most fault detection systems built to date [1–3] are inflexible (meaning they are application specific) and unreliable. Therefore, they are not general-purpose anomaly detection platforms. Given the ever-accelerating development/deployment pace of new type of network services and new network-enabled applications, new types of application specific anomaly detectors are constantly required. Therefore, the lack of flexibility and generality in current fault detection systems may hinder their usefulness. On the algorithmic side, not all the algorithms designed [1–5,25–27] have been subject to controlled testing with realistic anomaly injection, which could have validated their effectiveness (e.g., detection hit rates, false positive rates, and so on). Instead, they were tested and optimized against historical network and service data and their corresponding historical fault information (usually in the form of trouble tickets) [1–5,25–27]. These fault information sources are notoriously hard to collect and unreliable. Even if available, they are not specific enough to enable vigorous testing and optimization. In our previous work [1,2], this problem was addressed (in a best effort way) by collecting very low-level, highly specific, and real-time trouble ticketing information for algorithmic verification. Nevertheless, the drawbacks were apparent [1,2].

Motivated by these algorithmic and system drawbacks in previous work, we recently designed a set of IP network/service anomaly detection algorithms, implemented a real-time distributed anomaly detection platform, and vigorously tested them. This platform is called the IP network and service anomaly detector (IP NSAD). Specifically, IP NSAD is:

- *Capable of adaptive and automated detection of anomalies in IP networks and their services in real time. NSAD uses as inputs SNMP based standard network/service observables such as MIB2 and RMON1/2 variables [31],*
- *Capable of objective driven and highly effective anomaly detection. In this case, anomaly detection is performed on performance objective functions (as opposed to raw network observables) which are algebraic functions of standard based network/service observables (MIB2, RMON1/2, etc.),*
- *A flexible platform on which pre-constructed components (such as network samplers, data filters, rule generators, and anomaly detectors, etc.) can be*

*mixed and matched (through an intuitive graphical user interface, GUI) for building application specific anomaly detectors,*

- *A fully distributed system in which system components can be distributed to different platforms, and*
- *A reliable real-time system in which components are dynamically self-recovering.*

This paper is structured as follows. An overview of the anomaly detection algorithms is presented in Section 2. Section 3 details the system architecture and implementation of the IP NSAD platform. Section 4 summarizes test results of IP NSAD. Finally, Section 5 provides a summary.

## 2 Algorithms for IP Network/Service Anomaly Detection

This section provides a summary of the anomaly detection algorithms, which is an extension of our previous work [1,2]. The anomaly detection algorithms can be grouped into three categories: (1) sampling and filtering algorithms, (2) statistical analysis and rule generation algorithms, and (3) anomaly detection algorithm.

A network anomaly detector is a real-time program that adaptively analyzes performance data of managed networks to detect "abnormal" changes (relative to historical baselines or "expected" behavior) in traffic and performance. These abnormalities are signatures of soft and hard faults. For IP networks, an anomaly detector analyzes SNMP based network observables (i.e., MIB2 and RMON1/2 variables [31]) to identify fault location, raise alarms, and generate control signals upon detection of performance anomalies and network faults.

The three steps of adaptive network anomaly detection are:

1. Network data sampling and filtering
   *For best effort correction of stochastic effects in network monitoring and for handling missing data.*

   MIB2 or RMON1/2 counter (or gauge) values [31] generated by network elements (e.g., routers, switches, etc.) or probes (RMON probes) are retrieved periodically (in a best effort way with predefined time intervals) through SNMP. This network performance sampling uses a "overstepping" algorithm which forces the time stamps of the return SNMP PDUs to be slightly (bounded) later than the predefined (or theoretical) retrieval time stamps, taking into account the stochastic network delays on the SNMP PDUs. This in effect minimizes error interpolation. The time stamps of the resulting counter values are closely aligned, but not exactly, to a regular schedule. This misalignment is due to stochastic fluctuations in network delay, which affect the arrival times (with respect to the regular schedule) of the SNMP PDUs. These counter values are interpolated to form a set of exactly regular time series. Interpolation is used to synthesize missing counter values for missing regions whose sizes do not exceed predefined bounds.

First and higher order derivatives of counters can be computed directly from their regular time series.

2. Temporal-based performance thresholds
   *For predicted or "expected" baselines and their fluctuations of network performances.*

By exploiting the temporal performance regularities of networks, performance baselines and thresholds of IP networks can be built for their MIB2 or RMON1/2 counters. These baselines and thresholds can be classified into four classes: weekdays, Saturdays, Sundays, and holidays. Historical data of service classes are used to construct these adaptive thresholds for each monitored MIB2 or RMON1/2 counter.

For each of the four threshold groups, a set of adaptive thresholds are built to predict the expected performance of network services on weekdays, Saturdays, Sundays, and holidays, respectively. Each set of dynamic thresholds (upper and lower thresholds) is composed of a predicted baseline $\tilde{I}_s\left(T_{n,s}\right)$ and tolerance

$$\text{upper\_threshold} = \tilde{I}_s\left(T_{n,s}\right) + 2\tilde{\sigma}_s\left(T_{n,s}\right)\Big|_{\substack{\text{wkdys}\\ \text{sats}\\ \text{suns}\\ \text{holiday}}} \tag{1}$$

$$\text{baseline} = \tilde{I}_s\left(T_{n,s}\right)\Big|_{\substack{\text{wkdys}\\ \text{sats}\\ \text{suns}\\ \text{holiday}}} \tag{2}$$

$$\text{lower\_threshold} = \tilde{I}_s\left(T_{n,s}\right) - 2\tilde{\sigma}_s\left(T_{n,s}\right)\Big|_{\substack{\text{wkdys}\\ \text{sats}\\ \text{suns}\\ \text{holiday}}} \tag{3}$$

$\tilde{\sigma}_s\left(T_{n,s}\right)$ (note: "~" denotes "predicted") as follows

The baseline $\tilde{I}_s\left(T_{n,s}\right)$ and tolerance $\tilde{\sigma}_s\left(T_{n,s}\right)$ are computed from historical MIB2 or RMON1/2 data (i.e., counters) through one-dimensional time series analysis and are classified into the "weekday", "Saturday", "Sunday", and "holiday" classes [1,2]. The $\tilde{I}_s\left(T_{n,s}\right)$s represent the predicted "average" counters, while the $\tilde{\sigma}_s\left(T_{n,s}\right)$s represent the predicted "average" fluctuations of the corresponding counters. Both $\tilde{I}_s\left(T_{n,s}\right)$s and $\tilde{\sigma}_s\left(T_{n,s}\right)$ are updated periodically to account for the evolution in network traffic.

The baseline $\tilde{I}_s\left(T_{n,s}\right)$ and tolerance $\tilde{\sigma}_s\left(T_{n,s}\right)$ can also be computed for objective functions, which are algebraic functions of raw network observables. These performance based objective functions provide sensitive measures of application specific performance. For example, an objective function can measure the traffic inbalance between the inbound traffic flowing into a network region and the outbound traffic. This objective function is

$$f_{obj}(t) = \frac{d}{dt}\left[\sum_{\text{interfaces}}(ifOctetIn + ifOctetOut)\right],\qquad(4)$$

where *ifOctetIn* and *ifOctetOut* are MIB2 counters that register byte counts into an out of an router interface. Finally, the summation is performed over all interfaces related to the network region. The resulting objective function (Equation 4) enables detection of traffic inbalance anomalies.

3. Anomaly detection
*For comparing expected baselines/fluctuations with current network states to measure departures from predicted performances, which are signatures of anomalies.*

Expected performance of IP networks are predicted through the above thresholds, and deviations (in both magnitude and duration, as defined by a set of fault criteria) from the expected are indications of network/service anomalies [1,2].

In anomaly detection, an alarm is raised that signaling the onset of a network/service anomaly if (1) the measured (in real-time) $I_{s,measured}(T_{n,s})$ at time $T_{n,s}$ deviates from the thresholds by more than $a$ from the predicted baseline, and (2) the previous condition persists and for more than $T_{persist}$, i.e.,

$$\left|\sum_{T}^{T_{persist}}E_s(T_{n,s})\right| \ge \sum_{T}^{T_{persist}}2\tilde{\sigma}_s(T_{n,s}),\qquad(5)$$

where

$$\text{if } I_{s,measured}(T_{n,s}) \le \left[\tilde{I}_s(T_{n,s}) - 2\tilde{\sigma}_s(T_{n,s})\right] - a\tilde{I}_s(T_{n,s}):$$
$$E_s(T_{n,s}) = I_{s,measured}(T_{n,s}) - \left[\tilde{I}_s(T_{n,s}) - 2\tilde{\sigma}_s(T_{n,s})\right] - a\tilde{I}_s(T_{n,s})\qquad(6)$$
$$\text{if } I_{s,measured}(T_{n,s}) \ge \left[\tilde{I}_s(T_{n,s}) + 2\tilde{\sigma}_s(T_{n,s})\right] + a\tilde{I}_s(T_{n,s}):$$
$$E_s(T_{n,s}) = I_{s,measured}(T_{n,s}) - \left[\tilde{I}_s(T_{n,s}) + 2\tilde{\sigma}_s(T_{n,s})\right] + a\tilde{I}_s(T_{n,s})\qquad(7)$$

The choice of the parameters in the above criteria ($a$ and $T_{persist}$) are determined experimentally. Finally, the detected anomaly is written to a diagnosis log that identifies the "guilty" elements and the possible cause(s) of anomaly. This information is presented to network operators through a graphic user interface (GUI).

# 3 System Architecture and Implementation of NSAD

In this section, the system architecture of the IP NSAD is presented. The corresponding implementation is also detailed.

The overall system architecture of the IP NSAD platform is shown in Figure 1, which presents the various system components that make up an anomaly detector. As will be explained in detail, these components are responsible for gathering network performance data from network elements or probes (samplers), numerically and arithmetically processing the gathered data (filters), statistically analyzing the gathered data (rule generators), and finally performing real-time anomaly detection (detectors). These components are monitored and controlled by a centralized master controller, which can distribute the above system components to different machines connected by LAN(s) or WAN(s). Thereby, computationally and network-bandwidth intensive operations (such as rule generation of predicted baselines and thresholds, and network sampling, respectively) can be distributed to a set of processors and network segments for load balancing and for enhancing reliability. Further, local traffic reduction (by distributing some of the filters) reduces the bandwidth required for subsections of the system and reduces the managed scope. This is especially important when configuring data collection and anomaly detection for a wide area network, in which firewalls or other policy managed domains may need to be traversed. Currently, platforms supported by the core NSAD components and their master controller include Sun's Solaris 7 and Microsoft's Windows NT 4.0. Human interaction with the NSAD platform is conducted through a graphical user interface (GUI), which enables system construction (i.e., building anomaly detectors from system components), configuration, and advanced performance/anomaly visualization of IP networks.

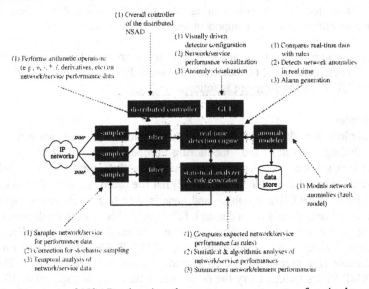

**Fig. 1.** Architecture of NSAD, showing the system components of a single anomaly detector.

In real applications, multiple anomaly detectors can be controlled and distributed by a master controller. For example, in an E-Commerce infrastructure composed of servers, routers, and Fast Ethernet switches, one detector may be used for web server anomaly detection (server overload, denial of service, etc.), while others may be configured to detect traffic anomalies by sampling router and switch performance data. This deployment of interrelated detectors in multiple points of a network is a key to effective performance monitoring and fault detection.

The architecture of NSADS is implementation-independent. It relies on a small number of behavioral and communication conventions. It consists of a number of simple system components (Figure 1) which are interconnected by communications links and provide time-stamped values (according to a fixed schedule) for further processing. The current implementation is in C for maximal efficiency. A Java version is planned and Inferno, CORBA and even hardware implementations are envisioned.

A detector instance is a configuration of an arbitrary number of these components, connected in a directed a-cyclic graph. The instance computes an objective function of the input observables, which can then be statistically modeled (Figure 1). Instances are configured from templates that describe generic versions of each supported detector type.

The user selects a supported type of fault detector interactively, then instantiates actual detectors with a minimal specification of bindings to the target network. Once instantiated and launched the detector is robust and generally requires no further user intervention, even in the presence of network failures. Adaptation to network growth is accommodated with simple editing of existing configurations. Scalability is provided by redistribution of component instances across the network.

The core system components of the NSAD platform include the (1) samplers, (2) filters, (3) rule generators, (4) detectors, (5) anomaly modeler, (6) master controller, and (7) GUI. Their functions are as follows.

- *Sampler*
  Samplers are data retrieval units that periodically poll network elements (including servers) and monitoring probes (e.g., RMON probes) for network/service performance data. Currently, they support (1) SNMP based (variable based and table based) and (2) flat file based retrieval. Therefore, MIB2 variables, RMON1/2 variables, and generic data (e.g., web server logs) can be retrieved periodically or on demand. Effectively, this module implements the first part of the anomaly detection algorithms outlined in Section 2. For periodic retrieval (i.e., with a fixed frequency), SNMP PDUs are generated on a fixed schedule (for example every 10 seconds starting at 0:00:00 GMT). The return SNMP PDUs (which carry the performance data) are not spaced at 10 seconds

interval, owing to the stochastic delay of the network(s) involved. Therefore, a "overstepping" algorithm is used to guarantee that every return PDU is displaced (time-wise) slightly later than the ideal 10 second time grid, without divergence (running over into the next time bin). Interpolation is used to realign the data back to a 10 second spaced (regular) time series. In addition, algorithms are provided to handle missing data. This sampling schedule (interval and start time) generate the clock for the entire system.

- *Filter*
  Filters perform numerical and arithmetic computation on sampled network data. Supported numerical operations include derivative calculations. Supported arithmetic operations include summation, difference, multiplication, and division. Using these filters, network observables (such as individual MIB2 or RMON1/2 variables) can be combined into performance objective functions for more effective anomaly detection. For example, traffic inbalance between inbound and outbound octet rates of a router can be measured and computed in real time.

- *Rule generator*
  Rule generators are the modules that implement the statistical analysis algorithms (second part of the algorithms outlined in Section 2) for generating predicted baselines and fluctuations of the performance variables or their objective functions. They analyze the stored historical performance data or their composite objective functions (filter outputs) of networks periodically, and compute the predicted baselines of these. Predicted fluctuations of the corresponding baselines are then computed. Rule generators are executed periodically, and infrequently compared to the frequency of real-time sampling. Typically, they are executed a few times per day (in our present system, every 12 hours). This means baselines and fluctuation rules for variables or objective functions are predicted for 12 hours periods on an ongoing basis (12 hours ahead of their use).

- *Detector*
  Detectors are executed in real time to detect network and service anomalies. They compare the predicted rules (in terms of baselines and their fluctuations) against their corresponding real time network data (or their objective functions) with respect to a set of anomaly criteria. These criteria are in the form of the algorithms outlines in Section 2 (part 3 of the set). Violations of the criteria are interpreted as anomalies. Degrees of violation are mapped to conditional probabilities, i.e., how likely the detected violations are real anomalies.

- *Graphic User Interface (GUI)*
  The GUI provides users the following functions. First, it provides advanced visualization capabilities for users to graphically view raw network performance, their statistical summaries, and network anomalies. Second, it enables users to graphically build anomaly detectors from components. Third, it allows the user to set system parameters (e.g., the machines on which to execute specific system components and the data sampling schedule). A screen shot of the NSAD GUI is shown in Figure 2, highlighting the detector construction and anomaly visualization functions. The GUI is written in Java, and is therefore platform independent. It can be remotely invoked through a web browser or executed as a standalone Java application (Figure 2).

- *Controller*

  A controller runs on each machine that will execute anomaly detector components. Typically, it is automatically initiated on machine boot. It launches and monitors all other components except rule generation. Failed components are re-spawned as necessary. Controllers communicate with one another on a well-known TCP port and mediate all communication between the GUI and other components.

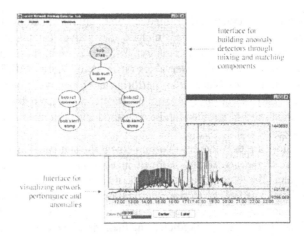

**Fig. 2.** A snapshot of the NSAD GUI.

The primary recovery mechanism provided by NSAD handles the loss of inter-component connections and file system unavailability. If a component detects the loss of a connection to any of its downstream or upstream connections, it simply terminates. This causes a cascade of terminations through the entire configuration. Even components hosted on other machines are cleanly shutdown so recovery can be initiated. Since the topmost component in any configuration is connected to the local controller, its termination initiates the recovery. If this connection is lost, the controller reinitiates the configuration using an exponential backoff strategy for repeated failures. If the controller fails, it is relaunched and then relaunches the components.

The combination of configuration files and controllers provides a mechanism for partitioning recovery. Any portion of a detector can be converted into a separate configuration. The topmost component of the new configuration will only terminate if it loses a downstream connection or the connection to the controller. This can be used to limit the downstream propagation of failures. When the upstream components have recovered from a non-local failure, they will reconnect to the subsystem.

If the local file system becomes unavailable, local components are prevented from recording their values. Instead, they queue values in available memory and log requests for operator intervention. If the rule bases are unavailable, the detector logs the problem and becomes quiescent.

Scalability is provided through the distributed nature of the detector and the use of remote aggregation to limit the quantity of data which must be moved upstream over any single link.

## 4   An Application and Preliminary Test Results

This section provides an example of IP anomaly detection, and a summary of some initial test results performed in our specially developed controlled testbed, where anomalies are injected to test the algorithmic performance of the IP NSAD.

Construction of anomaly detector(s) can be done intuitively through the GUI by a series of drag-and-drop steps, and the filling in of some system related and functional parameters (e.g., IP addresses for data polling and polling frequencies, respectively). Figure 3 shows an example of constructing an anomaly detector through the NSAD GUI. In this case, an anomaly detector is constructed to monitor the overall (summation of inbound and outbound) traffic (byte count) rate tranversing a router interface. The objective function being monitored is rate of the summation of the inbound-outbound interface octet counts, i.e.,

$$f_{obj}(t) = \frac{d}{dt}(ifOctetIn + ifOctetOut), \tag{8}$$

which is a sensitive measure of the traffic and load conditions on a subnetwork, as well as the health of a router interface.

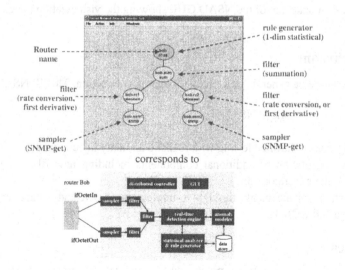

**Fig. 3.** A snapshot of the NSAD GUI, showing the detector construction .panel, and the corresponding anomaly detector.

In this case, the rule generator generates the dynamic baselines and fluctuations of the objective function (Equation 7). Figure 4 shows traffic anomalies detected by the detector.

To enable controlled testing of IP NSAD, we have constructed a special-purpose network testbed. This generates realistic background traffic, and can inject anomalies of different classes (e.g., web server overload, traffic storm, etc.) [32]. Preliminary results indicate that NSAD is capable of highly accurate anomaly detection. For example, in anomaly detection of web servers, the average hit rate exceeds 98%, with 2% of false positives.

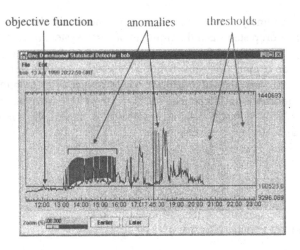

**Fig. 4.** A snapshot of the NSAD GUI, showing the visualization panel.

## 5   Conclusions

We have developed a general platform for IP anomaly detection. This IP NSAD

Ongoing and future work IP NSAD include:

- Vigorous controlled testing with realistic anomaly injections,
- Implementation of additional components including new filters, samplers, and rule generators, and
- System enhancements through re-implementing selected components with Java and CORBA.

## References

1.   Ho, L.L., Cavuto, D.J., Papavassiliou, S., Hasan, M.Z., Feather, F.E., Zawadzki, A.G., "Adaptive Network/Service Fault Detection in Transaction-Oriented Wide Area Networks," *Proceedings of the Sixth IFIP/IEEE*

*International Symposium on Integrated Network Management (IM'99)*, Edt. M. Sloman, S. Mazumdar, and E. Lupu, (IEEE Press), to appear in May 1999.

2. Ho, L.L., Cavuto, D.J., Papavassiliou, S., Zawadzki, A.G., "Adaptive and Automated Detection of Network/Service Anomalies in Wide Area Networks," *Journal of Network and Systems Management*, to appear in 1999.

3. Thottan, M., Ji, C., "Fault Prediction at the Network Layer using Intelligent Agents," *Proceedings of the Sixth IFIP/IEEE International Symposium on Integrated Network Management (IM'99)*, Edt. M. Sloman, S. Mazumdar, and E. Lupu, (IEEE Press), to appear in May 1999.

4. Hood, C. and Ji, C., `` Intelligent Processing Agents for Network Fault Detection", *IEEE Internet Computing*, Vol. 2, No. 2, March/April 1998

5. Hellerstein, J.L., Zhang, F., Shahabuddin, P., "An Approach to Predictive Detection for Service Management," *Proceedings of the Sixth IFIP/IEEE International Symposium on Integrated Network Management (IM'99)*, Edt. M. Sloman, S. Mazumdar, and E. Lupu (IEEE Press), to appear in May 1999.

6. Huberman, B.A., Lukose, R.M., "Social Dilemmas and Internet Congestion," *Science*, Vol. 277, p. 535, July 1997.

7. Held, G., *LAN Testing and Troubleshooting: Reliability Tuning Techniques*, John Wiley & Sons, 1996.

8. Ballew, S.M., *Managing IP Networks*, O'Reilly & Associates, 1997.

9. Miller, M.A., *Troubleshooting Internetworks*, M&T Publishing, 1991.

10. Espinosa, R., Tripod, M., Tomic, S., *Cisco Router Configuration & Troubleshooting*, New Riders, 1998.

11. Kumar, V.P., Lakshman, T.V., Stiliadis, D., "Beyond Best-Effort: Gigabit Routers for Tomorrow's Internet," *IEEE Communications Magazine*, V36(5), p152, May 1998

12. White, P.P., "RSVP and Integrated Services in the Internet: A Tutorial," *IEEE Communications Magazine*, V35(5), p100, 1997.

13. Reininger, D., " A Dynamic Quality of Service Framework for Video in Broadband Networks," *IEEE Network*, V12(6), p22, 1998.

14. Lazar, A.A., Wang, W., Deng, R., "Models and Algorithms for Network Fault Detection and Identification: A Review," *ICC Singapore*, Nov. 1992.

15. Parulkar, G., Schmidt, D., Kraemer, E., Turner, J., Kantawala, A., "An Architecture for Monitoring, Visualization, and Control of Gigabit Networks," *IEEE Networks*, p.34, Sept/Oct, 1997.

16 Katzela, I. Schwartz, M., "Schemes for Fault Identification in Communication Networks," *IEEE/ACM Trans. Networking*, Vol. 3(6), p.753, Dec, 1995.

17. Aidarous, S. (Edt.), Plevyak (Edt.), "Telecommunications Network Management: Technologies and Implementations," *IEEE Series on Network Management*, (IEEE Press, 1998).

18. Aidarous, S. (Edt.), Plevyak (Edt.), "Telecommunications Network Management into the 21st Century: Techniques, Standards, Technologies, and Applications," (IEEE Press, 1994).

19. Yemini, S., Kliger, S., Mozes, E., Yemini, Y., Ohsie, D., "High Speed and Robust Event Corrrelation," *IEEE Communication Magazine*, May 1996.

20.  Wang, C., Schwartz, M., "Fault Diagnosis of Network Connectivity Problems by Probabilistic Reasoning," *Network Management and Control Volume Two* (Ed. Frisch, I.T., Malek, M., Panwar, S.S.), p.67, (Plenum Press 1994).

21.  Dawes, N., Altoft, J., Pagurek, B., "Network Diagnosis by Reasoning in Uncertain Nested Evidence Spaces," *IEEE Transactions on Communications*, Vol. 43, p.466, 1995.

22.  Cortes, C., Jackel, L.D., Chiang, W., "Limits on Learning Machine Accuracy Imposed by Data Quality," *Proceedings of NIPS94 - Neural Information Processing Systems: Natural and Synthetic Pagination*, p. 239, (MIT Press 1994).

23.  Cox, R.M., "Detecting Lost Billing Records Using Kalman Filters," *AT&T Labs Preprint* (submitted), Oct. 1997.

24.  Feather, F.E., Siewiorek, D., Maxion, R., "Fault Detection in an Ethernet Using Anomaly Signature Matching," *ACM SIGCOMM'93*, 23(4), 1993.

25.  Maxion, R., Feather, F.E., "A Case Study of Ethernet Anomalies in a Distributed Computing Environment," *IEEE Transactions on Reliability*, 39(4), Oct 1990.

26.  Hood, C., Ji, C., "Proactive Network Fault Detection," *IEEE Trans. Reliability*, Vol. 46, No. 3, p.333, 1997.

27.  Hood, C., Ji, C., "Proactive Network Fault Detection," *Proceeding IEEE INFOCOM*, 1997.

28.  Jakobson, G., Weissman, M.D., "Alarm Correlation," *IEEE Network*, p. 52, Nov 1993.

29.  Katker, S., Paterok, M., "Fault Isolation and Event Correlation for Integrated Fault Management," *Proceedings of the Fifth IFIP/IEEE International Symposium on Integrated Network Management*, p. 583, 1997.

30.  Hasan, M.Z., Sugla, B., Viswanathan, R., "A Conceptual Framework for Network Management Event Correlation and Filtering System," *Proceedings of the Sixth IFIP/IEEE International Symposium on Integrated Network Management (IM'99)*, Edt. Edt. M. Sloman, S. Mazumdar, and E. Lupu, (IEEE Press), to appear in May 1999.

31.  Stallings, W., "SNMP, SNMPv2, SNMPv3, and RMON 1 and 2," (Addison-Wesley, 1999).

32.  Ho, L.L., Macey, C., Hiller, R., *in preparation*, 1999.

# Session 2

# Management Components and Multi-domain Management

*Chair: Seraphin B. Calo*
*IBM Research, U.S.A.*

# Integrating Service and Network Management Components for Service Fulfilment

David Lewis[1], Chris Malbon[1], George Pavlou[2], Costas Stathopoulos[3], Enric Jaen Villoldo[2]

1: Department of Computer Science, University College London, UK
{dlewis, cmalbon}@cs.ucl.ac.uk
2: Centre for Communications Systems Research, University of Surrey, UK
(g.pavlou, eexlej}@ee.surrey.ac.uk
3: Algo Systems, Athens, Greece
stathop@algo.com.gr

**Abstract.** Solutions in the network and service management layers of telecommunications management architectures are currently fragmented both in terms of standards and products. It is often, therefore, difficult for the developers of management systems to reuse and integrate management software from different sources in cost-effective solutions spanning the various TMN layers. This paper presents the analysis, architecture and design of a system that integrates service and network management building blocks in order to satisfy business process requirements for service order fulfilment. The presented system deals with network planning and provisioning according to network usage predictions based on customer subscription requests. It shows how component technology is used to provide a flexible and extensible telecommunication business solution.

**Keywords:** CORBA Components, TM Forum Business Processes, TINA Service and Network Architecture, Component Integration

## 1    INTRODUCTION

Mature telecommunication management standards exist largely at the element and network management layers of the TMN logical layer architecture but there is little in the way of standard information models or architectural guidance to those wishing to integrate management software across the network to service management layer boundary. One industrial body that has attempted to address both service and network management in an open and integrated way is the TeleManagement Forum (TM Forum). It has developed a business process model [1] that, based on surveys of major service providers, gives a detailed breakdown of the set of business processes that typically encompass a service provider's operations management activities. The interactions required between processes in different providers are also identified. This model, summarised in Figure 1, is intended for use as the basis for identifying the requirements for the ongoing development of agreements on common interfaces and information models within the TM Forum. The model is partitioned into processes that relate to customer care, to internal service development and maintenance and to the management of the provider's networks and systems. The processes are also grouped vertically into major service management areas, i.e. the fulfillment/delivery of the service, the assurance/maintenance of the service and the billing/accounting for the service. Individual processes are defined in terms of activities within the process and of input and output triggers to the process.

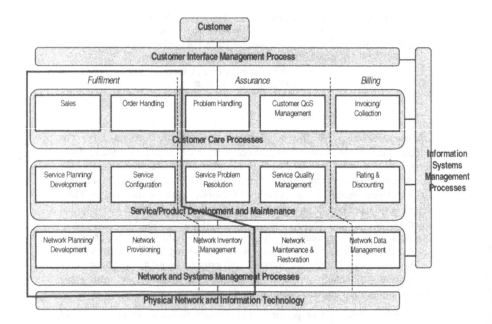

**Fig. 1.** TM Forum Business Process Model

Few of the information agreements that have emerged from the TM Forum to date have addressed vertical interactions between service and network level processes. However without guidance on how to develop open interfaces between management systems operating in different logical layers within a TMN there will be a tendency for commercial solutions to be proprietary stovepipes, e.g. between network level accounting and service level billing software.

A similar situation exists in the Telecommunications Information Networking Architecture Consortium (TINA-C). This group has aimed to develop a comprehensive architecture for telecommunications control and management based on Open Distributed Processing principles as defined by ITU-T in [2]. It generated detailed models for the integrated control and management of multimedia services and broadband networks based on existing concepts from TMN, IN and ATM. Service Management, principally subscription and accounting management, has been addressed in the TINA Service Architecture [3]. Network Management has been addressed in the Network Resource Architecture [4], which draws heavily on existing network management models, e.g. M.3100, in the structure of its Network Resource

Information Model (NRIM) [5]. Both these architectures have exploited ODP concepts and component-oriented models to integrate management functionality with service and network control. However, the only area where management interaction between the two architectures is currently well defined is connection management, which really is addressing control plane concerns.

A telecommunications management system developer faced with the need to integrate service and network management systems can use the TM Forum business process model to analyse their high level requirements. They can then draw on ITU-T, TM Forum or TINA-C specifications for specific service or network level management interfaces. However, there is little available guidance on the integration of such open solutions across business processes that reside in both the service and network management layers. The development of such guidance is the subject of research in the EU ACTS funded FlowThru project. FlowThru is developing guidelines to aid management system developers to construct systems assembled from reusable components that implement business process interactions. In addition, these guidelines will address how system assembly can be supported by new technologies such as Workflow, Enterprise Java Beans (EJB), CORBA Components and management protocol gateways.

This paper describes the solution to a management problem spanning both the service and network management layers. It specifically addresses process interactions in the fulfilment area of the TM Forum's business process model, as outlined in bold in Figure 1. This involved the integration of subscription management with network planning and provisioning for a switched network service. The approach taken shows how a CORBA component-based approach has been used to integrate existing software components in a loosely coupled fashion and in an easily extensible manner. This solution involved applying TM Forum industry agreements to existing TINA specified components that were themselves the products of previous research projects.

The next section details the fulfilment problem being addressed and puts it in the context of existing TINA and TM Forum specifications. Section 3 reviews the features of the components that were assembled in developing the solution and how they were assembled and modified to satisfy the problem requirements. Conclusions are drawn in section 4.

## 2 PROBLEM ANALYSIS

The problem addressed by this work is the integration of management functions in the service and network management layers related to the fulfilment of customer orders. The problem analysis considers orders for a switched ATM service, though the outlined system is applicable to any communications service that involved the dynamic allocation of resources. A customer could range from a single-terminal, domestic users through to corporate users with switched ATM customer premises equipment, supporting a number of users via a single UNI.

In terms of the TM Forum's business process model, the problem domain focused on the fulfilment process and consisted of the following business processes:

- Customer Care Process: This involved the management of the interactions between the customer and the provider's management system, in particular translating customer requests and queries into appropriate system operations.
- Order Handling: This involved the receipt, processing and tracking of orders for services from a customer and their translation into corresponding requests for network configuration changes.
- Service Configuration: This involved the installation and configuration of a service for a specific customer, including any customer premises equipment.
- Network Provisioning: This involved the reconfiguration of network resources so that network capacity is ready for the provisioning of services.
- Network Planning and Development: This process was responsible for designing the network capability to meet specified service needs at the desired cost and within operational constraints (e.g. QoS requirements), determined principally by service level agreement with customers.
- Network Inventory Management: This involved the installation of physical equipment in the network, i.e. trunks, subscriber lines, switches.

Though the Service Planning and Development is included by the TM Forum in this area of the business process model, it did not play a part in this solution. Within the context of TINA, the problem may be expressed in terms of business roles and reference points between these roles as defined in [6]. A mapping had already been suggested in [7] between the business roles defined by TINA-C and the business processes in the TM Business Process Model. Based on this, Figure 2 shows the overall business context of the problem being addressed in terms of the business roles played by the organisations involved, the business processes undertaken by those roles and the TINA reference points that exist between those roles. This mapping aided system developers understand where existing models from TINA and the TM Forum could be applied, as well as helping them position the resulting solutions for contribution to future standards.

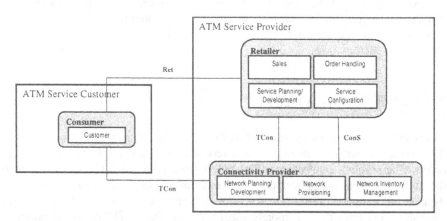

**Fig. 2.** Business Process to Business role mapping for ATM Service Fulfilment problem.

As the business problem under examination did not involve multiple providers, the federation reference points between the roles within the ATM Service Provider (available in the full TINA business model) were dropped. As the focus of this work was on the development of functions in the management plane, aspects of network and service control were assumed but not analysed or developed any further. The TCon reference point, which dealt with control of network level interconnection, was not examined on the assumption that existing UNI protocols would be used for connection set-up. Instead, the focus was placed on the management interactions that occurred across the Ret and ConS reference points. The Ret reference point was derived from the TINA service architecture that included a detailed model of how customer subscriptions and user's individual profiles could be managed as described in the section on the subscription management component below. ConS was extended with additional network configuration and planning management features as specified by the REFORM project and described in the sections on Configuration Management and Network Planning [8].

Existing TINA-specified models provided a core set of concepts that could be used in further analysing the requirements of the ATM service fulfilment business problem and the requirements for interactions between the business processes identified as being relevant to this problem. The key concepts were:

- Network Access Point (NAP): This is the representation within the service provider of the point on the network via which the customer uses the switched ATM service. This offers a UNI to the customer and can support multiple simultaneous connections.
- Class of Service (CoS): To restrain the complexity of the network dimensioning problem while at the same time offering useful service definitions to the customer, the notion of CoS is introduced to quantise the space made up by ATM QoS types and the parameter ranges they may exhibit.
- Service Usage Group (SUG): This is derived from the TINA subscription management model and represents a group of users who may use a particular type of service, defined as a service profile. It also defines the set of network access point from which this group of users can access this service profile.

To analyse the problem further, business roles within the business stakeholders were analysed to determine the responsibilities they have with respect to each other. Based on these responsibilities, use cases were drawn up documenting the functionality of the whole business system from the perspective of the actors who play the business roles. The use cases effectively defined the scope of the scenarios being addressed. They were restricted to the following:

- Adding and withdrawing a class of service to/from those that a customer may use when subscribing to the ATM service.
- Customer ATM service subscription: providing contractual and accounting information on the customer; specifying the physical sites from where the customer will use the service together with lists of users at each site; the classes of service they will use and under which service level agreement parameters they will use them.
- Adding or removing a site from which the customer's users may use the services.
- Authorising or barring a user from being able to use the service.

However, much direct analysis of the internal business processes, intra-component interactions still had to be identified. This was solved by breaking down individual use cases into separate activities that could be represented in a UML activity diagram, see Figure 3. By representing TM Forum business processes as a set of swim lanes and placing each activity in the appropriate lane, activities could be grouped by business process. As each business process could be encapsulated by a component, intra-component interactions were determined by examining the information exchange required to progress from one activity to the next.

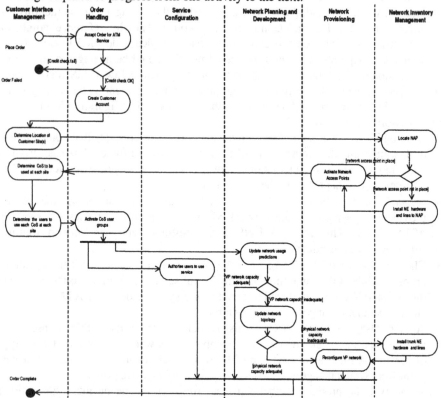

**Fig. 3.** Activity diagram for subscribe customer to ATM service use case

The next section presents how this analysis was mapped onto the design of existing management components and the identified interactions with respect to the outlined use-cases.

# 3 INTEGRATED SYSTEM DESIGN

The development of the system analysed in the previous section was driven by the fact that most of the required functionality was already available as existing components, the re-use of which was a key concern. These components were the results of previous research projects that had implemented and extended portions of the TINA specification set, implementing systems focusing in either the service or the network management layer.

The need for reuse and integration of existing software led to a component-based development approach. Typically, components can be defined as independently deliverable packages of software services. It is worth noticing that component-based development can co-exist with OO analysis and development. While the later is focusing on analysing and designing systems under a specific business problem, at the same time it is useful to perform the packaging of the developed system into a set of self-descriptive, application-independent components using the modelling constructs of a component technology.

This section describes how elements of the emerging CORBA component model [9] were used for modelling, packaging and seamlessly integrating the components of our system. It shows how the utilisation of a component technology provides easy component assembly and integration in a system designed using the OO development methodology. Three components (cf. Table 1) were identified, modelled and integrated according to a subset of the CORBA component model.

| Components | Business Process |
|---|---|
| Subscription Management | Order Handling<br>Service Configuration |
| Configuration Management | Network Provisioning<br>Network Inventory Management |
| Network Planner | Network Planning/Development |

**Table 1.** Building Blocks and their mapping to relevant Business Processes

Before describing how the merits of the component technology were exploited, the functionality of the components is outlined in the next subsection. Based on this high level description of the functionality of the components, **Table 1** shows how they mapped onto the TM Forum business processes relevant to the fulfilment problem.

## 3.1 Components

### 3.1.1 Subscription Management

The Subscription Management component comprises all the management functions needed in order to define service offerings, administer customers and users, and manage the details of service provisioning. The design is based on the subscription model developed in TINA [3]. The use cases implemented by the component cover the management of service offerings, of subscribers and of subscriptions. Management of service offering is concerned with the definition and adaptation of offered telecommunications services, from a management point of view. Management of subscribers consists of the creation and deletion of subscribers, the update of subscriber details, and the definition of subscriber's end-user groups and network sites. Finally, subscription management covers subscribing customers to services, update subscription details, cancel subscriptions, and the authorisation of end-users for specific services.

The component is decomposed into Computational Objects (CO). These define separate functional units needed to manage subscriber organisations and end-users, different types of services, and subscriptions to these services. The COs includes Service Template Handler, Subscriber Manager, Subscription Registrar, and Subscription Agent. The Subscriber Manager CO manages information associated to subscribers, e.g., subscriber details and user groups. The Service Template Handler CO is responsible for handling service templates that represent service capabilities provided by the provider. The Subscription Registrar CO acts on behalf of a provider in dealing with subscribers wishing to subscribe to a service and establish a service level agreement. The Subscription Agent CO is closely related to the User Agent CO that manages the access session of the TINA Service Architecture. A separate management application is typically used to allow customer administrators or provider administrators to access the subscription component.

The implementation of the subscription management component used for this problem was developed in the Prospect project, where it was reused in several different services. The definition of the component assumed a predominantly synchronous mode of operation in its interactions with users and other service control and management components. However, the analysis of the fulfilment problem in the previous section revealed that the overall fulfilment process involved unbounded delays due to network installations and reconfigurations. The subscription management component therefore had to offer an interface to users that would enable them to manage prolonged order processing by the provider's systems. A further CO, the Order Handler, was added to deal with the reception, tracking and possible cancellation of orders received from customers. The basic abstractions used in this component were taken from the TM Forum's Order Handling business agreement [10].

### 3.1.2 Configuration Management

The Configuration Management (CM) component spans the network and element management layers of the TMN hierarchy. Its scope is in general two-fold: to maintain a map of network resources both for inventory purposes and also for showing the topological relationships among resources; and to support the activation, deactivation, reservation and release of resources. The CM component presents a "server" interface to other components e.g. to Subscription Management and Network Planning and Dimensioning in the case of the fulfilment system described in this paper. In addition, it acts as a client to network nodes with management interfaces e.g. to ATM switches.

In TMN systems, configuration information is typically held in one or more hierarchically organised network Operation Systems (OSs), whose model conforms to the Generic Network Element Information Model [11] and to the emerging ITU-T Network Information Model. In the case of TINA, configuration information is split in two parts: dynamic information, concerning on-demand or semi-permanent trails, which is held in the Connection Management (CM) subsystem; and static information, which is held in the Resource Configuration Management (RCM) subsystem. In both cases, a client of the CM component may request the activation/deactivation of a resource, e.g. of a NAP for a particular subscriber, or the reservation and release of a resource, e.g. an ATM VP trail for planning and provisioning purposes.

The CM component in FlowThru comes from the REFORM and VITAL projects, which used TINA instead of TMN principles. Given the fact that TINA concentrates mostly on Connection Management which covers the equivalent control aspects, modifications and extensions were necessary. TINA prescribes the Network Resource Information Model [5], which is based on equivalent ITU-T models, but the associated information objects are "hidden" behind computational interfaces. The NRIM model was extended while a CORBA-based computational object with TMN Q3-like IDL interface was designed to provide access to those objects in a flexible fashion [12]. An additional important architectural consideration was that the distinction between static and dynamic resources was not considered appropriate.

The CM component comprises two computational objects: the ConfM Network Map (ConfM-NM), which acts in a similar fashion to a TMN configuration OS; and the ConfM Connection Manager (ConfM-CM), which establishes and releases VP trails. The ConfM-NM embodies the functionality of TINA RCM while the ConfM-CM embodies the functionality of TINA CM. The difference is that Conf-NM holds also dynamic resources, e.g. VP trails, providing a consistent view of all the necessary information for planning and provisioning purposes. An additional interface to the ConfM-NM object is being developed in FlowThru for presenting a customised facility for NAP management to the Subscription Management component.

### 3.1.3 Network Planning and Dimensioning

The Network Planner (NP) component is located at the network management level of the TMN hierarchy. From a TM Forum's viewpoint, it maps to the "Network Planning and Development" process.

More specifically, the Network Planner consists of the following three subsystems:
- The Class Of Service Model (CoSM) subsystem.
  The CoSM maintains a repository of the CoSs supported by the network. Each CoS is defined in terms of its bandwidth characteristics, performance targets and restoration characteristics. It should be noted that the CoSM restricts, yet is based on, the services offered to users through the Subscription Management component.
- The Predicted Usage Model (PUM) subsystem.
  The functionality of the PUM encompasses the maintenance of a valid model of the anticipated traffic to the network. Based on this model, the PUM supplies the VPC_TD (see below) with traffic predictions, required for the design of the VP layer. The VP layer (set of VPCs) and the static aspects of the VC layer (set of admissible routes per source-destination and CoS) are constructed so that to satisfy the predicted traffic demand.
  - Anticipated traffic is modelled in terms of the numbers of connection requests per CoS between source-destination pairs. The anticipated traffic model will be acquired from information regarding the subscribers of the network. This

information is given by the Subscription Management component and it describes: the number of users that are subscribed to use the network; the specific sources (i.e. the customer's NAPs) that generate traffic; and the specific CoS characteristics of the traffic. The information regarding the CoS being used is extracted by the Subscription Management component by mapping the QoS characteristics of the services (as in SLAs) to network CoSs.

Additionally, data regarding historical network traffic will be taken into account in order to make predictions as accurate as possible. Normally, the model needs to be validated and modified against actual network usage. However, this is not considered within the context of FlowThru.

- The VPC Topology Design (VPC_TD) subsystem.

The objective of VPC_TD is to design and redesign, whenever necessary, working VPCs and sets of admissible routes taking into account the existing CoSs. In addition, the existing component also designs suitable protection VPCs and allocates the appropriate amount of protection resources, thus providing for a resilient network design. VPC_TD's task is based on the predicted traffic and the physical constraints (e.g. connectivity, capacity of ATM links) of the network. These input parameters are subject to changes over the lifetime of a network. VPC_TD offers a certain level of flexibility to adapt to such changes.

The tasks of designing VPCs and routes based on them are not seen in isolation as they are tightly coupled; routes are based on VPCs; and VPCs are defined for routing. Along with these tasks, the tasks of designing appropriate protection VPCs and subsequently allocating protection resources across the network is considered. All these tasks are part of an iterative process involving complex optimisation problems aiming at providing cost-effective design solutions. The optimisation targets are set according to the business policy of the network operator. Part of this process will be to identify all possible routes between source and destinations and to choose a certain subset of these, according to the performance targets of the CoSs to be carried.

## 3.2 Component Interactions and Modelling

Each component possessed a set of pre-defined IDL interfaces that had to be preserved to maintain access to its core services. Additional component functionality and the information that needed to pass between the components was analysed using activity diagrams detailing each use-case. The identified component interactions are summarised below:

- The Subscription requires information on the available network-level CoSs to: create service records to which a customer can subscribe; define a set of QoS parameter limits to offer different SLAs for each service
- The Configuration Manager must know what NAPs are needed by a customer so that existing NAPs can be activated or new NAPs installed if none currently existed
- The Network Planner needs to be informed as new NAPs are activated for subscribed customers so that the Predicted Usage Model can be recalculated

- The Network Planner requires information on both the number of users at each NAP and the CoS to which they are subscribed, both influence the Predicted Usage Model
- NAP and user updates must be acknowledged by the Network Planner to indicate to what level each request can be accommodated within an existing SLA
- A user application for the service customer was required. This sends various subscription orders to Subscription Management and needs to be informed of changes in the status of these orders as they go through the various stages of fulfillment.

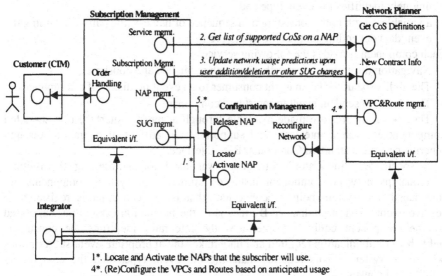

1*. Locate and Activate the NAPs that the subscriber will use.
4*. (Re)Configure the VPCs and Routes based on anticipated usage
5*. Release NAP(s) that the subscriber no longer uses (or when unsubscribed)

**Fig. 4.** Interactions sequence for a subscriber's lifecycle

Figure 4 depicts the component interactions and the integration approach followed. The sequence of interactions between the subscription management, the configuration management, and network planning components for a subscription lifecycle are given in Figure 4. These interactions and the accompanying IDL definitions could form additional management segments to the TINA ConS reference points. The interactions 3, 4 and 5 can repeatedly happen through the lifetime of a subscription as the customer adds or removes new users and sites.

To promote loose coupling of the components an asynchronous event-based approach to component interaction was taken. An event-based approach was also seen as essential for the Order handler CO in the Subscription Manager which had to mediate the progression of orders between the customer application and the other components.

To better support these interactions, the existing components were modelled by means of a CORBA-based component model. As work towards the specification of a CORBA Component Model is still ongoing (cf. [9]), current CORBA platforms do not provide support for building components as of this writing. However, a subset of the forthcoming component model suitable for our purposes was implemented. More specifically, part of the event model, as well as navigation through supported events, as in [9], was implemented. The consumer/publisher terminology introduced in the same specification is also used throughout.

The design borrows heavily from the Model-View-Controller classes used to build user interfaces in Smalltalk-80 and described in [13] as the Observer design pattern, and more recently deployed in the JDK 1.0+/JavaBeans Delegation Event Model and the CORBA component specification [9].

- An event is described by a simplified version of the Structured Event, specified in the CORBA Notification Service [14], and comprises a fixed-length header that uniquely identifies the event type and
- a variable-length body consisting of a sequence of name-value pairs, containing the event data depending on the type of the event.

Each component provides the following services

- Navigation through the events that are both published and consume.
- The ability to subscribe an event consumer to an event publisher of a component.
- The ability to send an event to registered components.

The above features are made available through a generic interface (the so-called component equivalent interface) and support a standard set of operations through inheritance from a standard ComponentBase interface.

A specialised "integrator" component was used for configuring the runtime relationships between component instances. Initially, all system components are introduced into system being unconnected (that is, no consumer is registered to receive events from a publisher). By means of the navigation capabilities supported by the component equivalent interfaces the integrator identifies the consumer-publisher communication required and undertakes the appropriate event subscriptions within the system. This requires matching the event types that the components publish and consume.

In our prototype component model implementation, the run-time environment is rather simple, providing for no Containers. However, even with this prototype it is possible to easily plug our components in different systems. The separation of the integrator component enables this role to be played in future system by software configuration applications or possibly workflow based systems with knowledge of event types and component features.

In the above example, design coupling between components is better targeted compared to components with synchronous interfaces by employing standardised event registration and message passing interfaces. An event consumer uses a well-known registration interface to notify a publisher of its desire to receive the latter's events. Events are passed from event publisher to event consumer via a standardised message-passing interface. This enables components to exchange information with only knowledge of the individual event they are interested in, rather than having to bind to an interface definition that may contain many operations that are not of interest.

New functionality in the form of additional event protocols can be created without impacting existing component design couplings. Also, it is possible to introduce components that may be interested in consuming events for reasons other than their original intention, for instance some of the events from our system could be monitored by additional systems measuring the response times to customer order requests.

Components that receive events for which they have no semantic understanding may simply choose to log them or perform some other generic processing on them. We were able to exploit this final point by creating an event listener capable of demonstrating real-time information exchanges occurring in the system. Because the event listener was registered with all event publishers, each publisher notified the listener whenever it emitted an event. Registration was performed so that there was no need for publisher and consumer to enter into the normal event protocol dialogue, the event listener merely recorded and displayed events. Frameworks can be deployed to expose event interfaces and connect them to consuming components in the same way as our simple integrator component. This allows the flow of information and control between components to be managed more flexibly, being less tightly-coupled to the design of the components themselves. This feature is compatible with the workflow-based approach to OSS integration. Threading ensures that a component is not suspended pending a reply to a given request. This avoids locking problems that may occur in synchronous systems as they are expanded with chains of synchronous requests. The event-based approach still embodies some design coupling between components. In order to process an emitted event a consumer must know how to process a known set of event types. This is a fact from which no component can escape - a consumed event must trigger some predicted action even if this is to ignore it.

## 4   CONCLUSIONS

This paper shows how problems spanning both the service and network management layer can be analysed using a combination of business processes (as advocated by the TM Forum) and business roles and reference point segments (as advocated by TINA-C).

The paper further shows, through an example, how such analysis is compatible with the construction of software solutions from existing components. Moreover, it illustrates how the use of UML Activity diagrams mapped to TMF advocated business processes can aid the design of those component extensions needed to effect successful inter-connection.

We have shown that the flexible reuse and integration of off-the-shelf software is possible through the exploitation of current component technology, particularly its asynchronous event-messaging. At a practical level, system functionality was extended through the introduction of event logging and monitoring components.

The use of the integrator object demonstrates how dynamic event identification and configuration can also be used to further improve flexibility by reducing component coupling to a runtime configuration issue. This can be enhanced through the development of component and event repositories: a component repository providing a central location within which component interfaces details are stored; an event repository performing a similar task by enabling events to be defined at runtime.

Furthermore, event adapters can be deployed between producers and consumers to further customise the event messaging at the component level.

Event coupling is unavoidable, an event is designed to trigger some action in a recipient. However, by using a non-blocking asynchronous event model, coupling can be reduced to a set of generic message passing and registration interfaces. The identification of common event types within a given problem domain would be one approach to reduce event coupling. International bodies such as the TM Forum being instrumental in this through further analysis and development of their business process model to encompass the definition of common event types between processes.

## ACKNOWLEDGEMENTS

The work presented in the paper was conducted with partial funding of the European Commission under the FlowThru project (AC335). The views expressed here are not necessarily those of the FlowThru consortium.

## REFERENCES

[1] NMF Telecoms Operations Map, NMF GB910, Stable Draft 0.2b, April 1998.

[2] Information Technology- Open Distributed Processing- Reference Model- part 1: Overview, ITU-T Draft Recommendation X.901/ ISO/IEC Draft International Standard 10746-1, 1995.

[3] Service Architecture, ed. L. Kristiansen, TINA-C, version 5.0, 1997.

[4] Network Resource Architecture Version 3.0, TINA-C baseline document, Feb. 1997.

[5] Network Resource Information Model Specification, TINA-C baseline document TB LR.010 2.1 95, 1995

[6] Reference Points and Business Model, TINA-C, Version 3, June 1996.

[7] Lewis, D., A Development Framework for Open Management Systems, Interoperable Communication Networks, vol 2/1, Baltzer Science Publishers, March 1999

[8] Final REFORM System Specifications and Architecture, The REFORM Consortium, July 1998.

[9] CORBA Components: Joint Revised Submission. OMG TC Document orbos/99-02-05, Draft, March 1999.

[10] SMART Ordering SP to SP Interface Business Agreement, NMF 504, issue 1.00, September 1997.

[11] Generic Network Information Model, ITU-T Recommendation M.3100, 1992.

[12] Pavlou, G., Griffin, D., Realizing TMN-like Management Services in TINA, Journal of Network and System Management (JNSM), Special Issue on TINA, Vol. 5, No. 4, pp. 437-457, Plenum Publishing, 1997.

[13] Gamma, E., Helm, R., Johnson, R., Vlissides, J., Design Patterns: Elements of Reusable Object-Oriented Software, Addison-Wesley, 1995

[14] Notification Service: Joint Revised Submission. OMG TC Document telecom/98-06-15, June 15 1998.

# Distributed Connection Management Architecture for Optimal VPC Provisioning on Hierarchical ATM Transport Network

Won-Kyu Hong , Dong-Sik Yun

Telecommunications Network Lab., Korea Telecom
463-1, Junmin-dong, Yusung-gu, Taejeon, Korea
{wkhong, dsyun}@kt.co.kr

**Abstract.** It was impossible to find a globally optimal route on hierarchical transport network because of the successive subnetwork partitioning and network topology abstraction. So, this paper proposes a hierarchical routing model that provides a globally optimal route on hierarchical ATM transport network. In addition, this paper proposes distributed connection management architecture adopting the proposed routing model. The hierarchical routing model and the distributed connection management architecture are specified in terms of information, computational and engineering viewpoints of RM-ODP. We implement the proposed routing model and the distributed connection management architecture, and show that the proposed connection management architecture always provides a globally optimal route with admissible performance by empirical performance analysis.

## 1 Introduction

ITU-T G.805 defines the generic transport network architecture from the perspective of the information transfer capability and defines especially the functional and structural architecture of transport networks independent of networking technology [1]. G.805 layering concept can be applied not only to transmission networks but also to switching networks. For example, there are ATM VC layer network, ATM VP layer network and SDH transmission layer network. A Layer Network (LNW) can be partitioned into Subnetworks (SNW) connected by Topological Links (TL). Each SNW can be successively decomposed into smaller SNW that is equivalent to a single switching element.

The deployment of hierarchical transport network based on the concepts of ITU-T G.805 layering and partitioning provides some strength in telecommunications network management. For one example of ATM VP connection service provisioning, SNW partitioning of VP layer network can narrow down the management scope of connection control, restoration, fault localization, performance monitoring, and so on. However, it gives a disadvantage that hardly finds a globally optimal path. In the partitioned subnetwork architecture, every subnetwork can view only its own subordinate subnetwork partitioning topology that is used for routing.

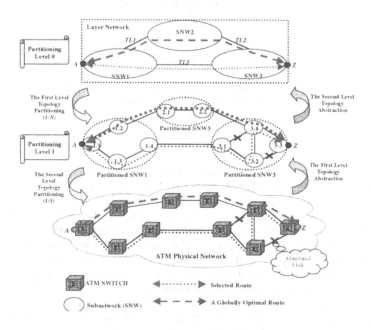

Fig. 1. Layer Network Partitioning

Fig. 1 describes a VP layer network partitioning structure and a route selection scheme based on ITU-T G.805 [1] and TINA-C NRIM [2]. A layer network and each subnetwork can select only the locally optimal path with their topology information that is composed of sets of subnetworks and topological links.

At the partitioning level 0, optimal routing path from *A* to *Z* is the direct link of TL3 between SNW1 and SNW3. Subsequently the optimal path selected by SNW1 traverses SNW1.1, SNW1.3 and SNW1.4. The optimal path selected by SNW3 traverses SNW3.1, SNW3.2, SNW3.4, and SNW3.3. Therefore the selected route by SNW1 and SNW3 at the partitioning level 1 is not a globally optimal path from the perspective of the physical network. According to this hierarchical routing model, the optimal path selected at upper partitioning level is different from the optimal path selected at the lower partitioning level.

To solve this problem, this paper proposes a new hierarchical routing model that is composed of several routing information objects: *Routing Information Base (RIB), Routing Metric (RM), Routing Table (RT), and Internal Cost and Reachability Table (ICRT)*. This paper also proposes distributed connection management architecture to provide a globally optimal route on hierarchical transport network and to adopt the generic telecommunications networking system functions: addressing, routing and switching.

This paper specifies the proposed routing model and distributed connection management architecture using the RM-ODP information, computational and engineering viewpoint [12]. We implement the proposed hierarchical routing model and distributed connection management model. Our empirical performance analysis shows that the performance of the proposed distributed connection management model is nearly same as traditional TINA-C hierarchical connection management model in spite of providing the globally optimal route.

## 2 Hierarchical Routing Information Model

To describe the generic transport network topology, ITU-T G.805 [1] and TINA-C [2] defines several information objects that are mainly composed of Subnetwork (SNW), Topological Link (TL) and Link Termination Point (LTP). Subnetwork represents the node or the administrative and routing scope. Topological link represents the topological relationships between two subnetworks and the potential connectivity between the subnetworks. Link termination point represents an ending point of a topological link. According to the partitioning concept, a layer network is decomposed into subnetworks. Each subnetwork may be decomposed into smaller subnetworks until the subnetwork is equivalent to a single network element (switch or cross-connect). The subnetwork that is corresponding to a single network element is called as Element Management Layer Subnetwork (emlSNW). The subnetwork that is decomposed into smaller subnetwork is named as Network Management Layer Subnetwork (nmlSNW).

With these information objects, we can not provide a globally optimal route because of successive subnetwork partitioning and topology aggregation as depicted in Fig. 1. To solve this problem, we newly define four information objects: *Routing Information Base (RIB), Internal Cost and Reachability Table (ICRT), Routing Metric (RM) and Routing Table (RT)* as depicted in Fig. 2.

*Routing Information Base (RIB)* information object represents the network topology largely based on the weighted graph model. It is defined from the perspective of network topology to construct routing table and is composed of ribNode to represent SNW, ribPort to represent LTP and ribLink to represent TL as depicted in Fig. 2. Every ribLink has a state measured by the QoS metric of concern. Every ribNode also has a state defined by the *Internal Cost and Reachability (ICR)* metric that takes a key role to provide a globally optimal route.

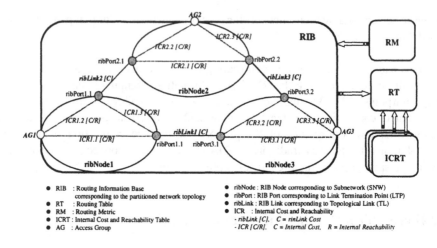

Fig. 2. Proposed Hierarchical Routing Model

We adopt the *Access Group* (AG) information object of ITU-T G.805 that is defined as a group of co-located "trail termination" functions that are connected to the same "subnetwork" or "link"[1]. We extend it to minimize routing table size. There is one AG in the ribNode that can be termination node to calculate routing path by routing algorithm. It physically represents the route path termination and logically represents all the access ribPorts in a ribNode. Because the source and destination to calculate route path are AGs not ribPorts, the routing table size can be remarkably reduced. AG can be comparable with the Internet routing mechanism that most hosts and routers use a default route in order to avoid routing entries for every possible Internet destination

*Routing Metric (RM)* information object maintains the necessary information to assign cost to ribLinks and to keep optimal route selection criteria. In order to assign ribLink cost we define three states: bandwidth, delay, and reliability. It also maintains the administrative weight (hop count) that is used to trim the routes to exceed the assigned hop count from the perspective of network administration. This is very useful to moderate the size of computed routing table and subordinate route information propagation complexity. Let's assumes that $B_d$ is the degree of residual bandwidth, $R_d$ is the degree of reliability, $H_c$ is the cost of hop count, $D_d$ is the degree of transit delay and $W_{lnw}$ is administrative weight applied to VP LNW. We allocate cost to ribLink ($L_c$) with the following criteria. If a ribLink is in fault, we allocate $\propto$ to $L_c$.

$$L_c = B_d + D_d + R_d + H_c, \quad where \quad H_c \geq B_d + D_d + R_d. \tag{1}$$

*Routing Table (RT)* information object contains all possible route information at any partitioning level. Most of existing routing algorithms rely on Dijkstra's algorithm to create a shortest-path route to the destination, based on a single quantity or metric. In ATM networks, links and connections are characterized by several metrics. It makes Dijkstra's algorithm unsuitable to apply to ATM network. Our routing algorithm adopts the pre-computed path driven approach to meet various kinds of QoS requirements and to provide a globally optimal route. At any partitioning level, if there are $n$ ribNodes, there are $n(n-1)/2$ route path entries. For example, at partitioning level 0 of Fig. 1, there are three AGs per ribNode: AG1, AG2, and AG3. We compute all possible routes among all combination of AGs. So there are three route entries: AG1 to AG2, AG1 to AG3, and AG2 to AG3.

Because we compute all possible routes on all combination of AGs in RIB, the complexity of route computation is very high. Fortunately, most of the large scaled backbone networks like VP layer network is connected each node with duplicated full mesh. It is also manifested that the more hop count is increased, the more the end-to-end transit delay is increased. So one should determine the reasonable end-to-end transit delay that is accomplished by the administrative weight ($W_{lnw}$) in Routing Metric (RM) information object. $W_{lnw}$ represents the maximum hop count of every route. We trim the routes that exceed the $W_{lnw}$ off in the process of route computation to moderate route computation complexity and to provide the optimal VPC that meets the end-to-end transit delay.

*Internal Cost and Reachability Table (ICRT)* information object contains the summarized subordinate RT information. In line with the network topology of Fig. 1, there are three other RIBs and RTs that are corresponding to the partitioned SNW1, SNW2, and SNW3. The summarized subordinate RTs of SNW1, SNW2, and SNW3 are composed of source/destination AG pair and the cost and reachability of its first priority route. Our routing information model can be represented using the generic model of Rumbaugh OMT diagram [15] like Fig. 3.

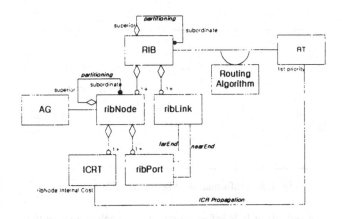

Fig. 3. Routing OMT Diagram

To provide a globally optimal route with the proposed information objects, we do following steps:

1. construct RIB with partitioned network topology information at every partitioning level
2. assign cost to every ribLinks using the Routing Metric (RM)
3. if RIB is composed of ribNodes corresponding to emlSNWs
   - prepare summarized RT information and propagate it to its superior partitioning level
   - otherwise, wait until it receives summarized RT information from all subordinate partitioning level
4. if RIB is composed of ribNodes corresponding to nmlSNWs,
   - construct ICRTs with the propagated summarized RT information from its lower partitioning level
5. when a source and a destination are specified,
   - make relation between ICR in ribNodes and summarized RT information cost of ICRT,
   - calculate total cost of all routes pertaining to the specified source and destination AGs, and
   - assign priority to all routes according to the total cost of each route.

The total cost of a $k$-hop path P is

$$C(P) = \sum_{i=1}^{k} Lc + \sum_{i=1}^{k+1} ICR_{(n)}, \text{ where } n = \text{ribNode that traverse the route P.} \quad (2)$$

If the specified source and destination are respectively $A$ and $Z$ in Fig. 1, the RT of partitioning level 0 will be changed to reflect the ICR information of subordinate partitioning level. $A$ implies the AG-A and $Z$ implies AG-Z in Fig. 4. So, we adjust cost and priority of routes in AG-A and AG-Z route entry to reflect the ICRT information. Reflecting the ICR information to each ribNodes, the total cost and priority of routes are changed as depicted in Fig. 4.

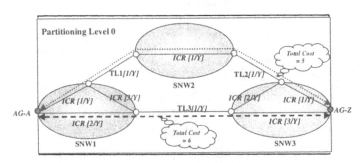

Fig. 4. RIB information to be applied ICR information

As a result of reflecting ICR information, we can select a route that traverses TL1 and TL2 as a globally optimal route to the contrary of Fig. 1. If we do not consider the ICR in the process of route selection, the route along the TL3 will be the optimal route. However, if the ICR is reflected into the process of selection, the route along the TL1 and TL2 will be more optimal route than the route along the TL3.

Network status is dynamically changed due to transient load fluctuation, connection in/out, and links up/down. As a result of above, the ribLink cost is subsequently changed, and so the pre-computed route cost and priority are adjusted. Then, if the pre-computed route of the highest priority is changed, subordinate route information should be propagated to superior partitioning level, else it needs not propagate.

## 3 Distributed Connection Management Computational Model

This paper fully adopts the TINA-C computational models of connection management and configuration management [3]. However, this paper describes the extended computational model in terms of generic networking system functions: addressing, routing, and switching. We define VP connection management architecture that is restricted within EML and NML of the TMN functional layering architecture. Our proposed distributed connection management computational model is like Fig. 5.

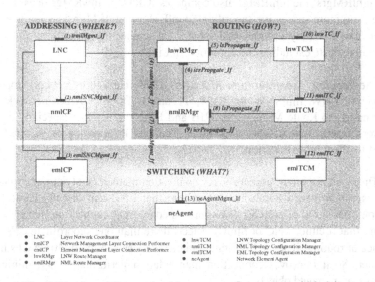

Fig. 5. Distributed Connection Management Computational Model

The *Layer Network Coordinator (LNC)* takes the role of establishment or release of trails within a layer network. We newly allocate addressing function to it. Our addressing function can be broken down two categories: resolving end user address (E.164) to network resource name (LTP) and selecting proper subordinate nmlCPs or emlCPs as a result of routing. There is one LNC for each administrative domain of every layer networks.

The *Connection Performer (CP)* provides interconnections of termination points of a subnetwork. There are two CPs of nmlCP (Network Management Layer CP) and emlCP (Element Management Layer CP). The nmlCP is allocated to every nmlSNW and selects proper subordinate nmlCPs or emlCPs as a result of routing, as does LNC. On the other hand, the emlCP interacts with neAgent in order to control switch. The emlCP is allocated to every emlSNW.

The *Network Element Agent (neAgent)* takes the roles of mapping between our network transport entity and switch resource entity, issues operation to control switch and receives various kinds of notification from switches. Especially the switching function can be achieved by the mutual interaction between emlCP and neAgent.

The *Layer Network Route Manager (lnwRMgr)* and *Network Management Layer Route Manager (nmlRMgr)* take the role of routing function. They gather network topology information from lnwTCM or nmlTCM in order to compose RIB and make routing table using this RIB. The lnwRMgr is only one, but nmlRMgr can be more than one according to the network partitioning. lnwRMgr is allocated to every LNW and nmlRMgr is assigned to every nmlSNW. lnwRMgr makes ICRTs with the propagated ICR information from subordinate nmlRMgrs. If there are successive subordinate nmlRMgrs, the nmlRMgr also composes ICRTs, as lnwRMgr does. However, if there is no more successive subordinate nmlRMgrs, nmlRMgr does not make ICRTs. It provides not only optimal path at normal connection setup procedure but also alternative route excluding the abnormal ribLinks.

The *Topology Configuration Manager (TCM)* configures network topology resources of LNW, nmlSNW, emlSNW, TL and LTPs. It provides network topology information to Route Manager for RIB and RT construction. Especially it monitors network resource status and gives Route Manager information of changed resource status to affect route selection.

There are important aspects of our connection management computational model. One is subordinate CP selection procedure that LNC can directly control emlCPs without mediation of nmlCPs. The other is concurrent connection management procedure that if either LNC or nmlCP selects more than one subordinate CPs in consequence of routing, it sends SNC manipulation requests to the multiple CPs in current manner. So it improves connection manipulation performance and minimizes the number of managed objects.

Table 1. Computational Object Interfaces

| Interfaces | Role of Interface |
|---|---|
| *trailMgmt_if* | Create, delete, modify and reroute Trail |
| *nmlSNCMgmt_if* | Create, delete, modify and reroute nmlSNC |
| *emlSNCMgmt_if* | Create, delete and modify emlSNC |
| *RouteMgmt_if* | Provide optimal route and alternative route including CAC |

| icrPropagate_if | Gather subordinate summarized RT information (ICR) |
|---|---|
| lsPropagate_If | Receive link State that will be effect the ribLink cost calculation<br>Modify RIB and Re-construct RT only when the network topology is changed |
| lnwTC_If | LNW resource provisioning (LNW, nmlSNW, LTP, TL) |
| nmlTC_If | nmlSNW resource provisioning (nmlSNW, emlSNW, LTP, TL) |
| emlTC_If | emlSNW resource provisioning (emlSNW, LTP) |
| neAgentMgmt_If | Adaptation between management objects and switch dependent objects |

## 4 Engineering Model and Implementation

### 4.1 Engineering Model

We have implemented our VP connection management model with the proposed hierarchical routing model. The network topology and connectivity related information objects are modeled as the *Persistent Engineering Objects (PEO)* to be kept in spite of system failure. It is realized into C++ objects and its information is stored into Oracle Database for persistency. On the other hand, the information objects related routing are realized into the *Transient Engineering Objects (TEO)* to be not kept in case of system failure, instead can be rebuilt based on the persistent engineering objects. All routing information objects are defined as TEOs because it can be reconstructed with the SNW, LTP and TL PEOs in case of route manager system failure.

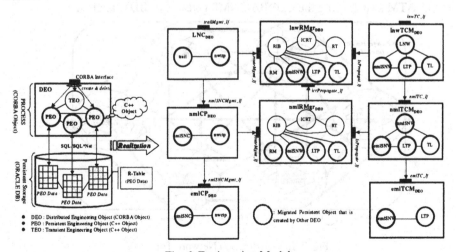

Fig. 6. Engineering Model

All computational objects are described with IDL and realized into the CORBA distributed objects of *Distributed Engineering Object (DEO)* executing on the distributed platform. It creates, modifies and deletes the necessary PEOs or TEOs on which operations are called by client DEO. After creating a PEO, its information is stored into database and deleted from memory at end of transaction. However, the TEOs for routing is not stored into database but kept only in memory after the end of transaction.

The connection management DEOs of LNC, nmlCP and emlCP create connectivity PEOs and store their information into database at the end of transaction. The network topology configuration management DEOs of lnwTCM, nmlTCM and emlTCM create network topology related PEOs and store their information to database, as connection management DEOs do. The routing management DEOs of lnwRMgr and nmlRMgr create RIB, ICRT and RT TEOs and keep their information only in memory.

The engineering model supports the object migration concepts of CORBA. Though the SNW, LTP, and TL PEOs are created and managed by topology configuration manager DEOs, these can be migrated to Route Manager DEOs when Route Manager does CAC or rebuilds routing related TEOs after system crash.

## 4.2 Implementation and Empirical Performance Analysis

For implementation, we choose IONA Orbix distributed platform for enhancing the distribution transparency. In order to support object persistency, we choose Oracle and store all PEOs into this database. We configure ATM backbone network with the FORE ASX200 switches and connect them with OC-3C links. We implement the neAgent that plays the role of adaptation between our management system and FORE ATM switch using the CORBA/SNMP gateway of JIDM approach.

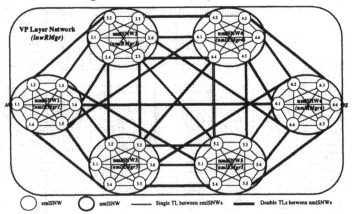

Fig. 7. Implementation Network Topology

The network topology for implementation is depicted in Fig. 7. There are one VP layer network, six nmlSNWs and thirty-six emlSNWs. The LNC, lnwRMgr and lnwTCM are allocated to VP layer network. The nmlCP, nmlRMgr and nmlTCM are allocated to every nmlSNWs. The emlCP and emlTCM are assigned to every emlSNWs and the neAgent is allocated to every ATM switches. All route and connection management DEOs is implemented with thread for current connection management. We use seven UTLASPARC workstations that every workstation is allocated to each Route Manager. One is for LNC, lnwRMgr and lnwTCM DEOs, others are for nmlCP, nmlRMgr and nmlTCM DEOs.

This paper describes implementation experiences on connection manipulation and route management compared our connection management architecture with traditional TINA-C connection management architecture. We analyze the performance of routing table construction and connection setup of both of one to propagate ICR information and the other to not propagate.

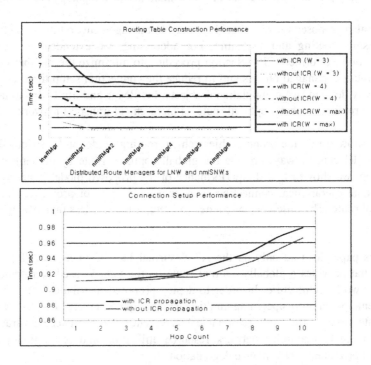

Fig. 8. Route and Connection Management Performance Evaluation

Inferring from Fig. 8, we learn that complexity of routing table construction including ICR metric propagation totally depends on the number of subordinate nmlRMgrs and the administrative weight ($W_{LNW}$). The complexity of routing table construction of all nmlRMgrs that has no any successive subordinate nmlRMgrs is similar without regard to it that they propagate ICR information to superior route manager or not, as they do not create ICRTs. On the other hand, the lnwRMgr shows a prominent performance gap depending on whether lnwRMgr gathers ICR information and constructs its correspondent ICRT or not.

From the perspective of connection setup, there is no prominent performance gap without regard to it that the Route Manager chooses the proposed end-to-end optimal path selection mechanism or not. The slight gap in connection setup time is mainly caused by the route cost calculation to reflect ICR cost of route manager.

## 5 Conclusion

This paper proposed hierarchical routing model that always provides a globally optimal route on the hierarchical transport network architecture. It has been proved that the model provides a globally optimal path using the information objects newly defined. Among them, ICRT is key information object to resolve the problem to hardly find optimal route because of subordinate network topology abstraction.

We also proposed the distributed connection management architecture to integrate addressing, routing and switching. For addressing, we extended the subordinate Connection Performer (CP) selection procedure to minimize the number of connectivity related managed objects and to reduce the connection setup time. For routing, we newly defined two computational objects: lnwRMgr and nmlRMgr to take a key role to provide a globally optimal route on hierarchical transport network.

We showed that the proposed hierarchical routing model and distributed connection model could always provide the globally optimal route by implementation. In addition, we showed that the performance of the proposed model is nearly same as traditional hierarchical connection management in spite of providing the globally optimal route. The difference of connection setup time was less than 5% by our experience.

This paper focused only on the ATM Virtual Path Connection (VPC) management that provides a globally optimal route on the G.805-based hierarchical transport network architecture. In order to deploy proposed distributed connection management model into upcoming multi-layer and multi-service network, we should evaluate what is the most reasonable convergence point between abstraction and partitioning to maximize network resource utilization and restoration probability without prominent performance degradation.

## References

1. ITU-T Recommendation G.805, "Generic Functional Architecture of Transport Networks," November 1995.
2. Network Resource Information Model Specification, Document No. NRIM_v2.2_97_10_31, October 31, 1997.

3. Network Resource Architecture, Document No. NRA_v3.0_97_02_10, TINA-C, February 1997.
4. ITU-T Recommendation M.3100, "Generic Network Information Model," July 1995.
5. ITU-T Recommendation M.3010, "Principles for a Telecommunications Management Network," May 1996.
6. ITU-T Recommendation I.311, "B-ISDN General Network Aspects," March 1993.
7. ATM Forum, "PNNI Specification 1.0," af-pnni-0055.0000, March 1996.
8. Hui Xie and John S. Baras, "Performance Analysis of PNNI Routing in ATM Networks: Hierarchical Reduced Load Approximation," February 1996.
9. Tsong-Ho Wu and Noriaki Yoshikai, "ATM Transport and Network Integrity," Academic Press, 1997.
10. P. Lauder, R.J. Kummerfeld, and A. Fekete, "Hierarchical Network Routing," IEEE Conference on Communications Software, April 1991.
11. IONA Technologies Ltd., "Orbix Programming Guide – Release 2.0," November 1995.
12. OMG, "CORBAServices: Common Object Service Specification," March 31, 1995.
13. OMG, "The Common Object Request Broker: Architecture and Specification," July 1995.
14. ISO/IEC CD 10746-1, "Basic Reference Model of Open Distributed Processing – Part 1: Overview and Guide to Use", July 1994.
15. James Rumbaugh, Michael Blaha, William Premerlani, Frederick Eddy and WilliamLorensen, Object-Oriented Modeling and Design," Prentice Hall, 1991.

# A Multi-agent Paradigm for the Inter-domain Demand Allocation Process

M. Calisti and Boi Faltings

Laboratoire de Intelligence Artificielle
Swiss Federal Institute of Technology
CH-1015 Lausanne, Switzerland
{calisti, faltings}@lia.di.epfl.ch
http://liawww.epfl.ch/ calisti

**Abstract.** Market liberalisation and increasing demands for the allocation of services which span several networks are pushing every network operator to evolve the way of interacting with peer operators. The Inter-domain Demand Allocation (IDA) process is a very complex task for several reasons: there are different actors involved, end-to-end routing must take into account QoS requirements, network resources and information are distributed, etc. In this paper we address the problem of the QoS-based multi-domain routing, and more specifically a multi-agent paradigm for supporting the IDA process is defined. We show how Artificial Intelligence methods for distributed problem solving supply a compact way to formalise the multi-domain routing process, and how this formalism enables an agent middle-ware to route demands across distinct domains.

**Keywords:** Inter-domain routing, service demand allocation, constraint-based routing, agents, network provider.

## 1 Introduction

Today's networks are controlled at various organisational and functional layers by human managers, in particular the management of end-to-end services across different telecom operators is largely non automated. What seems more suitable for the future scenarios, is a management solution based on static and/or mobile software entities [19], collecting network state information and which have the ability to directly invoke effective changes to switch controllers, without the interaction of a human operator. Such a dynamic and active (reactive and proactive) paradigm would improve both intra-domain and inter-domain routing capabilities.

The main factors that are pushing Network Operators, NOs, to evolve the way they interact with each other are: the market liberalisation, the technological rate of change, the need for reducing time to market for new services, the aim to enable end-to-end managements of services, the co-ordination of multi-vendors and multi-jurisdictional environments, the need for scalable and flexible systems for future development.

There are several approaches to multi-domain connection management[1], e.g., TINA with LNFed reference points [2], the TMN X-interface [12], [6], [7], the mobile agent paradigm using OMG's MAF [8] (Object Management Group, Mobile Agent Facility). Furthermore, extensive work has been devoted for supporting the inter-working between CMIS/GDMO and interfaces specified in the Interface Definition Language (for good references check [9]). Nevertheless, more study is needed for the definition of agent-oriented APIs (Application Programming Interfaces) for the translation of TMN or TINA terms and the associated information models. Additionally, there are still open issues regarding procedures and interactions to achieve connectivity across several domains indipendentely on the under-laying network technology.

Our work aims to address these open issues. This paper examines the correlation between intra- and inter-domain routing, and proposes a mechanism to make local routes consistent with inter-domain constraints. In particular it introduces the use of Artificial Intelligent techniques together with multi-agent system technology, in order to face the *Inter-domain Demand Allocation*, IDA, problem. Agents (static and mobile) can be deployed for dynamically configuring the resources of switches and cross-connects [13]. Agents inside distinct domains can run different routing algorithms, which can be modified by the agents themselves (e.g., changing, adding or modifying metrics). Furthermore, agents can actively modify the strategy they adopt for inter-domain routing.

Section 2 describes the problem we address. Section 3 presents the *Network Provider Interworking*, NPI, paradigm and shows how to apply the Distributed Constraint Satisfaction techniques to formalise the IDA process. Section 4 focuses on the solving algorithm. Some first evaluation results are shown in Section 5. In Section 6 we initiate a discussion on a possible deployment of NPI in a real scenario. Some final remarks and comments on future work are given in Section 7.

## 2 The problem

The IDA process is a very complex task for NOs for several reasons: there are distinct entities involved (final customers, service providers, service brokers, etc.), the routing must take into account QoS requirements, network resources and information are distributed, a trade-off between the profit optimisation and the end-user satisfaction is required. Figure 1 shows the principal entities involved in this process. An end user is represented by an End User Agent (EUA). This entity can contact one or several Service Provider Agents , SPAs, specifying a service demand and optional negotiation parameters, such as for example a target timeout to receive back an offer. Every SPA can then contact one or several Network Provider Agents, NPAs. Whenever the service demand spans several network domains, several NPAs must interact. A Mask Agent, MA, represents a

---

[1] We refer the establishment of semi-permanent connections through the management plane.

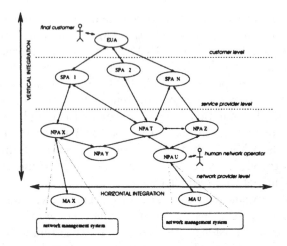

**Fig. 1.** Dynamic service provisioning scenario.

wrapper for the non-agent-based Network Management System: gateway functionalities must be performed for converting Agent Communication Language messages to, for instance, CMIP (Common Management Information Protocol) primitives.

In the short term such a scenario could be introduced through software tools supporting human operators, for example proposing alternative choices, evaluating prices, QoS and topology constraints, and summarising offers from other operators[2]. This would improve the providers negotiation strategy and would support a more dynamic multi-domain service demand allocation.

Focusing on the interaction among Network Providers every network is represented as a set of nodes and links (Figure 2). Two main sub-problems need to be addressed: (1) Finding the routes which satisfy connectivity and QoS constraints. (2) Selecting a specific route by negotiating with the other providers. This paper focuses on the former sub-task that can be more precisely expressed as it follows. A network operator receiving a demand has:
- To detect the source and the destination network domains. Whenever the destination node resides in a remote network the *inter-domain routing* must be started.
- To compute an abstract path $P$. An *abstract path* is an ordered list of distinct network provider domains between the source and the destination network domains.
- To contact all the network providers along $P$.
- To compute the *local routes*, i.e., intra-domain routing inside every network along $P$.
- To make the set of local routes consistent within inter-domain constraints. All

---

[2] For an automated version of such a framework more time is required for a larger deployment of agent technology in telecom environments. However, several research activities are focusing on suck kind of scenario [20], [17]

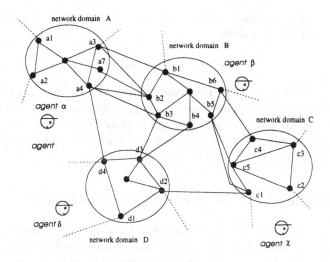

**Fig. 2.** Network formalisation.

local routes which violates such constraints are discarded.
- To negotiate with the providers along $P$ for allocating a *global route*, i.e., the end-to-end connection consisting of local routes and inter-domain links interconnecting them.
- If an agreement is found the network resources are reserved
- Otherwise the service demand is rejected.
If no answer has been found before a certain timeout, the overall allocation process fails.

## 3  Network Provider Interworking paradigm

The inter-domain routing requires the coordination of distributed NPAs. All knowledge about the resources needed to allocate a demand cannot be gathered into one single network provider, for various reasons. Fundamentally, for reasons of both scalability and security, network operators do not reveal details of their internal structure. Instead, every network advertises only a summary, or aggregated view, of the costs and availabilities associated with traversing them (this is also proposed by the ATM PNNI standard).

Hence, every NPA assigns a part of the global route, namely the local part inside its network, and then it negotiates with others in order to interconnect its local solution to form a global route.

The interconnection of different providers' network is modelled as a connected abstract network graph $G=(Nodes, Links)$. A node can correspond to a network node (such as switches and routers), to sub-networks or, at the highest level of abstraction, to networks. The links represent both the connections existing inside every network domain, *intra-domain links*, and the connections to other providers domains, *inter-domain links*. In our framework a communication demand $d_k$, or *demand*, is specified by a triple:

$$d_k ::= (x_k, y_k, qos_{req,k})$$

where $x_k$ is the source node, $y_k$ the destination node[3], and $qos_{req,k}$ the required QoS by the demand. We assume that the $qos_{req,k}$ expresses the bandwidth (peak bandwidth) needed by the service. Taking into account other parameters, such as the delay or the number of hops, which are additive metrics, implies to introduce additional constraints in the solving algorithm[4].

## 3.1 Formalising the route allocation process as a DCSP

Constraint satisfaction is a powerful and extensively used Artificial Intelligence paradigm [21]. *Constraint satisfaction problems* (CSP) involve finding values for problem variables subject to restrictions (constraints) on which combinations of values are acceptable. CSP are solved using search (e.g., backtrack) and inference (e.g., arc consistency) methods.

Finding a route for allocating service demands that cross distinct networks, can be considered as a Distributed Constraint Satisfaction Problem [16], DCSP, since the variables are distributed among agents and since constraints exist among them. We assume that: (1) every agent has exactly one variable, (2) all inter domain constraints are binary, i.e., they involve two variables, (3) there is at least an agent for every domain, (4) all the agents in the scenario know each other, (5) agents communicate using messages.

The *variable* every agent handles is a "local path" (actually it is not a path since it expresses just the two end points of it) specified as a couple:

$$p ::= (inputpoint, outputpoint)$$

The values for each variable are all the possible combinations of boundary points, i.e., input-output points to/from every network, which represent the possible local routes to allocate the demand. Note that only *simple paths*, i.e., loop-free, are considered. The set of all the possible input-output points combinations is the *domain* for each variable. Consider the example depicted in Figure 2. Agent $\alpha$ receives a demand $d_k = (a_1, b_6, qos_{req})$ The variable for agent $\alpha$ is the couple $p_\alpha = (i, o)$ and the domain of $p_\alpha$ is $D_{\alpha,k} = \{(a_1, a_3), (a_1, a_4), (a_1, a_7)\}$. Agent $\alpha$ selectes the abstract path A - B. The domain for agent $\beta$ is: $D_{\beta,k} = \{(b_1, b_6), (b_2, b_6), (b_3, b_6)\}$. The domains of the variables are dynamically computed for every specific demand. The dynamical re-computation allows

---

[3] We assumed that a service request corresponds to a single point to point connection request.

[4] There must be a centralised control, for instance performed by the agent in the network provider which first receives the service demand from a service provider, which checks if the sum of all delays along the path does not exceed the delay requirements. These issues are still under investigation.

first to update the variable domains according to the network state, and also to reduce the search space.

There are essentially two categories of constraints: the QoS constraints, that depend on the type of the service requested by the user, and the policies applied by the providers . The first kind of requirements are explicited as $qos_{req}$ in the in the demand (see above). The second class of constraints includes the policies applied by the providers, which correspond to a set of inference rules that can be either static or dynamic. Some of those rules depend on the technology inside every network domain, some others on how the availability of network resources is managed, and finally some others can take into account the past experiences.

Our paradigm does not force the use of any specific intra-domain policy[5]: although distinct network providers can deploy different policies the NPI mechanism is still valid. In our framework the global constraints (QoS and connectivity) are locally translated in constraints between the boundary points, that neighbour network domains use for the inter-domain routing.

## 4  Solving the IDA process

The *Distributed Arc Consistency* algorithm is based on the use of arc consistency techniques [14], that are used to narrow the space of possible choices before actually performing search. The main principle is that for every existing constraint between two variables $i$ and $j$, all the values of the variables $i$ and $j$, that are not consistent with the given constraint, are eliminated. The algorithm consists of the following steps:

1. An agent $\alpha$ receives a demand $d$.
2. Agent $\alpha$ detects the destination and the source network domains.
3. Based on a global view of the network scenario, which is updated dynamically by the agents, an abstract path $P$ for $d$ is computed. None, one or several paths can exist. If none, the demand is rejected . If more than one path exists the optimal one is selected.
4. Agent $\alpha$ contacts every agent along $P$. From now on several agents run in parallel similar routines.
5. Each agent defines the variable domain $D$ and the set of constraints $C$. $C$ is determined considering the available QoS on the inter-domain links interconnecting every provider network with its neighbours.
6. Based on $qos_{req}$ every agent reduces $D$ by performing *node consistency*. Every local path that cannot support the $qos_{req}$ is eliminated from $D$. The node-consistency process can be supported by the Blocking Island, BI, techniques [15]. The BI formalism allows to quickly detect if there exists a route connecting the input point with an output point guaranteeing the $qos_{req}$. If the input point $i_\alpha$ and the end point $o_\alpha$ belong to the same $\beta$-BI level with

---

[5] The use of the Blocking Island paradigm, see Section 4, inside every modelled network is not mandatory, although in our opinion it represents a very efficient instrument to check the internal resource availability.

$\beta \geq qos_{req}$, then $(i_\alpha, o_\alpha) \in D$, i.e., there is a local route which guarantees the $qos_{req}$[6].

If one agent has an empty variable domain $D$ a failure message is sent to all agents along $P$. A new abstract path can be searched (backtrack to step 3).

7. Establishing arc consistency. Every agent determines all the values of its variable domain which are compatibles with the values contained in the variable domains of the neighbours. If an agent obtains an empty variable domain, a failure message is sent to all agents along $P$. Then, backtrack to step 3.

8. At least one solution, i.e. one route along $P$, exists. In order to be sure that a solution will still exist after the negotiation, we assume that there exists a pre-reservation mechanism of the negotiated resources required by the demand $d$. If network failures or physical changes occur the guarantee of having a solution is not valid any more. In this case every agent is notified by the Network Management System and the algorithm backtracks to 3.

9. If the negotiation is successful the resources needed are reserved and the service demand can be allocated, otherwise a failure message is sent to all the agents involved along $P$ and the algorithm goes to 3.

In the worst case scenario, the complexity of the arc consistency algorithm is $O(|P| N^6)$, with $|P|$ being the number of networks involved along $P$ and $N$ the maximum number of boundary nodes of a network along $P$[7].

## 4.1 Visualizing the DAC mechanism

The DCSP formalism allows to easily visualize which are the links in the scenario that can support the $qos_{req}$. After the arc consistency propagation, the only links considered are the ones which guarantee the $qos_{req}$ and which satisfy the inter-domain constraints. Consider that NPA A receives the demand d=(a1, b6, 15) (Figure 2). Figure 3 (A) shows the situation before any computation. The routes inside every domain are specified as couples of end-points, e.g., (a1, a3) inside the network domain A. Figure 3 (B) indicates all the links, intra and inter domain, that satisfy the $qos_{req}$. This is the configuration after every agent has performed steps 5 and 6 of the DAC algorithm. At step 5 the link l3 is excluded since it cannot guarantee the $qos_{req}$=15. At step 6 every agent checks the node consistency: the local path (b2, b6) is pruned out from the variable domain $D_\beta$. Finally, (B) shows $D_\alpha$={(a1, a3),(a1, a4),(a1, a7)} and $D_\beta$={(b1, b6), (b3, b6)}. Figure 3 (C) depicts the situation after the arc consistency propagation (step 7 of the DAC algorithm). The variable domains are : $D_\alpha$={(a1, a3),(a1, a4)} and $D_\beta$={(b1, b6),(b3, b6)}. The value (a1, a7) is pruned out from $D_\alpha$ since (a1, a7) is not consistent with any value in $D_\beta$.

---

[6] **Frei:** *A $\beta$-BI for a node $x$ is the set of all nodes of the network reachable from $x$ using links with at least $\beta$ available resources, including $x$.*

[7] More detailed considerations about the completeness and the complexity of DAC can be found in [4].

There are two solutions in the end: (a1, a3)-l1-(b1, b6), (a1, a4)-l4-(b3, b6). The agents can now start the negotiation to select which solution to adopt (for brevity's sake the negotiation aspects are not addressed in this paper).

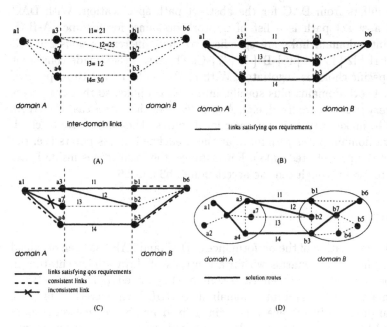

**Fig. 3.** DAC visualization.

## 4.2 Global path computation and selection

Every NPA computes the list of abstract paths [8]. The computation is based on Dijkstra's algorithm modified in order to find out the "optimal" paths. An abstract path is *optimal* if there exists no other abstract path that is strictly better in terms of price and that meets bandwidth requirements. The price of an abstract path is the sum of the prices of the abstract links which compose the path itself. The bandwidth of an abstract path is given by the minimum bandwidth value of tits component abstract links. The abstract path computation algorithm takes as input a graph G=(N, L, C, d), where N is a finite non-empty set of nodes, L is the list of links between any two pair of nodes from N and C a function that returns the couple c:=(price, qos) associated with every link l ∈ L, and finally d is the demand to allocate. The output is the complete set of optimal abstract paths from the demand's source node to all the specified destination node.

The choice of an abstract path P for a service demand d is based on the following heuristics: (1) Eliminate all the paths that do not guarantee enough

---

[8] On-demand routing: the end-to-end route is computed upon connection request.

bandwidth. (2) Among the paths left select the cheapest (i.e, minimum price). (3) If still more than one path exists, chose the path which has, after having accepted the incoming demand $d$, the largest bandwidth left.

We also tested a different algorithm , the *Fixed Access Points*, FAP, algorithm that mainly differs from DAC for the abstract path specification. With DAC the selected abstract path is a list of network domains: for instance A-B-C. No specific inter-domain links are specified, so that different options are still possible: A-{ l1 | l2 | l3 | l4 | l5}-B-{ l6 | l7}-C. This set is then made consistent and next a specific choice is negotiated. With FAP the abstract path is specified as a list of network domains plus specific inter-domain links, so that the access points for every network are fixed, e.g., A-l2-B-l6-C. In this latter case the NPAs do not need to make arc consistent their local routes. They only have to check that the intra-domain paths terminate at the predefined access points (i.e, the end-points of the pre-selected links). For instance, the local routes inside B are constrained to pass through the the access points b2 and b6.

# 5 Results

A quantitative evaluation of the performance of DAC and FAP has been obtained by simulating network scenarios within a centralised[9] Java implementation of the two algorithms. A typical scenario is composed of a fixed number of network provider domains (NPDs) and inter-domain links (IDLs), characterised by price and QoS parameters. Inside every domain a fixed number of network nodes are connected by intra-domain links. We estimated the time needed by the two different mechanisms to determine if none, one or many solutions exist (i.e., excluding the negotiation step). The negotiation aspects will play a major role in the distributed multi-agent version of NPI, which is currently under development. Figure 4 compares the time performance of the two mechanisms for the same simulated scenario, that contains 6 providers' networks and 16 inter-domain links randomly distributed between them. Case A and B differ for the set of demands that have to be allocated (see X-axis). For both mechanisms there are common constraints: same global abstract routes, i.e., same network domains to cross, and same QoS requirements. However, within FAP the search space is further reduced because of additional constraints, i.e., the fixed pre-selected access points. This means that if the failure probability, $P_f(P)$, along a global route P is small a conclusion is found faster with FAP than with DAC, (case A). With FAP in fact no arc-consistency takes place, so that there is a time gain. This remains valid as long as no other abstract paths are available. When the $P_f(P)$ increases, DAC performs better (case B). In fact, DAC expresses a set of possible solutions: alternative choices can be available along a pre-selected abstract path, although some access points may have been excluded by the arc consistency. The failure probability along P, $P_f(P)$, is determined by two main factors: the

---

[9] The resolution of the service demand allocation is performed by a unique agent, that knows about the other domains, so that is the only handling variables and constraints.

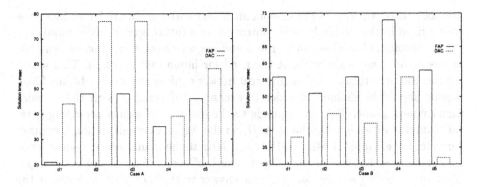

**Fig. 4.** DAC visualization.

difference $d_{av}$ between the QoS available along $P$ (inter-domain links) and $qos_{req}$, and the internal configuration of the network domains. The higher the $d_{av}$ is, the more capable the networks along $P$ are (i.e., the intra-domain routing is less likely to fail) and the smaller is $P_f$. The critical point is that it is not realistic to assume that a network operator is able in advance to exactly compute $P_f(P)$, since a knowledge about the internal topology of competitors domains would be required. However, another major element makes finally DAC more appealing than FAP. In many of the analysed cases, FAP terminates faster because the demand is rejected (no further backtracks are possible so that the algorithm terminates), while DAC is successfully going on for computing a solution through the arc consistency propagation.

In all studied cases DAC terminates in less than 0,1 msec. However, these results are dependent on the simulated scenarios. The crucial area for further work is getting more realistic data input and testing DAC more exhaustively within the distributed NPI architecture.

A distributed version of DAC, which is currently under test, will give a more precise estimation of the time needed for finding a solution to the IDA problem, following the NPI paradigm. The current simulations, with NPAs-Java agents distributed over different local hosts (SUN Sparc stations), terminate in few seconds (from 5 to 10 seconds without considering the negotiation). However, more work is required in order to give more stable and proper results.

## 6  Discussion

Currently many aspects of the interworking are statically fixed by contracts and many steps of the interaction are regulated by human operators by fax, e-mail etc. The NPI paradigm can be considered as a high level service which could be deployed in two different ways: in a short term period as a smart support for human operators, in a long term perspective as an autonomous system acting on behalf of humans and working at the connection management level. The first version would offer a valid support for human operators: it could compute local routes guaranteeing the $qos_{req}$ and it could automatically verify which ones are not consistent with the inter-domain constraints (which are for instance the routes fixed in the currently used contracts). In a future scenario NPI could supply an automated mechanism to route and negotiate the allocation of demands across distinct networks without the need for human intervention. This would require the integration of NPI in a real network infrastructure[10]. *Ad hoc* Mask Agents should be defined in order to exchange information with the network management plane. This corresponds to the creation of agents providing gateway functionalities for translating to/from the Agent Communication Language from/to, for example, CMIS/GMDO and IDL at the management system level.

We believe that one of the main strength of the NPI paradigm is the capability of supplying a rapid and efficient answer to the IDA process, without the need for different operators to reveal a substantial amount of internal information. The data to be exchanged concerns the set of possible access points that a network provider can use for a specific demand. We believe that is reasonable to assume that providers which need to interoperate must exchange a minimal amount of data, such as topology aggregated view.

Furthermore, the mechanism for achieving interconnectivity is valid independently on the specific underlying technology, i.e., it does not depend on how the QoS is provided, or on the specific networking mechanisms for reserving resources and for starting the connection. Such kind of paradigm is based on the idea that the complexity of protocols and technical details are hidden by the Mask Agents.

There are several reasons for the choice of agents. They enable abstractions from technical details, they recognise changes in the environment, they react to external events and they can create goals and plans. However, the real strength of agents is based on the community of multi-agent system and the negotiation mechanism and coordination facilities. A dynamic agent-based negotiation phase would allow to flexibly adapt prices and connectivity configuration to changes occurring inside and outside a single provider network. Automated and standardised information exchanges between software agents compared to the exchange of possibly ambiguous faxes, non punctual phone calls and sometimes unpredictable e-mails between humans, seems a valid argument for relying on software mediators.

# 7 Conclusion and future work

This paper has described a multi-agent paradigm to support the QoS-based inter-domain routing problem in a flexible and dynamic way without the need of human intervention. In particular the paper shows how the DCSP formalism provides a powerful and intuitive way of expressing the QoS-based inter-domain routing problem and a way of solving the problem which have been so expressed.

In our view, the increased flexibility of the NPI approach provides for new opportunities in the area of network inter-operability. In a future scenario NPI

---

[10] For instance telecommunications architectures such as TINA, IN gaiti, or more generically TMN [1] compliant environments.

agents could program the behaviour of network nodes (switches and/or routers) in order to automate the inter-domain routing process. Furthermore, agents could supply a flexible and dynamic negotiation framework.

We have built prototypes to test many of the concepts outlined in this paper and preliminary considerations enforce the use of DCSP techniques to support the inter-domain routing process. In order to validate the NPI paradigm we are continuing to test it by constructing more realistic scenarios and designing negotiation protocols around them, a problem that is complicated by the fact that the interworking process is itself in flux and no stable data is available.

# References

1. I-ETSI 300 653. "Telecommunication Management Network (TMN). Generic managed object class library for the network level view", 1996.
2. "TINA Reference Points", The TINA Consortium, Version 3.1, June 1996.
3. B. Awerbuch, Y. Du, B. Khan and Y. Shavitt, "Routing Through Networks with Hierarchical Topology Aggregation". Technical Report, DIMACS, n. 98-16, 1998.
4. M. Calisti, C. Frei, B. Faltings, "A distributed approach for QoS-based multi-domain routing" AiDIN'99, *AAAI Workshop on Artificial Intelligence for Distributed Information Networking*, 1999.
5. T. Przygienda, O. Crochat, J. Y. Le Boudec, "A Path Selection Method in ATM using Pre-Computation". In: *Proceedings of IZS96*, February 1996.
6. A. Galis and C. Brianza and C. Leone and C. Salvatori "Towards Integrated Network Management for ATM and SDH Networks Supporting a Global Broadband Connectivity Management Service", Mullery A (Eds.)- Springer Verlag, Berlin, 1997, ISBN 3-540-63145-6.
7. D. Griffin, G. Pavlou, T. Tin, "Implementing TMN-like Management Services in a TINA Compliant Architecture: A Case Study on Resource Configuration Management". Lecture Notes in Computer Science, vol. 1238, 1997.
8. "Mobile Agent System Interoperability Facilities Specification", OMG TC Document orbos/97-10-05.
9. A. Galis, D. Griffin, "A comparison of approaches to multi domain connection management", available at the URL http://www.misa.ch/.
10. A. Hopson, R. Janson, "Deployment Scenarios for Interworking". TINA Consortium. TP-AJH.001-0.10-94 TINA-C, 19 January 1995.
11. Gacti D., Pujolle G., "TMN, IN, and DAI". In: *Proceedings TINA'93*, II/111-121, 1993, L'Aquila, Italy.
12. ACTS-MISA project documentation, http://www.misa.ch
13. M. Breugst, T. Magendanz, "Mobile-Agents- Enabling Technology for Active Intelligent Network Implementation". *IEEE Network Magazine, Special Issue on Active and Programmable Networks, May/June 1998, Vol. 12(3)*.
14. V. Kumar. "Algorithms for Constraint satisfaction Problems: A Survey", *Appeared in AI Magazine 13(1): 32-44, 1992*.
15. Frei, C. and Faltings, B. "A dynamic hierarchy of intelligent agents for network management". In *Proceedings of Workshop on Artificial Intelligence in Distributed Information Networks IJCAI'97*, 1997.
16. M. Yokoo, E. Durfee, "Distributed Constraint Satisfaction for Formalising Distributed Problem Solving", *12th IEEE International Conference on Distributed Computing System '92, 614-621*.

17. FACTS project. http://www.labs.bt.com/profsoc/facts/
18. FIPA 97 ver. 2, Specifications, http://www.fipa.org/spec/fipa97.html
19. T. Magendanz, K. Rothermel, S. Krause, "Intelligent Age nts: An emerging Technology for the Next Generation Telecommunications?", INFOCOM'96.
20. P712 project: http://www.eurescom.de/Public/Projects/p700-series/P712-/P712.HTM
21. E. Tsang, "Foundations of Constraint Satisfaction", 1993, Academic Press, London, UK.

# Panel 1

# Providing Managed Services to End-Users

*Organizers: Metin Feridun[1], Burkhard Stiller[2]*
*[1]IBM Research, Switzerland, [2]ETH Zürich, Switzerland*

# Providing Managed Services to End-Users

## Abstract

End-users, whether at home, within an enterprise, or mobile, require managed Internet services, specially in a model, where Internet Service Providers (ISP) are characterized as service sellers and end-users as service buyers. Today, ISPs acting in similar roles (seller/buyer) establish peering agreements between them to manage services. Can these schemes developed for managing inter-ISP services be extended to managing Internet services to large numbers of end-users?

Today, Internet service provisioning determines a market, where legal contracts between users and providers are essential. Effective and efficient combinations of fine-grained monitoring and charging functions are a key to successful service provisioning for end-users. However, it is not clear how these functions will be provided in technical and economical terms.

The panel will discuss a number of open issues:

- Do we need managed services for end-users, especially including charged services?
- Is there a need to charge differently for different services?
- How fine-grained can efficient monitoring be?
- What are the types of technical parameters, such as bandwidth, error rates, and delay, which can be used for pricing services?
- How can service level agreements be specified within a contract so that they can be monitored and enforced by both the seller and the buyer?

The goal of this panel will be to develop an understanding of issues and approaches for the support of Internet services from the perspective of a large set of end-users.

# Session 3

## The Future of SNMP-based Management

*Chair: George Pavlou*
*University of Surrey, Guildford, U.K.*

# Next Generation Structure of Management Information for the Internet

Jürgen Schönwälder and Frank Strauß

Technical University Braunschweig
Bültenweg 74/75, 38106 Braunschweig, Germany,
{schoenw|strauss}@ibr.cs.tu-bs.de

**Abstract.** Management Information Bases (MIBs) for use with the Simple Network Management Protocol (SNMP) are defined in a language called the Structure of Management Information (SMI). This language, based on an adapted subset of ASN.1 (1988), has been a constant source of confusion for Internet MIB designers, MIB implementors and users of network management products. This paper presents work towards a new SMI, tentatively called SMIng, which addresses some of the shortcomings of the current SMI. We describe the design of an embeddable C library to access SMI definitions as well as some tools using this library.

## 1  Introduction

The Internet Structure of Management Information (SMI) defines the language for describing Internet Management Information Bases (MIBs). The SMI is primarily used to define managed objects together with their data types and the notifications that can be emitted.

There are currently two versions of the SMI [1]. The first version of the SMI, called SMIv1, is defined in RFC 1155 [2], RFC 1212 [3] and RFC 1215 [4]. Work on SMIv1 started in 1988 and completed in 1991 with the publication of the SMIv1 specifications as Internet Standards.

The second version of the SMI, called SMIv2, is defined in RFC 2578 [5], RFC 2579 [6] and RFC 2580 [7]. SMIv2 was approved as a full Internet Standard in January 1999 and it will replace the SMIv1 standard. SMIv2 is an evolution of SMIv1 and offers some new features that were not part of SMIv1. Among the new features are macros to define conformance requirements for MIB modules and macros to describe implementation capabilities. The SMIv2 specifications also contain a set of general purpose data types (so called textual conventions).

The Internet Engineering Task Force (IETF) established a policy in 1994 which requires that all new MIB modules published in RFCs must use the SMIv2 format. This rule forced many vendors to add support for SMIv2. Furthermore, the possibility of automated conversion of SMIv2 MIB modules into SMIv1 MIB modules raised the acceptance of SMIv2 outside the IETF. Many vendors now use SMIv2 internally for maintaining their MIB modules, even if they distribute SMIv1 MIB modules to their customers.

Within the IETF, there are currently about 100 MIB modules on the standards track with definitions for several thousand managed objects and about hundred notifications. Additional MIB modules are still being developed within the IETF and other standardization bodies. Some vendor specific MIB modules reach the size of all IETF MIB modules taken together. These numbers clearly show that there is a non-trivial investment in MIB module definitions, and more important, MIB implementations. Future network management protocols are therefore forced to interface with Internet MIBs in order to protect the investment made during the past 10 years.

This paper is structured as follows. We first take a critical look at the current SMIv2 in Section 2. In Section 3, we present the core concepts of a proposed new SMI, tentatively called SMIng. Some examples of SMIng definitions are discussed in Section 4. A portable implementation of an SMI library which can be embedded into a broad range of management applications is described in Section 5. We relate our work with other approaches to describe management information in Section 6 before we conclude with some remarks about the current status of the SMIng effort and some thoughts about the future of SMIng.

## 2  Problems of SMIv2

The SMIv1 was defined at a time when the Abstract Syntax Notation One (ASN.1) [8] was the protocol specification language of choice. ASN.1 was selected as the base for the SMI, not realizing that ASN.1 with its syntactic rules is problematic as a data definition language. Furthermore, the decision to base the SMI on ASN.1 made the SMI standard depend on the ASN.1 specification, which is under control of the International Organization for Standardization (ISO). In fact, SMIv1 and SMIv2 are both based on the 1988 version of ASN.1, which is no longer available from the official ISO standards sources. This dependency makes it difficult for MIB developers or implementors to find answers to questions concerning the syntactical rules of the SMI language.

During the development of SMIv2, it was decided that pure ASN.1 is not sufficient to define SMIv2. New constructs were introduced as part of the definition of SMIv2 which are outside of ASN.1. Hence, the SMIv2 is now officially based on an "adapted subset of ASN.1 (1988)." This implies that it is not possible to use generic ASN.1 tools to process MIB definitions. In fact, the authors are not aware of a single MIB parser which is implemented using generic ASN.1 tools.

Existing MIB parsers are usually implemented from scratch. This requires to translate the SMI definition into a Backus-Naur Form (BNF) grammar and a set of lexical rules in order to use them with scanner and parser generators. Some programmers avoid this translation (since it is difficult to obtain and read the relevant ASN.1 specification) by implementing "fuzzy" MIB scanners that do not really check whether a given MIB module conforms to the SMI rules or not. As a consequence, we are faced with many erroneous MIB modules and it is relatively common that end users have to edit MIB definitions in order to feed them into management applications.

Another drawback of the current SMI is the insufficient ability to be parsed efficiently. This makes it unacceptable for most management applications, especially for those with short expected runtime or the need of a huge amount of management information, to parse MIB modules during startup. In consequence, many applications use proprietary intermediate file formats to store management information more efficiently and reduced to the main items, usually the numerical object identifier values together with associated descriptors, type information and probably display hints. Other information from the original MIB modules is usually not accessible from these files. Intermediate formats are generated as the output of MIB compilers like mosy or SMICng. By using intermediate files, detailed MIB parsing is no longer required on each application startup.

Another problem area is the lack of extensibility of the current SMI. Within the IETF, there is occasionally a need to define new management information that does not fit into macros provided by SMIv2. An example is the definition of protocol identifiers for RMON-2 probes [9]. There is also a desire to augment MIB definitions. One of the well known examples is the assignment of severity levels for notifications[1]. Some management systems actually use quite complex annotations to map SMI notifications into OSI alarm records. The lack of an annotation mechanism in SMIv1/SMIv2 forces people to store annotations either in SMI comments or in DESCRIPTION clauses. This leads to MIB maintenance problems in multi-vendor environments since end users are now forced to manually merge modifications made by different vendors.

Finally, there are several issues with programmatic access to SMI definitions. Advanced SNMP toolkits and management platforms require fast access to large amounts of SMI definitions, e.g. to implement basic type checking, to convert enumerations to labels, to convert object identifier values to descriptors, or to apply display hints. User interfaces use SMI information to format tables or to display values together with their units. Since an application needs to deal with thousands of SMI definitions, it is necessary to load MIB modules fast and to balance the memory usage for storing MIB definitions against the time needed to locate a particular piece of information. There are currently no generally accepted APIs that address this issue. Instead, users are faced with several intermediate formats used by the various management tools in use. This makes the task of maintaining MIB modules on large management systems complex and error prone and it makes the implementation of custom management tools more complex than necessary.

## 3 SMIng Design

The first goal of the SMIng design was to overcome the dependency on external standards and to make the SMIng definition self-consistent. This includes the requirement to define SMIng formally in a BNF grammar to simplify the imple-

---

[1] Although frequently used in practice, this example is questionable since the severity of a notification generally depends on the current state of a network and is not static.

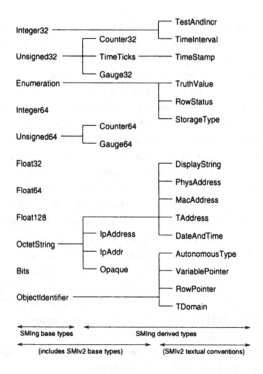

**Fig. 1.** SMIng base data types and fundamental derived data types

mentation of SMIng parsers. A decision was made to use the Augmented BNF (ABNF) [10] which is pretty powerful and under control of the IETF.

The second requirement for SMIng was to simplify the language where possible. An SMIng file simply contains a sequence of SMIng statements. Every SMIng statement starts with a leading lowercase keyword identifying the statement followed by a number of arguments. Statements are terminated by a semicolon. An argument may be quoted text, an identifier, a value of any base type, a list of identifiers enclosed in parenthesis or a statement block enclosed in curly braces. Since statement blocks are valid arguments, it is possible to nest statement sequences. These few rules build the core SMIng grammar rules and simplify the implementation of parsers. The strict statement separation by semicolon characters enables easy error recovery in parsers. SMIng uses case sensitive identifiers. Uppercase identifiers identify SMIng types and modules while lowercase identifiers identify statements, named numbers or nodes in the registration tree. Case sensitive identifiers simplify the conversion between SMIng and SMIv2 since ASN.1 identifiers are also case sensitive.

SMIng generally disallows forward references except in those cases where forward references are unavoidable (table indexing). Syntactic elements and the names of keywords were chosen to make MIB modules more understandable for the average network operator and programmer. Furthermore, SMIng definitions are compact since related definitions are not distributed over several locations within a MIB module. SMIng also avoids redundant definitions and it mandates a certain order of the statements in a MIB module.

The third goal was to overcome the current restrictions on SMI base data types. There is a long standing need for a more complete set of base data types (especially a complete set of 64 bit types) and SMIng provides them. The base types supported by SMIng as well as core derived data types are shown in Figure 1. Since the SMIng base types are not compatible with existing SNMP versions, a mapping needs to be defined from SMIng base types to the types available in a particular version of the SNMP protocol. The SMIv2 has been very close to the SNMP protocol. In fact, the protocol imports from the SMI definition. However, we believe that there are benefits in decoupling the SMI from SNMP since it is likely that MIB data will be carried by several different protocols in the future.

The fourth goal for SMIng was to support future SMI extensions without breaking deployed SMIng parsers. The solution adopted for SMIng achieves this goal using two simple mechanisms. First, the ABNF grammar contains productions that allow the parser to skip unknown statements. Second, the SMIng has an extension statement which can be used to define an SMIng extension. No attempts have been made to define the syntactic or even semantic aspects of an SMIng extension in order to keep SMIng simple by staying away from a meta level which adds considerable complexity and is likely to lead to implementation problems. However, having an identification of extensions is necessary so that parsers which "understand" a particular extension can decide whether a given statement is such an extension or not.

Finally, the fifth goal was to provide a mechanism to annotate SMIng definitions. MIB annotations have been used in several management systems to add information to a particular MIB definition. The SMIng provides an annotation construct which separates annotations from the annotated definition. This construct is actually defined through the SMIng extension mechanism and thus not part of the SMIng core.

## 4  SMIng Examples

This section presents some fragments of an SMIng MIB module. The examples are taken from the IF-MIB [11] converted into SMIng format.

Figure 2 shows the head of the IF-MIB module definition in SMIng. The first difference from SMIv2 is that module meta information (organization, contact, description, revision) is directly associated with the module. The ifMIB identifier in the module statement and the oid statement can be used to provide the information necessary to translate the SMIng module meta information into an invocation of the SMIv2 MODULE-IDENTITY macro. Another difference from SMIv2 is the absence of an explicit last update timestamp. SMIng uses the topmost revision statement to indicate the timestamp of the last modification. Figure 2 also shows the import statements for the IF-MIB module. It is generally not necessary to import SMIng constructs. However, derived SMIng types such as Counter32 must be imported from the relevant SMIng module.

```
module IF-MIB ifMIB {

    import IRTF-NMRG-SMING-TYPES (Counter32, Gauge32, Counter64, TimeTicks
                                  DisplayString, PhysAddress, TruthValue,
                                  RowStatus, TimeStamp, AutonomousType,
                                  TestAndIncr);
    import IRTF-NMRG-SMING (mib-2);
    import SNMPv2-MIB (snmpTraps);
    import IANAifType-MIB (IANAifType);

    oid          mib-2.31;

    organization "IETF Interfaces MIB Working Group";
    contact      "  Keith McCloghrie
                    Cisco Systems, Inc.
                    170 West Tasman Drive
                    San Jose, CA  95134-1706
                    US

                    408-526-5260
                    kzm@cisco.com";
    description  "The MIB module to describe generic objects for
                  network interface sub-layers.  This MIB is an updated
                  version of MIB-II's ifTable, and incorporates the
                  extensions defined in RFC 1229.";

    revision {
      date         "1996-11-03 13:55";
      description "[Revision added by libsmi due to a LAST-UPDATED clause.]";
    };
    revision {
      date         "1996-02-28 21:55";
      description "Revisions made by the Interfaces MIB WG.";
    };
    revision {
      date         "1993-11-08 21:55";
      description "Initial revision, published as part of RFC 1573.";
    };

    //...
};
```

**Fig. 2.** Module definition in SMIng

Figure 3 shows a type definition. The statements in the typedef block define
the base type including a range restriction, the display format and a description.
Note, there is no status statement for this definition. The absence of a status
statement associates the default status current with an SMIng definition.

SMIng allows to derive new types from any existing type, no matter whether
the existing type is a base type or a derived type. Type definitions can use a
units statement to define the units associated with that type. This is different
from SMIv2 which only allows UNITS clauses in OBJECT-TYPE definitions.

SMIng makes a distinction between scalar objects and columnar objects.
Figure 4 shows the definition of the scalar ifNumber and fragments of the definition of the table ifTable. Note that column statements are nested into a row
statement which is itself nested into a table statement. This nesting naturally
expresses the table registration structure and it avoids redundant definitions as
can be found in SMIv2.

```
typedef InterfaceIndex {
  type        Integer32 (1..2147483647);
  format      "d";
  description "A unique value, greater than zero, for each interface
               or interface sub-layer in the managed system.  It is
               recommended that values are assigned contiguously
               starting from 1.  The value for each interface sub-
               layer must remain constant at least from one re-
               initialization of the entity's network management
               system to the next re-initialization.";
};
```

**Fig. 3.** Type definition in SMIng

```
scalar ifNumber {
  oid         interfaces.1;
  type        Integer32;
  access      readonly;
  description "The number of network interfaces (regardless of their
               current state) present on this system.";
};

table ifTable {
  oid         interfaces.2;
  description "A list of interface entries.  The number of entries
               is given by the value of ifNumber.";

  row ifEntry {
    oid         ifTable.1;
    index       (ifIndex);
    description "An entry containing management information applicable
                 to a particular interface.";

    column ifIndex {
      oid         ifEntry.1;
      type        InterfaceIndex;
      access      readonly;
      description "A unique value, greater than zero, for each
                   interface.  It is recommended that values are
                   assigned contiguously starting from 1.  The
                   value for each interface sub-layer must remain
                   constant at least from one re-initialization of
                   the entity's network management system to the
                   next re-initialization.";
    };
    // ...
  };
};
```

**Fig. 4.** Scalar and table definition in SMIng

The table definition in Figure 4 is incomplete, which is indicated by a comment. Comments in SMIng start with the character sequence // and end at the end of the line.

Notifications are defined using the SMIng notification statement, which is very similar to the SMIv2 NOTIFICATION-TYPE macro. Figure 5 shows the definition of the linkDown notification.

```
notification linkDown {
    oid         snmpTraps.3;
    objects     (ifIndex, ifAdminStatus, ifOperStatus);
    description "A linkDown trap signifies that the SNMPv2 entity,
                acting in an agent role, has detected that the
                ifOperStatus object for one of its communication links
                is about to enter the down state from some other state
                (but not from the notPresent state). This other state
                is indicated by the included value of ifOperStatus.";
};
```

**Fig. 5.** Notification definition in SMIng

Object or notification definitions can be grouped using the group statement as shown in Figure 6. SMIng does not distinguish between notification groups and object groups. It is allowed to group notifications and objects together within a single group statement in SMIng. However, mixing notification and object definitions in an SMIng group makes it impossible to translate the SMIng module to SMIv2 automatically.

```
group ifCounterDiscontinuityGroup {
    oid         ifGroups.13;
    members     (ifCounterDiscontinuityTime);
    description "A collection of objects providing information
                specific to interface counter discontinuities.";
};
```

**Fig. 6.** Group definition in SMIng

Figure 7 shows parts of a compliance definition in SMIng. The compliance statement requires that all identifiers appearing in a compliance definition are locally defined or properly imported. This is different from SMIv2 which introduced special rules for resolving naming scopes in the MODULE-COMPLIANCE macro.

Finally, Figure 8 shows an IF-MIB annotation which makes the discontinuity indicator for counter objects machine readable. The ifTableDiscontinuity annotation uses an SMIng extension called discontinuity which is imported from the TUBS-IBR-EXTENSIONS MIB module. The target and description statements are part of the annotation extension and therefore not explicitly imported.

```
compliance ifCompliance {
    oid         ifCompliances.1;
    status      deprecated;
    description "The previous compliance statement for SNMPv2 entities
                which have network interfaces.";

    mandatory   (ifGeneralGroup, ifStackGroup);

    // ...

    optional ifPacketGroup {
      description "This group is mandatory for all network interfaces
                  which are packet-oriented.";
    };

    // ...

    refine ifAdminStatus {
      type        Enumeration ( up(1), down(2) );
      access      readonly;
      description "Write access is not required, nor is support for the
                  value testing(3).";
    };
};
```

**Fig. 7.** Compliance definition in SMIng

```
module TUBS-IBR-EXTENSIONS {

  //...

  extension discontinuity {
    description "Indicates the discontinuity indicating object for a
                given set of targets. The intended usage of this
                extension is within an annotation statement which
                identifies the targets. The ABNF definition for this
                extension is:

                    discontinuityStatement = discontinuityKeyword sep
                                                qlcIdentifier optsep ';'
                    discontinuityKeyword = 'discontinuity'
                ";
  };
};

module TUBS-IBR-IF-MIB-ANNOTATION {

  imports IRTF-NMRG-SMING-EXTENSIONS (annotation);
  imports TUBS-IBR-EXTENSIONS (discontinuity);

  //...

  annotation ifTableDiscontinuity {
    targets       (ifInOctets, ifInUcastPkts, ifInNUcastPkts,
                  ifInDiscards, ifInErrors, ifInUnknownProtos,
                  ifOutOctets, ifOutUcastPkts, ifOutNUcastPkts,
                  ifOutDiscards, ifOutErrors);
    discontinuity ifCounterDiscontinuityTime;
    description   "The discontinuity indicator for the ifTable.";
  };
};
```

**Fig. 8.** Annotation and extension in SMIng

## 5  SMI Library libsmi

There is no common way for management applications to access MIB definitions, neither in form of a standardized API to access SMIv1/SMIv2 files nor in form of a standardized intermediate file format. This section describes the design and implementation of a portable and reusable C library called libsmi providing access to all definitions contained in SMIv1, SMIv2 or SMIng MIB modules, except agent capability statements. In particular, the libsmi API provides access to:

- module definitions (struct SmiModule) including all revision information (struct SmiRevision),
- type definitions (struct SmiType) including named numbers in case of enumerated types like Bits and Enumeration (struct SmiNamedNumber) and size and range subtyping restrictions (struct SmiRange),
- all kinds of nodes in the registration tree defined by module, node, scalar, table, row, column, notification, group, compliance statements, or their SMIv1/v2 equivalents (struct SmiNode),
- all information associated with notifications, tables, groups, and compliance statements.

Figure 9 provides an overview over the data structures exported by the libsmi API.

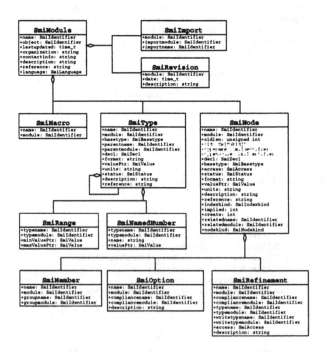

**Fig. 9.** Data structures exported by the SMI library

The access methods provided by the libsmi API include direct access functions by key values (e.g. names or object identifiers) as well as iterators like get-first/get-next functions to retrieve all available structures of a certain kind within a module. The library also provides functions to initialize and configure the behavior of libsmi and a function to add a module to the set of modules known by the application. Figure 10 shows a simple example program which prints an indented list of all nodes defined in a given module.

```
#include <stdio.h>
#include <smi.h>

int main(int argc, char *argv[])
{
    SmiNode *smiNode;

    if (argc != 2) {
        fprintf(stderr, "Usage: smitree module\n");
        exit(1);
    }

    smiInit();
    smiLoadModule(argv[1]);

    for(smiNode = smiGetFirstNode(argv[1], SMI_NODEKIND_ANY); smiNode;
        smiNode = smiGetNextNode(smiNode, SMI_NODEKIND_ANY)) {

        printf("%*s%s::%s\n", smiNode->oidlen * 2, " ", smiNode->module, smiNode->name);

    };

    return 0;
}
```

**Fig. 10.** Example usage of the SMI library

The internal library design consists of two layers as shown in Figure 11. The upper layer implements the API and the internal data structures that are used to store management information internally in memory. This layer retrieves the information through one or more backends residing on the lower layer of libsmi. The libsmi currently supports two parsers that are implemented using flex and bison, the improved GNU implementations of lex and yacc. One parser is derived from the SMIv1 and SMIv2 specifications. The other one strictly follows the SMIng ABNF grammar. Both parser backends resolve imports automatically by recursively parsing imported MIB modules.

The libsmi library includes two applications, a MIB checker and a MIB dump program. The MIB checker (smilint) uses the verbosity level of the underlying SMIv1/SMIv2 and SMIng parsers to generate errors and warnings about illegal or inadequate definitions in a MIB module. The MIB dump program (smidump) iterates through the definitions of a given module and writes the retrieved structures in one of several output formats. The supported output formats include SMIv1, SMIv2, SMIng, the mosy file format, a tree structure of recursively imported MIB modules, a tree structure of derived type definitions,

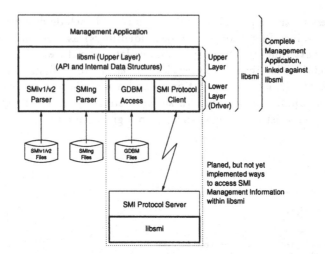

**Fig. 11.** Internal structure of the SMI library

a tree structure of node definitions, and CORBA IDL according to the JIDM specification translation rules [18].

The concept of backends and dump formats enables the conversion of MIB modules, e.g. dumping an SMIng module that is read by the SMIv2 parser backend and vice versa.

# 6 Related Work

Management Information Bases within the ISO management framework are defined using a set of templates, usually known as the Guidelines for the Definition of Managed Objects (GDMO) [12]. The GDMO language is very close to ASN.1 although it does not fully conform to the ASN.1 standard [13]. GDMO has similar problems like SMIv1/SMIv2 due to a close but not absolute relationship to ASN.1. The nine GDMO templates can be used to create very modular MIB definitions which enhances re-usability. However, the price for the modularity is that a reader of GDMO MIB definitions must follow several references in order to understand a managed object class definition. Instead, all existing SMI versions try to keep the relevant pieces of an object definition close together in order to enhance readability.

The Common Information Model (CIM) [14] is a relatively new management information model defined by the Desktop Management Task Force (DMTF). CIM schemas are used to define management information following an object-oriented approach. Schemas are stored in files using the Management Object Format (MOF). This format was inspired by the CORBA IDL language [15] but has substantial differences. The CIM model and the corresponding file format have an extension mechanism based on qualifiers. CIM distinguishes between meta, standard, optional and user-defined qualifiers. This allows to extend the

CIM and the MOF file format over time. However, user-defined qualifiers must be embedded in CIM schema files and are generally not recommended. There are currently no clear rules how to allocate qualifiers in an ordered way to avoid ambiguities. Recent work within the Web-Based Enterprise Management initiative aims to replace the MOF format with an XML [16] Document Type Definition (DTD) [17]. Using XML makes in our view a CIM schema definition less readable due to the space needed for the XML mark-up. However, the XML format allows developers to use off-the-shelf XML converters to produce hypertext versions for use with Web browsers. On the other hand, using XML means that the CIM file format depends on a technology not under control of the DMTF. This may result in derivations from the XML standard in the future, similar to the current situation with the derivation of the SMIv2 from ASN.1.

The CORBA standards of the Object Management Group (OMG) [15] have received quite some attention in the network management area. However, the Interface Definition Language (IDL) has so far not been used to standardize management information bases. This probably just shows the lack of an organization willing to standardize management information directly in IDL. It may also indicate that CORBA IDL is already too close to implementations and does not support the machine readable definition of other types of modeling information. The Joint Inter-Domain Management project (JIDM) has developed specifications how GDMO and SMI MIB modules can be translated into CORBA IDL definitions [18]. However, some machine readable information is usually lost during the translation since it shows up only in IDL comments and it is not possible to access this information at runtime easily.

# 7   Conclusions and Future Work

This paper proposes a new Structure of Management Information called SMIng for use with the Internet management framework. We presented the motivation and the requirements for SMIng. The main features of SMIng are the independence from ASN.1, a minimal and complete set of core data types, provisions for SMI extensions and annotations, compactness and simplicity. The specification of the SMIng has been submitted to the Network Management Research Group (NMRG) of the Internet Research Task Force (IRTF) for further development.

This paper also describes a reusable and portable C library which provides access to MIB definitions. It supports parser backends for SMIv1, SMIv2 and SMIng and hides the differences between the SMI versions as much as possible. Two applications using the libsmi library have been written to validate MIB definitions (smilint) and to convert MIB definitions between SMIv2, SMIng and other formats (smidump).

The implementation of the SMI library is freely available[2]. We plan to integrate the library into other open source management software packages (e.g. the UCD SNMP distribution) and to provide bindings to languages such as Tcl,

---

[2] http://www.ibr.cs.tu-bs.de/projects/libsmi/

Python or Java. Future work may also result in additional backends for the libsmi. Currently two ones are planned: A client libsmi might access management information through a protocol from a management information repository server that holds a large set of MIB modules, while clients do not have to load any modules, and consequently reach very short startup times. Another backend is planned to use a classical database file format like gdbm to store the management information. This will lead to short application startup times and low memory usage at the expense of slower libsmi function calls. Both plans require caching techniques in the library's upper layer and have to handle some problems with iterating access functions.

# References

[1] D. Perkins. SNMP Versions. *Simple Times*, 5(1), December 1997.

[2] M. Rose and K. McCloghrie. Structure and Identification of Management Information for TCP/IP-based Internets. RFC 1155, May 1990.

[3] M. Rose and K. McCloghrie. Concise MIB Definitions. RFC 1212, March 1991.

[4] M. Rose. A Convention for Defining Traps for use with the SNMP. RFC 1215, March 1991.

[5] K. McCloghrie, D. Perkins, J. Schönwälder, J. Case, M. Rose, and S. Waldbusser. Structure of Management Information Version 2 (SMIv2). RFC 2578, April 1999.

[6] K. McCloghrie, D. Perkins, J. Schönwälder, J. Case, M. Rose, and S. Waldbusser. Textual Conventions for SMIv2. RFC 2579, April 1999.

[7] K. McCloghrie, D. Perkins, J. Schönwälder, J. Case, M. Rose, and S. Waldbusser. Conformance Statements for SMIv2. RFC 2580, April 1999.

[8] D. Steedman. *Abstract Syntax Notation One (ASN.1): The Tutorial and Reference*. Technology Appraisals, 1990.

[9] A. Bierman and R. Iddon. Remote Network Monitoring MIB Protocol Identifiers. RFC 2074, January 1997.

[10] D. Crocker and P. Overell. Augmented BNF for Syntax Specifications: ABNF. RFC 2234, November 1997.

[11] K. McCloghrie and F. Kastenholz. The Interfaces Group MIB using SMIv2. RFC 2233, November 1997.

[12] ISO. Information technology — Open Systems Interconnection — Structure of Management Information — Part 4: Guidelines for the Definition of Managed Objects. International Standard ISO 10165-4, ISO, 1992.

[13] M. Sloman. *Network and Distributed Systems Management*. Addison-Wesley, 1994.

[14] DMTF. Common Information Model (CIM) Specification Version 2.0. CIM Standards, Desktop Management Task Force, March 1998.

[15] J. Siegel. *CORBA Fundamentals and Programming*. Wiley & Sons, 1996.

[16] T. Bray, J. Paoli, and C. M. Sperberg-McQueen. Extensible Markup Language (XML) 1.0. W3C Recommendation, Textuality and Netscape, Microsoft, University of Illinois, February 1998.

[17] DMTF. Specification for the representation of CIM in XML Version 1.0.1. CIM Standards, Desktop Management Task Force, January 1999.

[18] The Open Group. Inter-domain Management: Specification Translation. Preliminary specification p509, The Open Group, March 1997.

# An XML-based Framework for Dynamic SNMP MIB Extension

Ajita John, Keith Vanderveen, and Binay Sugla

Bell Labs Innovations, Lucent Technologies,
101 Crawfords Corner Rd
Holmdel, NJ 07733, USA,
{ajita,vandervn,sugla}@research.bell-labs.com

**Abstract.** Current SNMP-based management frameworks make it difficult for a network administrator to dynamically choose the variables comprising the MIB at managed elements. This is because most SNMP implementations represent the MIB implicitly as part of the agent code - an approach which impedes the runtime transfer of the MIB as a separate entity to be easily shipped around the network and incorporated into different applications. We propose the use of XML to represent MIBs at managed elements. We describe a network management toolkit which uses XML and the Document Object Model (DOM) to specify a MIB at runtime. This approach allows the MIB structure to be serialized and shipped over the network between managers and agents. This use of the DOM for MIB specification facilitates dynamic MIB modification. The use of XML also allows the MIB to be easily browsed and seamlessly integrated with online documentation for management tasks. XML further allows for the easy interchange of data between network management applications using different information models.

## 1 Introduction

Network management tools and applications which use the Simple Network Management Protocol (SNMP) tend to have low scalability and are inflexible and difficult to use. This is because, for most SNMP agents, the Management Information Base (MIB) is not a self-contained module but is instead dispersed throughout the agent code [16, 19]. This makes it difficult to modify or replace the MIB without replacing the agent, which causes the MIB to be out of date with respect to the needs of the network administrator.

The network administrator is often faced with a situation where some required information is not available in the MIB. This is illustrated in the following scenario: Hearing of the epidemic spread of an e-mail virus through the Internet, the administrator of an enterprise network wants to add some additional monitoring capability to his company's e-mail servers. Knowing that the virus replicates by e-mailing multiple copies of itself to addresses in the address book of a victim, the administrator decides to monitor the ratio of the number of e-mails received by users in his company to the number of e-mail senders. The decision to choose this ratio is based on the presumption that address books of people within an enterprise contain many addresses within the enterprise and a small number of infected users would send out email messages to a large number of people within the enterprise. If this ratio becomes higher than usual, a virus infection may be occurring. The number of stored e-mails is available as mta-StoredMessages from the Mail Monitoring MIB [12], but the number of e-mail senders is not in this MIB. This leads to the situation depicted in Figure 1(a) where the administrator searches for a variable #ESenders (number of e-mail senders) in a MIB but finds that #ESenders is not in the MIB. Current solutions to this problem either involve shutting the agent down and recompiling new instrumentation into the agent code [1] or spawning new sub-agents under a master agent [15]. Recompilation is inelegant and may not be feasible in all environments. The sub-agent approach is not scalable because each subagent runs as a separate process, and because of the overhead of sub-agent-to-master communication.

Another problem caused by the tight coupling of agent code and MIB is that there is no convenient way to transfer the MIB from an agent to another application. Determining an SNMP agent's MIB requires a MIB walk, which can take a number of network messages proportional to the size of the MIB [16]. Even after doing a MIB walk, variables from a part of the agent which are not working (because a sub-agent or the instrumentation for that part is not working) will not be visible [16] to a management application. We believe that transparent, efficient transfer of MIBs will become a necessity as we move towards larger networks, more complex and diverse network management applications, and multiple (possibly hierarchical) managers.

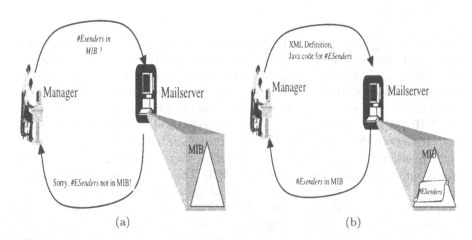

**Fig. 1.** Administrator (a) unable to get value of variable #ESenders (b) downloading definition and access code for #ESenders

We introduce XNAMI, an XML-based architecture for SNMP management with a *dynamically reconfigurable* or *eXtensible* MIB, to overcome the above-mentioned limitations of MIBs. In practice, there may be several MIBs per agent, e.g. MIB-II, the RMON MIB, the ATM MIB, etc. For simplicity of discussion, we group all these real MIBs into a single logical MIB that encompasses all the others. An XNAMI agent's MIB is represented as a document in XML [18], which allows the MIB structure to be serialized and shipped over the network between managers, agents, and other applications. The use of XML also allows the MIB representation to be easily browsed and seamlessly integrated with online documentation for management tasks. XML further allows for the easy interchange of data between network management applications using different information models, because of the widespread availability of tools to convert from one XML Document Type Definition (DTD) to another. Finally, XML's Document Object Model (DOM) [20] provides a convenient API which allows variables to be added to or deleted from the XNAMI MIB at runtime. In the preceding e-mail example, the administrator can write Java code which determines the value of *#ESenders* on most systems by scanning the files which hold mail for each user (on UNIX systems, this is usually in /var/spool/mail) and summing the results. If the mail servers are running XNAMI agents, the administrator can add the variable *#ESenders* to the MIB along with the associated Java access code (Figure 1(b)). The administrator can also add a *meta-variable* [7] which represents the ratio of the number of e-mails received by users in his company to the number of e-mail senders. The administrator can then monitor the ratio visually by displaying a graph of its value on a monitor, or set an SNMP trap to be triggered if the ratio rises above a certain threshold, or both.

To be able to add new instrumentation to an XNAMI MIB, a network administrator has to have both the skill to program the method code and access to the particular subsystem of the network element being instrumented. At present, most vendor-supplied network elements are closed boxes. However, by opening up at least a part of the internals of their products, network equipment vendors can help network providers achieve greater service differentiation. Therefore, we believe that network equipment will follow the trend toward open systems now being witnessed in the software industry.

The rest of this paper is organized as follows: Section 2 summarizes related work, Section 3 gives an introduction to XML and partial XML documents for some MIBs, , Section 4 describes the XNAMI agent and manager, and conclusions and directions for future work are given in Section 5.

## 2 Related Work

In a typical SNMP agent implementation, the MIB is hardwired into the agent code [16, 19]. That is to say, pointers to method routines for each MIB variable are stored in a data structure (usually a table of some sort), indexed by the OBJECT IDENTIFIER prefix that forms the name of the OBJECT-TYPE of the instance whose value is to be retrieved or changed. This data structure is compiled into the agent code, which necessitates a recompilation each time the MIB is changed. The only way provided by SNMP to see what variables are present in the MIB is to do a 'MIB-walk' by repeatedly invoking the get-next operation or the get-bulk operation on the agent, which requires many network messages and can be a time-consuming process [16].

Kalyanasundaram et al. describe an SNMP agent in which a part of the MIB is decoupled from the agent code [11]. Their agent contains a new kind of MIB module built around the notion of a spreadsheet, with data organized in two-dimensional tables of cells. Each cell contains an executable script which specifies how to compute the value of that cell from the values of other cells, or from data retrieved from other MIB modules or SNMP agents. A manager of the spreadsheet agent can create new cells by sending SNMP SET requests containing the scripts for computing the values in the new cells. A key difference between this spreadsheet agent and the XNAMI agent is that the spreadsheet cell values are derived, while in XNAMI new MIB variables may be defined which access system data directly. A related difference is that XNAMI provides control over the structure of the entire MIB residing at the agent, while the spreadsheet agent allows modifications only to the spreadsheet part of the MIB. The authors of [21] propose building a MIB on a remote agent using a scripting language, which is similar to the idea behind XNAMI. However, no implementation of this idea is described.

Wellens and Auerbach proposed using HTTP and HTML to access an agent's MIB [7]. The rationale behind their proposal was to replace UDP with HTTP as the transport protocol, thereby making retrieval of large amounts of data more efficient. They also proposed replacing the SNMP get, get-next, and get-bulk operators (and their set analogues) with get- and set-subtree operators that retrieve entire subtrees of an agent's MIB at once. Marvel [2] and the Push vs. Pull approach [14] are continuations of the Wellens and Auerbach work. Tsai and Chan implemented an SNMP agent which embodies these ideas but is 'bilingual' in that it can be accessed either through HTTP and HTML pages or SNMP [4]. Because HTML provides no way to define new elements, however, values of MIB variables have to be encoded in HTML documents either as binary data or using non-standard markup tags. Because XML allows the definition of new elements, XNAMI's representation of MIB variables uses just UTF-8 (which includes ASCII) characters and conforms to the XML standard. XNAMI also differs from both the Wellens et al. and Tsai et al. agents in that new variables can be added to the MIB at runtime by sending an XML description of the new variables, as well as code for the set and get methods. XNAMI's representation can also be extended to include new types of MIB variables and remain in conformance to the XML standard. Although XNAMI currently uses UDP as the transport protocol for communication between manager and agent, it could be modified easily to use HTTP.

HTML and HTTP have been used for network management applications which do not have SNMP MIBs at all [3, 17]. Among the advantages cited are reduced cost compared to SNMP/SMI MIB-based management applications and easy integration of displays of network information with on-line documentation or manuals. The HTML output of many of these systems is designed to be human readable, but not necessarily machine readable [3]. Another disadvantage of breaking with SNMP altogether is that new software must be written to communicate with SNMP-speaking agents and applications. XNAMI allows easy integration of MIBs into online documents without departing from the SNMP standard.

Recently, a new representation for management data called the Common Information Model (CIM) has been proposed [9]. CIM is based on the Unified Modeling Language (UML), and captures information about a network by modeling it as a collection of objects having certain relationships with each other. To date, no API or communication protocol has been defined for exchanging CIM information between applications. Like XNAMI, CIM will also use XML to exchange object definitions [9]. This makes it particularly easy to extend XNAMI's DOM MIB representation to represent CIM models as well. This would allow an XNAMI agent to be a CIM agent in addition to being an SNMP agent, as soon as a communication protocol for CIM is specified.

## 3 An XML Document Representation of MIBs

This section gives a brief introduction to the Extensible Markup Language (XML) and the Document Object Model (DOM) and presents a partial XML document for describing SMIv2 MIBs.

### 3.1 XML

XML is a *markup metalanguage*, i.e. a language for defining markup languages [6]. A *markup language* is a set of conventions used together for annotating text. The best known example of a markup language is Hypertext Markup Language (HTML), which is used to create web pages. HTML is defined using the markup metalanguage Standard Generalized Markup Language (SGML), a predecessor of XML [18]. XML is a simplified dialect of SGML which was designed to allow it to be served on the Web in a similar manner to HTML.

A self-contained piece of XML is called a *document*, and consists of storage units called *entities*, which contain either parsed or unparsed data. Parsed data is made up of characters, some of which form the character data in the document, and some of which form *markup*, a description of the document's storage layout and logical structure. Unparsed data may consist of characters or binary data, and contains no markup. Markup in XML (and SGML) consists of *elements*, which contain text or other elements. An example of an element is the list element in HTML, which is <li> ...some text... </li>. The element consists of a *start tag*, <li>, the contents ("...some text..." in the above example), and an *end tag*, </li>. Elements may also have *attributes*, which contain additional information about an element instance. An example of an element containing attributes is the following date element, in which YEAR, MONTH, and DAY are all attributes: <

date YEAR=1998 MONTH=07 DAY=28 />. This date element has no content because all of the information is present in the attributes, so the end tag is omitted and a backslash is placed just before the closing angle bracket instead.

To define a markup language using XML or SGML, one specifies the elements present in the language, the attributes which each element may or must have, and the relationships between elements (such as, that element type A may contain an element of type B, followed by an element of type C). These specifications occur in a *document type definition* (DTD). The SGML DTD for HTML may be found at [10]. Section 3.2 describes the DTD for the XML representation of the XNAMI MIB.

When an XML document is processed, it is typically parsed into a labeled directed graph where each node is an instance of an element, and node A has an arc to node B if element instance A has a relationship with element instance B. Examples of relationships which might be represented in this graph are "contains", "has as an attribute", "is an attribute of", and "is contained by". This graph is analogous to the parse tree produced by a parser of a high-level programming language such as C or Java. So that different XML applications can share this graph structure of a document with each other, a standard interface has been defined. This interface is known as the Document Object Model (DOM). DOM defines how the graph produced by parsing an XML document should look, and it also defines object interfaces to the nodes and arcs of this graph in OMG IDL [20]. A DOM instance of an XML document is realized by creating an object for each element of the document, using Java, DCOM, CORBA, or some other distributed object framework [20].

## 3.2  A Partial DTD Example

Unlike most SNMP agents, the XNAMI agent maintains an explicit runtime representation of its MIB, which is separate from and independent of the agent code itself. XNAMI maintains its MIB as a DOM representation of an XML document which reflects the structure of the OID tree. This representation is generated at startup by parsing an XML document describing the MIB. The objects in XNAMI's DOM representation are Java objects.

Figure 2 shows a Document Type Definition (DTD) for XML documents describing SMIv2 MIBs. A managed object is represented by an element *SMIV2-OBJECT* composed of five mandatory elements *NAME, OID, SYNTAX, MAX-ACCESS, STATUS, DESCRIPTION*, and three optional elements *REFERENCE, INDEXPART*, and *DEFVAL*. Element *NAME* contains an object name readable by people and is defined to be of type *PCDATA* (parsed text). Elements *OID* and *SYNTAX* also contain parsed text. *OID* provides an identifier of the object. *SYNTAX* refers to an abstract data structure corresponding to this object. Access information is given in element *MAX-ACCESS* consisting of exactly one of five possible subelements *not-accessible, accessible-for-notify, read-only, read-write*, or *read-create*. Each of these subelements are defined to be empty (i.e., they do not contain any text or elements). Element *STATUS* indicates whether this definition is current. *STATUS* includes one of three empty subelements *current, deprecated,* or *obsolete.* Elements *DESCRIPTION* and *REFERENCE* provide textual description and cross-reference for the object. Element *INDEX-PART* is used for instance identification when the managed object represents a conceptual row. *INDEXPART* consists of either subelement *INDEX* or subelement *AUGMENTS. INDEX* lists indexing objects described by optional empty subelement *IMPLIED* and subelement *OID. AUGMENTS* contains subelement *OID* that names the object corresponding to the augmented base conceptual row. Element *DEFVAL* defines an acceptable default value represented as parsed text.

```
<!ELEMENT SMIV2-OBJECT ( NAME,
                         OID,
                         SYNTAX,
                         MAX-ACCESS,
                         STATUS,
                         DESCRIPTION,
                         REFERENCE?,
                         INDEXPART?,
                         DEFVAL? )>
    <!ELEMENT NAME (#PCDATA)>
    <!ELEMENT OID (#PCDATA)>
    <!ELEMENT SYNTAX (#PCDATA)>
    <!ELEMENT MAX-ACCESS (not-accessible
                         | accessible-for-notify
                         | read-only
                         | read-write
                         | read-create)>
        <!ELEMENT not-accessible EMPTY>
        <!ELEMENT accessible-for-notify EMPTY>
        <!ELEMENT read-only EMPTY>
        <!ELEMENT read-write EMPTY>
        <!ELEMENT read-create EMPTY>
    <!ELEMENT STATUS (current | deprecated | obsolete)>
        <!ELEMENT current EMPTY>
        <!ELEMENT deprecated EMPTY>
        <!ELEMENT obsolete EMPTY>
    <!ELEMENT DESCRIPTION (#PCDATA)>
    <!ELEMENT REFERENCE (#PCDATA)>
    <!ELEMENT INDEXPART (INDEX | AUGMENTS)>
        <!ELEMENT INDEX (IMPLIED?, OID)+>
            <!ELEMENT IMPLIED EMPTY>
        <!ELEMENT AUGMENTS (OID)>
    <!ELEMENT DEFVAL (#PCDATA)>
```

**Fig. 2.** A DTD for SMIv2

*sysOREntry* is an SMIv2 object defined in [5]. Figure 3 presents *sysOREntry* as a XML document conforming to the DTD given above.

```
< ?xml version="1.0" encoding="UTF-8"?>
<!DOCTYPE SMIV2-OBJECT SYSTEM "smi-object.dtd">
<SMIV2-OBJECT>
    <NAME>
        sysOREntry
    </NAME>
    <OID>
        1.3.6.1.2.1.1.9.1
    </OID>
    <SYNTAX>
        SysOREntry
    </SYNTAX>
    <MAX-ACCESS>
        <not-accessible/>
    </MAX-ACCESS>
    <STATUS>
        <current/>
    </STATUS>
    <DESCRIPTION>
        An entry (conceptual row) in the sysORTable.
    </DESCRIPTION>
    <INDEXPART>
        <INDEX>
            <OID>
                1.3.6.1.2.1.1.9.1.1
            </OID>
        </INDEX>
    </INDEXPART>
</SMIV2-OBJECT>
```

**Fig. 3.** *sysOREntry* represented as an XML document.

## 4 XNAMI Architecture

XNAMI provides an elegant and flexible way to manage networks by supporting the following capabilities:

• New variables can be added to the MIB at a managed element. The definition and code required to access the new variable are downloaded from the manager to the agent.

- Unused variables can be deleted from the MIB at a managed element. The definition and code required to access the variable are removed from memory or disk, thereby conserving system resources.

- A view of the MIB for each managed element is available to a manager for browsing.

- Variables in the MIB at a managed element can be selected for monitoring. Each variable can have a customized monitoring patch which determines how the value of that variable will be displayed at the manager. A plotting chart is invoked for each monitored variable which displays the results of periodic polling of the value of the variable.

The entire XNAMI implementation is in Java. It uses the SNMPv3 protocol to send messages between the manager and the Agent. It also provides a web interface for the manager to send commands for adding, deleting, and monitoring variables to the Agent.

The requirements placed by XNAMI on the managed element are as follows:

1. There must be a Java Virtual Machine at the managed element.

2. The code to access an added variable in the MIB has to have the permission to execute at the managed element, i.e. must run with privileges if it needs to.

Figure 4 shows the architecture for the XNAMI system. It consists of three parts: the agent code which will reside on the managed element, the manager code which can reside on any system, and a web browser interface that the manager uses to interact with the agent. The remainder of this section describes the individual components of the manager and the agent, and describes how XNAMI uses XML to achieve MIB extensibility.

## 4.1 XNAMI MIB

An example of an XNAMI MIB tree is shown in Figure 5. Some of the upper-most nodes in the tree have been omitted for clarity. In the XNAMI MIB tree, leaf nodes represent items of management information which cannot be further subdivided (columnar or scalar objects in SNMP parlance). All other objects are internal nodes. The objects in a MIB actually represent classes of management information which may have one or more instances. In the XNAMI MIB, the code to perform a GET or SET on an instance of an object is stored in the node for that object. Any additional information concerning an instance of an object is stored in a cell of an array indexed by the instance number, and the array is stored at the object node. When XNAMI receives a GET or SET request, it takes the OID argument to the request and traverses the MIB tree until it finds the node having that OID. Because only instances of scalar or columnar objects can be the targets of GETs or SETs, this node must be a leaf node. XNAMI then retrieves the code (using Java's dynamic classloading capabilities) for performing the GET or SET and executes it, passing in the instance number as a parameter. The GET or SET code can use the instance number to access the array to retrieve information associated with the instance; in the extreme case, this could even be more code to execute, specific to that instance. A new

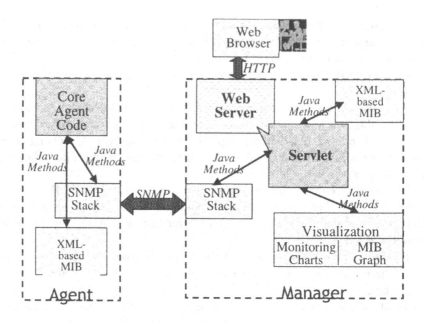

**Fig. 4.** Architecture for XNAMI

instance of an object can be created by doing a SET on the object with the instance number of the new instance.

To illustrate how objects are stored in an XNAMI MIB, consider tcpConnEntry, which is a composite object representing a TCP connection. It is composed of the objects tcpConnLocalAddress, tcpConnLocalPort, tcpConnRemAddress, and tcpConnRemPort. In the XNAMI MIB, tcpConnLocalAddresss is a leaf node, as are the other components of tcpConnEntry. tcpConnEntry itself is an internal node, with tcpConnLocalAddress and its other components as children. To retrieve the value of instance $n$ of tcpConnEntry, a manager would do GETs on instance $n$ for each of tcpConnEntry's components.

New MIB objects are added to the tree through the two leaf nodes shown in Figure 5, mib_proxy and methods_proxy. To add a subtree onto an agent's MIB, an XNAMI manager performs SET operations on the mib_proxy and methods_proxy objects. The structure of an SNMP SET PDU which performs this SET operation is shown in Figure 6. The PDU contains the OID for each proxy followed by a string containing the value to which it is set. Please note that there is nothing special about the structure of the PDU shown in Figure 6; strings are a common SNMP data type, and any SNMP SET PDU would look similar.

The value to which the manager SETs mib_proxy is a string containing a description in XML of the new objects in the subtree. This string is parsed in the same manner as the XML document describing the MIB at startup, and a DOM representation produced. This DOM representation of the new subtree is then grafted on to the MIB tree.

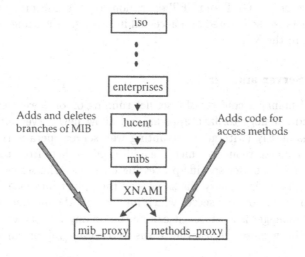

**Fig. 5.** Two new variables added to MIB

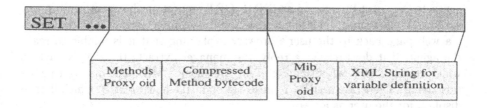

**Fig. 6.** SNMP PDU

The values which the manager passes to the methods_proxy object are strings containing compressed Java bytecode, one for each leaf node being added to the tree. The bytecode strings contain the code for doing GET and SET operations on the newly-added MIB objects. As the new MIB objects are created, the bytecode for each node is decompressed and loaded as a Java class containing two methods, one for a GET on the MIB object and the other for a SET. An instance of this class is then created and stored in the node created for the new MIB object. The use of compression necessitates an agreement between the manager and agent on the compression algorithm being used. If the bytecode sent to the agent or the data returned by the agent (see Section 4.2) does not fit into a single PDU, then it can be sent over multiple PDUs using a method similar to that described in [8].

Deletion of MIB objects is accomplished simply by performing a SET operation on mib_proxy. The XML string passed as a value contains the simple command "delete" and the OID of the node to be deleted. Deleting a node has the effect of removing the entire subtree rooted at that node.

The code for the GET and SET operations on the mib_proxy and method-s_proxy objects is itself stored and accessed in precisely the same way as for any other object in the MIB.

## 4.2 Web Server and Servlet

The XNAMI manager consists of a servlet running on on a web server. Servlets are server-side analogs to Java applets, and allow new server functionality to be added seamlessly (without interrupting web server operation) at run time. Servlets receive http requests which are addressed to them from the web server, and then do some servlet-specific processing on them. The servlet interface facilitates portability in exactly the same way the applet interface does, because a servlet should run on any server which implements the interface [13]. Because the XNAMI manager is a servlet, it can be run on any web server that supports servlets. We have chosen to use the Nexus web server [13] for our work because it is free.

To manage an XNAMI agent, the user enters the agent's address in an HTML form on a web browser and submits it to a web server running the XNAMI manager servlet. The web server passes the form to the XNAMI servlet, which then contacts the agent by sending an SNMP GET request on the agent's mib_proxy variable. If the manager doesn't receive a reply within a timeout period, it sends a web page back to the user's browser explaining that it is unable to reach the agent. If it does receive a reply, the manager extracts the reply's payload which contains an XML string describing the agent's MIB. The manager parses this string to generate a DOM representation of the agent's MIB, which it then displays for the user as a tree.

The user requests the addition or deletion of variables in an agent's MIB through HTML forms generated by the XNAMI manager and displayed on the user's browser. The manager then sends to the agent SNMP SET requests on the mib_proxy and methods_proxy variables to carry out these requests. In response to each SET on mib_proxy, the agent returns an XML string describing the state of its MIB after the SET is performed. This XML string is, in a sense, the 'value' of the mib_proxy variable, and it is consistent with SNMP semantics to return the new value of a variable whenever a SET is performed on that variable. The XNAMI manager uses these XML strings to update the user's graphical display of the agent's MIB, and also to generate new HTML forms for the user's browser which provide choices to the user as to which variables can be uploaded to the agent, deleted from the agent, or monitored. 'Monitored' variables have their values polled periodically by the manager and to the user.

## 4.3 Distributed Management Issues

In a distributed management scenario, there could be multiple managers for a managed element and the potential for confusion if one manager modifies variables being monitored by another manager. Such confusion can be avoided by using SNMP traps to notify managers if another manager has altered a part of an agent's MIB. The agent's MIB could also include a log of all the changes made to the MIB. Potential conflicts in OIDs for variables added to an agent's MIB by different managers in an organization can be avoided by having a central repository for OIDs or by giving each manager a separate subtree of the MIB.

## 5   Conclusions and Future Work

This paper describes the ideas and implementation behind an XML-based architecture for SNMP management of networks and applications. This architecture, called XNAMI, allows runtime MIB extension within the SNMP framework. The use of XML allows the MIB to be shipped over the network, browsed easily, and seamlessly integrated with online documentation for management tasks, especially configuration ones. XML also facilitates interoperability by allowing for the easy interchange of data between management applications using different information models.

We plan to extend the XML description of MIB objects in XNAMI to include suggestions to the XNAMI manager on how data for that object should be presented visually to the user. For example, an object such as the number of dropped packets at an interface might most logically be presented as a line chart and plotted with respect to time, while the up or down status of an interface could be presented using an icon which is either green (up) or red (down). The advantage to storing visual presentation cues such as these with the XNAMI agent is that managers will be able to more appropriately display data from MIB objects with which they have no familiarity. We also plan to explore the use of the XNAMI framework in various application management areas such as distributed program debugging where program variables in memory have to be monitored.

**Acknowledgements**
Sergey Gorinsky from The University of Texas at Austin helped in the design of the DTD presented in Section 3.2. Jean-Philippe Martin-Flatin from The Swiss Fed. Inst. of Technology, Lausanne (EPFL) helped with comments which improved the final version of the paper.

## References

1. AdventNet. http://www.adventnet.com.
2. N. Anerousis. A distributed computing environment for building scalable management services. In *Proceedings of the 6th IFIP/IEEE Integrated Management, Boston MA, May 1999.*, May 1999.
3. B.Bruins. Some Experiences with Emerging Management Technologies. *The Simple Times*, 4(3):9–12, July 1996. http://www.simple-times.org.
4. C.-W.Tsai and R.-S.Chan. SNMP through WWW. *International Journal of Network Management*, 8(2):104–119, March-April 1998.

5. J. Case, K. McCloghrie, M. Rose, and S. Waldbusser. *Management Information Base for Version 2 of the Simple Network Management Protocol (SNMPv2)*, January 1996. IETF RFC 1907.

6. C.M.Sperberg-McQueen and L.Burnard. Guidelines for electronic text encoding and interchange (tei p3). http://www-tei.uic.edu/orgs/tei/sgml/teip3sg/.

7. C.Wellens and K.Auerbach. Towards Useful Management. *ConneXions*, 10(9):2–9, September 1996.

8. J. Schoenwaelder D. Levi. *Definitions of Managed Objects for the Delegation of Management Scripts*, May 1999. IETF RFC 1902.

9. DMTF. Common Information Model Web page. http://www.dmtf.org/spec/cims.html.

10. I.Jacobs D.Raggett, A.Le Hors. Html 4.0 strict dtd. http://www.w3.org/TR/REC-html40/sgml/dtd.html#dtd.

11. P. Kalyanasundaram, A. Sethi, C. Sherwin, and D. Zhu. A Spreadsheet-Based Scripting Environment for SNMP. In *Integrated Network Management, V*, pages 752–765. Chapman and Hall, 1997.

12. S. Kille and N. Freed. *Mail Monitoring MIB*, January 1994. IETF RFC 1566.

13. Anders Kristensen. Nexus web server page. http://www.hplbwww.hpl.hp.com/people/ak/java/nexus.

14. J.P. Martin-Flatin. Push vs. Pull in web-based network management. In S. Mazumdar M. Sloman and E. Lupu (Eds.), editors, *Proc. 6th IFIP/IEEE International Symposium on Integrated Network Management (IM'99)*. IEEE Press, May 1999.

15. M.White and S.Gudur. An Overview of the AgentX Protocol. *The Simple Times*, 6(1), March 1998. http://www.simple-times.org.

16. D. Perkins and E. McGinnis. *Understanding SNMP MIBs*. Prentice Hall, 1997.

17. P.Mullaney. Overview of a Web-based Agent. *The Simple Times*, 4(3):12–18, July 1996. http://www.simple-times.org.

18. R.Cover. The SGML/XML Web Page. http://www.oasis-open.org/cover/sgml-xml.html.

19. S.Roberts. An Introduction to SNMP MIB Compilers. *The Simple Times*, 2(1), January 1993. http://www.simple-times.org.

20. W3C. The DOM Web page. http://www.w3c.org/DOM.

21. D. Zhu, A. Sethi, and P. Kalyanasundaram. Towards Integrated Network Management Scripting Frameworks. In *Proceedings of the Ninth Annual IFIP/IEEE International Workshop on Distributed Systems: Operations and Management*, pages 233–246, Newark, DE, October 1998.

# Directory Supported Management with SNMPv3

Salima Omari[1], Raouf Boutaba[2], Omar Cherkaoui[3]

[1] Laboratoire PRiSM, Université de Versailles, 45 avenue des Etats-Unies,
78 000 Versailles, France
osa@prism.uvsq.fr
[2] Computer Science Department, University of Waterloo,
Waterloo, Ontario, Canada, N2L 3G1
rboutaba@cs.uwaterloo.ca
[3] Laboratoire de téléinformatique, Université UQAM, CP 8888, Succursale Centre-Ville,
Montreal, Quebec, Canada, H3C3P8
cherkaoui.omar@ info.uqam.ca

**Abstract.** Data security and maintaining system integrity are the primary concerns pointed out by corporations and individuals when connecting to the Internet. To respond to this demand, the most recent agreed Internet management standard, SNMPv3, introduces new security features to make SNMP-based management ready for enterprise management. This is possible only if the SNMPv3 management framework is introduced properly in the enterprise, i.e., in such a way to respond efficiently to the management and security requirements specific to this enterprise. This paper proposes the use of standard directory service and protocol to configure SNMPv3 entities, to regulate SNMPv3 management exchanges and to customize security features according to the enterprise needs. It addresses in particular the configuration of access control parameters to be implemented by SNMPv3 entities according to enterprise security policies.

## 1 Introduction

Data security and maintaining system integrity are the primary concerns pointed out by corporations and individuals when connecting to the Internet. The recently agreed version of the Internet management standard, SNMPv3, overcomes the weakness of the previous versions of the protocol by allowing authentication, privacy and access control to be performed during the exchange of messages between SNMPv3 entities (i.e., SNMPv3 managers and agents). This functionality is performed within the entity subsystems, more precisely by the security subsystem and the access control subsystem. The modular architecture of the entity, as defined by the IETF (Internet Engineering Task Force), allows these subsystems to implement different security models. The models currently defined with SNMPv3 management are: USM (User-based Security Model) [6]; and VACM (View-based Access Control Model) [5]. These additions allow the SNMPv3 management platform to claim reliability and hence readiness to be introduced into enterprise network management. In current practices, configuration information and security parameters are maintained in distinct data stores, in multiple formats, and possibly by different managers. This may lead to inconsistent management decisions, which may lead, in turn, to the enforcement of conflicting security policies, and hence to jeopardizing enterprise information security.

This work aims at tackling the above-stated problem by using a uniform, enterprise-wide directory service to efficiently support SNMPv3 management applications. It aims in particular at implementing consistent models for security parameters within a logically centralized, physically distributed information store (the directory). In general, this approach will reduce the complexity of the task of managing large corporate networks. In particular, it will facilitate the proper configuration of SNMPv3 entities and ultimately its automation. Central to the proposed approach is the directory service used to store and access information about users, network devices, and applications including management applications. The adopted directory service allows various network applications and services to share information accessed through a uniform protocol, namely the Lightweight Directory Access Protocol (LDAP).

This paper emphasizes the use of a standard directory to store and access SNMPv3 security parameters used to configure and (re-)initialize SNMPv3 management entities. To promote interoperability between various management applications, SNMPv3 informational model is described according to the Directory Enabled Network (DEN) specification [3]. The DEN is an industry initiative standardized within the DMTF (Desktop Management Task Force) to provide a uniform model representing users, profiles, applications and network services within the directory through which management data from any source can be accessed in a common way. We extend the DEN specifications to integrate the SNMPv3 information model. SNMPv3 persistent information is maintained by the directory service and can be shared/reused by a variety of authorized management applications and tools.

This paper is organized as follows. Section 2, gives an overview of SNMP version 3 highlighting the security features, the subsystems of the SNMPv3 framework supporting these features, as well as the security models defined for these subsystems. Section 3, describes the usage of the directory for management purpose including the DEN specifications for enterprise network and systems management and the LDAP protocol commonly used as directory service and protocol. Section 4, introduces our proposal for SNMPv3 directory-enabled management. It presents an integrated SNMPv3 directory-enabled management architecture describes the LDAP classes related to the SNMPv3 entities. Section 5 describes our ongoing implementation and section 6 concludes the paper.

## 2  SNMPv3 Management Framework

Like the previous versions, the new generation of the Internet-Standard Management Framework (referred to as SNMP version 3) is based on the agent-manager model. However, it provides a new architectural model and new security features. The new features of SNMPv3 include security (authentication and privacy , as well as authorization and access control) and administrative framework (naming of entities, usernames and key management, notification destinations, proxy relationships, remotely configuration via SNMP operations).

The SNMPv3 specifications of the Internet-Standard Management Framework are based on a modular architecture [7]. As depicted by Figure 1, the SNMP entity, either manager or agent, consists of an SNMP engine and one or several associated applications.

The SNMPv3 engine consists of the dispatcher, the message processing subsystem, the security subsystem, and the access control subsystem.

The dispatcher coordinates the communications between the various subsystems. The message processing subsystem is responsible for preparing outgoing messages and for extracting data from received messages. It may support several message processing models, for example SNMPv1, SNMPv3, etc.

The security subsystem provides message security services such as integrity, authentication and privacy. Multiple security models may be supported by the security subsystem. For instance, the User-based Security Model (USM), described in RFC2574 [6], is the standard security model currently used with SNMPv3. It provides integrity, authentication and privacy services by computing message authentication codes, key management and data encryption. The access control subsystem constitutes a decision making point to allow or not a specific type of access (e.g., read, write, notify) to a particular object instance. Similarly, to the security services, the access control services can be provided by multiple access control models to allow future updates in case the security requirements change. The View-Based Access Control Model (VACM), described in RFC2275 [5], is one such model currently used within SNMPv3 access control subsystem. It basically allows restricting access to a subset of the management information referred to as a MIB view.

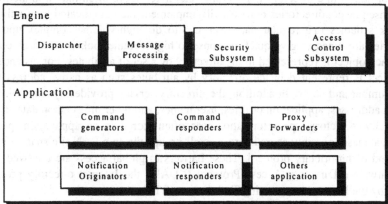

**Fig. 1.** Architecture of SNMPv3 entities

At the application level of the SNMPv3 entity, the various applications use the services provided by the SNMPv3 engine to accomplish specific tasks. According to the role of the SNMP entity (manager or agent), five dominant types of applications can be enumerated: command generators; command responders; notification generators; notification receivers; and proxy forwarders. The reader can refer to [8] for more details about these application types or other possible applications.

The subsystems, models, and applications within an SNMP entity may need to maintain their own sets of configuration information. Portions of the configuration information may be accessible as managed objects. The collection of these sets of information is referred to as an entity's Local Configuration Datastore (LCD).

As described in this section, the new SNMP framework offers an extensible architecture composed of a set of subsystems. Each subsystem may implement different mechanisms and support multiple models. Traditionally, security parameters are maintained in the MIBs encapsulated by the SNMP entities associated with the various network elements. This makes the maintenance of global security information difficult. Indeed, the various MIBs are distributed throughout the enterprise network and are more adapted for the storage of dynamic, frequently changing, information about the state of the devices. For persistent global management information such as enterprise security policies, a more appropriate repository is required. A directory service, that provides a logically centralized physically distributed database for enterprise wide information and global management strategies, is a more natural alternative. In this perspective, we introduce, in the next section, the use of a directory service for network management.

## 3 Directory Services for Network Management

A Directory can be considered as a special database that contains attribute-structured information. Such a database is more descriptive than traditional relational databases. The information in a directory is generally read much more often than it is modified. As a consequence, directories don't usually implement the complicated transaction or roll-back schemes that regular databases use to do high-volume complex updates. Directories are tuned to give quick-response to high-volume lookup or search operations. Each object is represented in the directory by a set of attributes. For instance, an user object is represented in the directory by attributes such as name, address telephone number and so on. In addition, the directory service provides dynamic binding between addresses, application profiles, user names, and other information data stores. Historically, directory-type information was often stored in an application-specific private database, possibly shared across small groups through LAN file sharing using some kind of proprietary protocol. These barriers to global access are removed with the Lightweight Directory Access Protocol (LDAP), the Internet directory protocol defined by the Internet Engineering Task Force (IETF).

LDAP is a strategic directory protocol that runs over TCP/IP [10] [11]. It defines a reasonably simple mechanism for Internet clients to query and manage an arbitrary database of hierarchical attribute value pairs. The LDAP directory service model is based on entries. An entry is treated as an object. An LDAP object is an entity that is described with attributes and has a unique name, Distinguished Name (DN), by which it is referred to when used along with other objects. LDAP directory entries are organized in a hierarchical, tree-like, structure that reflects corporate, geographical and/or organizational boundaries. For instance, the entries representing countries appear at the top layer of the tree.

The definition of an LDAP object class includes, a name that uniquely identifies the class, an OID that also uniquely identifies the class, a set of mandatory attributes types, a set of allowed attribute types, and a Kind (structural, auxiliary, or abstract).

The kind of the object class indicates how the class is used. Structural classes, for example, describe the basic aspects of an object. It can be used to place restriction on where an entry can be stored within the directory information tree (DIT). Most object classes are structural classes. Auxiliary classes do not place restriction on where an entry may be stored, and they are used to add a set of related attributes to an entry that already belongs to a structural class. Abstract classes are rare and are used only for classes needed to support LDAP's basic information model.

**Example of LDAP classes:**

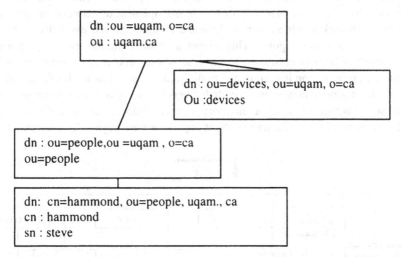

The version 3 of the LDAP protocol [12] requires that directory servers publish their supported schemas through LDAP itself. This allows directory client applications to programmatically retrieve the schema and adapt their behavior based on it. It also allows the protocol to be extended to support new operations, and controls may be used to extend existing operations.

The authentication process, when accessing the directory, is called *binding*. There are different types of binding methods. In a simple bind, the client presents a DN and a password in clear text to the LDAP server. The server verifies that the password matches the password value stored in the *userpassword* attribute of the entry and, if so, returns a success code to the client. The simple bind does send the password over the network to the server in clear. However, one can protect against eavesdroppers intercepting passwords by encrypting the connections, for example using secure sockets layer (SSL) or transport security layer (TLS) [14]. SSL and TLS allow encrypting all the data flowing between a client and a server. LDAPv3 also includes a new type of binding operation, the SASL bind. SASL[13] is an extensible, protocol-independent framework for performing authentication and negotiation of security parameters. With SASL, the client specifies the type of authentication protocol it wants to use (e.g. kerberos, S/Key). If the server supports the authentication protocol, the client and server perform the agreed-upon authentication protocol. Incorporating SASL into LDAPv3 means that new authentication methods can be easily implemented for LDAP without requiring a revision of the protocol.

After the server has verified the identity of the client. It can choose to grant additional privileges based on some site-specific policy thanks to the access control list (ACL). ACL provides information about the entities to which those rights are granted, and the directory entries to which those rights apply. For example, a more permissive policy allows some authenticated users to modify certain attributes of their own entries whereas other users (e.g. administrative staff) may modify any attribute of any entry.

Actual implementations of directory services support a wide scope of applications including electronic mail, printing services, and many others. The LDAP directory service has also been used as a support for the management of network equipment. It allows both network administrators and routers to store and retrieve network-related information from a single point. This allows a network administrator to manage a network more efficiently compared to the case where persistent information such as configuration information is maintained in different databases at the levels of individual devices. Sharing management knowledge between various management processes is another advantage of using a directory service. Indeed, the directory acts as a global repository storing information about objects that are physically distributed.

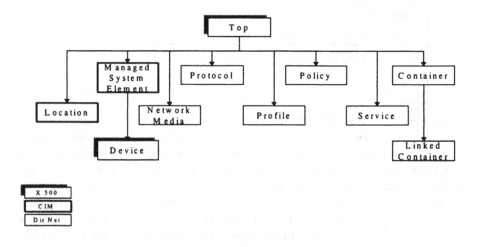

**Fig 2.** DEN Hierarchy Classes

Usually directory information has to be replicated in order to allow for efficient access from anywhere in the system as well as fault tolerance. It is the role of the directory service to ensure the consistency of the replicated information by reporting updates among the replicas. However, in order to permit a true exchange of network, system and service management data among heterogeneous management tools, a standard schema for describing these data is required. A recent initiative known as the DEN (Directory Enabled Network) standardized within the DMTF aims at enhancing the standard X.500 directory service to integrate enterprise network elements, services, and policies. The considered classes concern high-level management information such as routing policies or quality of service (QoS) parameters.

Fig.2. shows the main classes specified as part of the DEN initiative. It particularly shows how DEN is built upon CIM (Common Information Model) and X500 [9] to model the functional and management interfaces of network elements and services. The resulting common schema yields increased integration of management applications and tools.

## 4  Directory Support SNMPv3 Management

The objective pursued here through SNMPv3/DEN integration is the efficient configuration of SNMP entities. Rather than making a connection to each device and performing a one-by-one configuration of SNMPv3 entities, the network manager only places the appropriate configuration attributes into the node's entry in the directory server. When a SNMPv3 device is initialized, its associated LDAP client queries the directory server and obtains its configuration details. This allows configurations of the Local Configuration Data Store (LCD) with consistent information. The configuration is applied uniformly across different SNMPv3 entities.

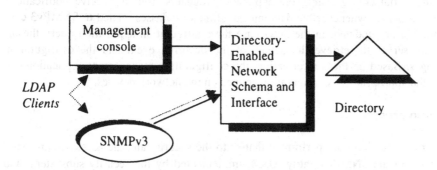

**Fig. 3.** LDAP-enabled SNMPv3 management

Another advantage of the directory-based SNMPv3 management is to enable various applications to share information on SNMPv3 entities through the directory. Fig. 3 illustrates the overall architecture including the directory service and SNMPv3-based management entities.

According to this architecture, the LDAP directory server contains the SNMPv3 LDAP classes. The Directory enabled network schema and interface consists of an API that allows clients to access the directory information.

There are two kinds of clients that access the directory:

- The administrator who populates the directory with data related to the snmpv3 entity. There are two types of data. The first type is related to the general configuration of the SNMPv3 entity subsystems, namely the security subsystem, the access control subsystem, the message processing subsystem, and the application part. These data are contained in the SNMPv3Modules class. The second type is related to "the existence" of the SNMPv3 agents and their individual configurations. A manager who wants to create an SNMPv3 agent must create a class with an engineID as distinguished name, and must decide its initial configuration. The references to the subsystems' configuration of this SNMPv3 agent are then made automatically.
- The SNMPv3 entity. At entity set-up, the SNMPv3 application acting as an LDAP client searches its initial configuration into the LDAP directory server using the engineID. The SNMPv3 obtains the initial configurations and then translates them into SNMPv3 MIB attributes.

### Dynamic configuration

To allow for dynamic and timely updates of SNMPv3-entities' configuration, the configuration process interacts with a monitoring service, which in turn interacts with the LDAP directory service. The provided event-based monitoring service allows to associate data from a variety of applications, and allows applications such as configuration management to capture the flow of information and respond to events as they occur. Directory principals, i.e. users, applications, and network devices, store event types in the directory and produce events that are stored in event queues. After setting up the initial configuration, the application registers itself to receive notifications from the server whenever the data into the directory classes related to SNMPv3 configuration are updated. In the latter case the configuration application query the directory server to retrieve the details of the occurred event and the configuration changes. Based on these information, the configuration management application can take the appropriate re-configuration actions on the network devices.

### Security services

Security procedures are performed thanks to the security and the access control subsystems in the SNMPv3 entity. USM, implemented by the security subsystem, and VACM, implemented by the access control subsystem, are the models currently standardized as part of the SNMPv3 framework. The USM model provides authentication, which checks the identity of data sources. It also provides privacy through a protection against disclosure of the message payload, and a protection against message delay or replay. Management operations using the USM model use the traditional concept of a per-user association of security information. An SNMP engine must have knowledge of any particular user from which authorized management operations are stemming prior to perform these operations. The VACM model allows checking if access for a given group is permitted to a set of MIB variables identified by a MIB View.

The use of a directory service in supporting SNMPv3 management should not threaten SNMPv3 security. The LDAP directory protocol must provide a sufficient security level so as not to jeopardize the SNMPv3 security feature. The LDAP security model relies on the connection-oriented nature of the LDAP protocol. This means that a LDAP client opens a connection with an LDAP server and sends a number of protocol data units on the same connection. The clients are responsible for initiating a communication to an LDAP server using the bind operation, which involves an authentication of the client. A client identifies itself by providing a distinguished name (DN) and a set of credentials. The server checks whether the credentials are correct for the given DN and, if they are, notes that the client is authenticated as long as the connection remains open.

## 4.1. SNMPv3-LDAP Objects

The integrated SNMPv3/DEN schema extends the DEN information model by adding classes that represent SNMPv3 entities. This integration facilitates the management of network devices offering SNMPv3 interfaces. The LDAP directory contains configuration parameters of SNMPv3 entities. These SNMPv3 data are searched and accessed (read/write operations) by management entities directly or by network administrators through a management tool capable of parsing and displaying the specific schema structure.

We have defined two kinds of LDAP object classes related to SNMPv3 management. The first one describes the SNMPv3 entities that must exist in the administrative Network. This object class, see fig.4, identified by the SnmpEngineID. The latter uniquely identifies the SNMPv3 entity and hence the representative object of the class. The attributes of the object class contain the description of the entity and its subsystems.

The second kind of object classes relates to the different model and subsystem that can compose the entity and their possible initial configurations. The manager has to select an initial configuration. These classes are ACM, SM, MP, D and Application classes which respectively correspond to the access control model subsystem, the security model subsystem, the message processing subsystem, the dispatcher subsystem, and the applications. Since each subsystem may contain several models, we define sub-classes, each of which corresponds to a given model. Examples of these sub-classes are the VACM and USM sub-classes. The MP class contains others sub-classes, each of which describes the message processing model, such as the one of SNMv1, SNMPv2, or SNMPv3. Fig.4 gives an overview of the LDAP object classes related to the SNMPv3 entity.

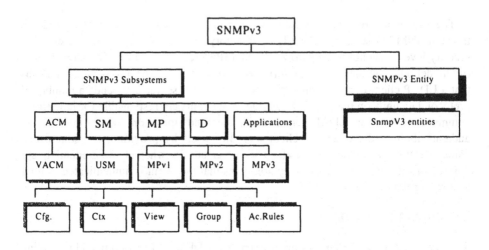

**Fig.4.** SNMPv3 LDAP object

The modularity of the SNMPv3 architecture and the object oriented modeling of information allow to add (respectively remove), in a flexible way, applications into (respectively from) an SNMPv3 entity either manager or agent. Our directory based management architecture allows to easily incorporating a directory service client (LDAP client) into the entity application part (see Fig.1). This new application is launched when the SNMPv3 entity is started within a device. It requests the directory service (LDAP server) for entity information such as entity configuration parameters or security parameters. Fig.5 shows the extension of the SNMPv3 entity architecture to include an LDAP client and thereby integrating directory service support for SNMPv3-based management applications.

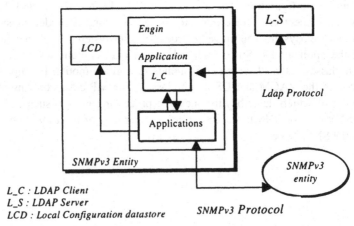

L_C : LDAP Client
L_S : LDAP Server
LCD : Local Configuration datastore

**Fig. 5.** SNMPv3 entity architecture

The implementation of the prototype is done at UQAM University as an extension of the ModularSNMPv3 project, which implemented a SNMPv3 platform in JAVA.

To configure the SNMPv3 entities we have used the Sun Directory which offers a global directory and naming service. The latter includes an LDAP server compliant with the LDAP v3 Internet standard. It provides options to encrypt the communications between clients and the server using SSL, and an authentication mechanism (CRAM MD5) during the binding operation through the SASL protocol. Also supported is the EXTERNAL mechanism when the SSL library is installed on the server, and the server is configured to support TLS security.

The Java Naming and Directory Interface (JNDI) [15] has been used for the implementation of the LDAP clients, the user interface and the SNMPv3-configuration application. JNDI provides directory and naming functionality to Java applications. It is defined to be independent of any specific directory service implementation. Consequently, a variety of directories already existing or upcoming can be integrated and accessed in a uniform way.

Finally, the EventDirContext method contained in the Javax.naming.event package provided by JNDI2.1 is used to permit the registration of clients' interest in the occurrence of certain events and their notification whenever these events occur. This way LDAP clients representing SNMPv3 entities are dynamically notified when configuration information is updated in the directory. The updates are then retrieved from the directory and the corresponding changes are performed as part of the entity reconfiguration.

## 5 Conclusion

This paper has shown the benefit of using a directory service to support SNMPv3 management applications and to promote interoperability between the various enterprise applications. It has shown how the directory can be populated with enterprise wide information that is relevant to secure SNMPv3 management. In particular, the directory has been used to store and access persistent SNMPv3 entities' configuration information. This approach allows customizing the access control and security models (VACM and USM) implemented by the entities according to the enterprise-specific security requirements. Interoperability is achieved on one hand by using the widely accepted LDAP standard protocol for interacting with the directory service and on the other hand by adopting a common schema for describing directory information. We have specified the SNMPv3 management entities using the LDAP classes. To integrate directory service support for our SNMPv3 management system, we have implemented LDAP clients within the application layer of our SNMPv3 entities. The configuration of an SNMPv3 engine, one or several of its subsystems, is conducted through the associated LDAP client application by accessing and retrieving configuration information from a logically centralized LDAP server.

The major addition to SNMP-based management that is brought by the new version of the protocol (SNMPv3) is the security feature. Therefore, we need to emphasize the security issue by using the directory service to store and access enterprise wide security policies and to configure access control and security subsystems of the

SNMPv3 management entities. In [4], we have defined a model for expressing and storing management policies as well as its mapping into SNMPv3 access control and security models, particularly VACM and USM. As a future work, we intend to use the directory service to store and maintain enterprise wide management policies. This will allow for enterprise policy-driven management and customized and flexible control of SNMPv3 management application. For example, security policies will be flexibly added, removed and modified by accessing the directory service, instead of being hard-coded into security management applications. The directory supported configuration service of SNMPv3 entities described in this paper will be extended to ensure the mapping of high-level enterprise security policies into SNMPv3 security parameters and to detect/resolve/prevent policy conflicts.

# References

1. Case, J., M. Fedor, M. Schoffstall, and J. Davin, "The Simple Network Management Protcol", STD 15, RFC 1157, University of Tennessee at Knoxville, Performance Systems International, Performance International, and the MIT Laboratory for Computer Science, May 1990.
2. Jeffrey D Russ Mundy David Partain Bob Stewart, «Introduction to Version 3 of the Internet-standard Network Management Framework» Draft, Octobre 1998.
3. Judd, S., Strassner, J., "Directory Enabled Networks - Information Model and Base Schema", Draft version 3.0c5, August 1998.
4. Omari, S., Boutaba, R., Cherkaoui, O, "Policies for SNMPv3-based management", IEEE /IFIP IM'99, Mai 1999.
5. Wijnen, B., Presuhn, R., and K. McCloghrie, "View-based Access Control Model for version 3 the Simple Network Management Protocol (SNMP)", RFC 2275, January 1998.
6. Blumenthal,U., Wijnen, B., "User-Based Security Model for version 3 of the Simple Network Management Protocol (SNMP)", RFC 2574, April 1999.
7. Harrington, D., Presuhn, R., and B. Wijnen, "An Architecture for describing SNMP Management Frameworks", RFC 2271, January 1998.
8. Levi, D., Meyer, P., and B. Stewart, "SNMPv3 Applications", RFC 2273, January 1998.
9. ITU-T Rec. X.500, "The Directory: Overview of Concepts, Models and Service", 1993.
10. Wahl, M.,. Coulbeck, A., Howles,T., Kille, S., "Lightweight Directory Access Protocol Attribute SyntaxDefinitions", RFC 2252, December 1997.
11. Howes, T, Smith, M, Good, G, "Understanding and deploying LDAP Directory services", MTP edition
12 Wahl, M., Howes, T, Kill, S., "Lightweight Directory Access Protocol (v3)", RFC 2251, December 1998
13. Myers, J., "Simple Authentication and Security Layer (SASL)", RFC 2222, October 1997
14. Dierks, T. and C. Allen, "The TLS Protocol Version 1.0", RFC 2246, January 1999
15. Java Naming and Directory Interface (JNDI)., www.java.sun/jndi

# Session 4

## Programmable SNMP-based Management

*Chair: Jürgen Schönwälder*
*Technical University Braunschweig, Germany*

# Remote Service Deployment on Programmable Switches with the IETF SNMP Script MIB

Jürgen Quittek and Cornelia Kappler

C&C Research Laboratories, NEC Europe Ltd.
Hardenbergplatz 2, 10623 Berlin, Germany
{quittek,cornelia}@ccrle.nec.de

**Abstract.** Some approaches to network programmability require control processes for network devices. Such control processes are executed at the device or at a control node locally connected to the device. This paper discusses the management of these control processes, which is part of configuration management.

Typically, similar or identical control processes have to be installed on several devices of the same network in order to realize a desired service. In such cases an automated remote installation and maintenance of control processes is desirable, especially when devices are located far away from each other.

The idea presented and evaluated in this paper is managing the control processes remotely with the IETF SNMP Script MIB. It is shown that the Script MIB provides sufficient means for installing, configuring, starting, updating, replacing, and terminating control processes for programmable network devices.

We applied our idea to GSMP control processes realizing an IP switching over ATM service. This case study demonstrates the feasibility, but also discusses practical problems and restrictions.

## 1 Introduction

Programmability of networks is becoming an important factor in business scenarios for network providers. Major reasons for this trend are the increased speed of the development of technology and standards, the specialization of providers, and the need for rapid service creation and deployment.

Currently, several approaches to network programmability are being discussed. They range from solutions with restricted programmability fitting into the existing networking frameworks, to very general and flexible approaches requiring new technologies and devices.

An example for the first kind of approaches is policy-based networking using the COPS protocol [1]. Here, access to networking services is controlled by policies which can be changed during operation of the network. Policies are stored at one or more policy servers which are asked for access decisions. They can e.g. be consulted by an IP router to decide the acceptance of an RSVP reservation.

An example for a radical new approach are active networks [2], where each packet sent via the network may carry code to be executed on its way. The code may just influence the way a packet is routed, but it may also implement a complex service, e.g. a multicast of a packet stream with a data compression adapting itself to the available bandwidth.

Approaches relevant to this paper are in-between the two extrema, using APIs or communication protocols for programming single network devices or even entire networks. They offer a high degree of programmability without requiring large investments in new technology. These approaches require *control processes*, using the protocol or the API for managing and controlling the network. The main topic of this paper is how such control processes in turn can be managed within the Internet management framework.

An example for the API approach is the proposed IEEE PIN standard for application programming interfaces for networks. It is being defined by the IEEE P1520 working group[1] which consists of three sub groups covering ATM switches, IP routers and switches, and SS7 systems. The API supports control of network services involving several devices, as well as settings of specific properties at single devices.

An approach using a communication protocol for controlling single switches is the General Switch Management Protocol (GSMP). The first versions have been proposed by Ipsilon Networks, Inc. as informational RFCs (RFC 1987 [3] and RFC 2297 [4]). In February 1999, an IETF working group has started producing a standard[2]. In May 1999, the Multiservice Switching Forum[3] (MSF) selected GSMP as its base line protocol.

GSMP is used for managing and controlling ATM switches including switch and port configuration, connection management, and monitoring. GSMP separates the control software from the switch fabric. They communicate with each other via a reserved ATM connection. This gives high flexibility to control software design.

Typically, for GSMP as well as for other protocol and API approaches, similar or identical control processes have to be installed on several devices of the same network in order to realize a desired network functionality. In such cases an automated remote installation and maintenance of control processes is desirable, especially when devices are located far away from each other. Usually, this is considered to be a part of configuration management.

We suggest to use the IETF SNMP Script MIB [5] for installing, starting, updating, replacing, and terminating control processes remotely. The Script MIB has been designed for delegating management functions as scripts to SNMP agents. As a case study we managed IPSOFACTO control processes. IPSO-FACTO [6] is an IP switching technology realizing IP services over ATM with GSMP control processes. It is currently being discussed as an multicast extension for MPLS [7]. Based on this experience, we discuss the benefits and problems of managing network control processes with the Script MIB.

---

[1] see http://www.ieee-pin.org/

[2] see http://www.ietf.org/html.charters/gsmp-charter.html

[3] see http://www.msforum.org/

The remainder of this paper is structured as follows. The Script MIB is introduced in more detail in section 2. Section 3 describes GSMP, particularly covering requirements for the control processes. A brief introduction to IPSO-FACTO is given in section 4. Section 5 describes our experiences with managing IPSOFACTO control processes with the Script MIB.

## 2 The IETF Script MIB

The Script MIB has been developed by the IEFT distributed management working group[4] and was published as proposed standard RFC 2592 in May 1999 [5]. The Script MIB supports starting, controlling, and terminating remote processes (scripts) within the SNMP management framework. It furthermore gives access to output of the scripts. The scripts may be implemented in arbitrary programming languages and code formats. The MIB provides the following capabilities:

- Transferring management scripts to SNMP agents at distributed locations.
- Transferring script arguments.
- Initiating, suspending, resuming and terminating management scripts at these locations.
- Transferring the results produced by running management scripts.

### 2.1 Overview of the Script MIB

The Script MIB consists of six tables, the main four tables are introduced below. In order to keep our overview clear and short, we omit some features, such as *language extensions* and *pushing* of scripts.

The *language table* provides information about the languages supported by a Script MIB implementation, e.g. the Java virtual machine or the Tcl interpreter.

The *script table* lists all scripts known by a Script MIB implementation. Scripts can be permanently installed, or downloaded (pulled) by the agent from a URL.

The *launch table* describes scripts that are ready to be launched. An entry defines the argument passed to a script and the owner indicating the permissions and credentials of the script during execution. A managed object in the entry called *launch button* allows a manager to invoke a script with a single SNMP set operation.

Finally, the *run table* lists all scripts that are currently running or that have terminated recently. It contains objects that allow a manager to

- retrieve status information from running scripts,
- control running scripts (suspend, resume, abort),
- retrieve the arguments passed to scripts at invocation,
- retrieve intermediate results of running scripts,
- retrieve results from recently terminated scripts,

---

[4] see http://www.ietf.org/html.charters/disman-charter.html

- retrieve starting and termination time of scripts,
- control the remaining maximum lifetime of a running script,
- control how long script results are stored in the MIB.

The Script MIB supports SNMPv3 including the User-based Security Model (USM) and View-based Access Control (VACM). A detailed discussion of Script MIB security can be found in [8].

## 2.2 Script MIB Usage and Communication Model

We explain the usage of the Script MIB by describing the steps required for running and controlling a script on a network node. Figure 1 illustrates these steps:

1. In order to install a script at the network node, the manager has to check which languages are supported by the Script MIB implementation. He retrieves this information at the language table.
2. Based on the information about supported languages, the manager selects an appropriate script from a script repository. The script has to be installed at a new row of the script table which the manager creates. Now, the manager writes the script URL to the script table and then requests the SNMP agent to download the script from the script repository.
3. When the desired script is installed, the manager creates an entry in the launch table indexing the script and describing an execution environment. For the same script, several entries can be created in order to start the script

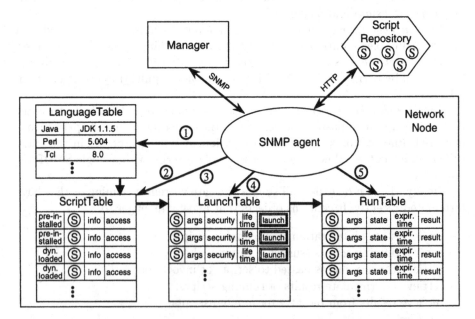

**Fig. 1.** Usage of the Script MIB. Circled digits refer to step numbers in section 2.2.

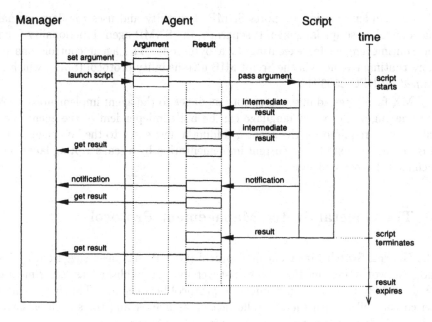

**Fig. 2.** The manager–script communication model

with different predefined arguments, or to run the script under different runtime security profiles.

With the entry in the launch table properly set, the manager can start a script by setting the launch button. By setting the launch button more than once, several concurrently running scripts can be started from the same row of the launch table. For each running instance of a script, an entry in the run table is created automatically.

4. The manager controls running scripts and retrieves intermediate or final results of running scripts by accessing the run table. The communication model between the manager and a running script is shown in Figure 2. The final result produced by the script is kept by the agent for a expiration time given by a managed object in the according run table entry. During this time the manager can read the result. The manager can clear the result anytime by setting the expiration time to zero.

## 2.3 Implementations

There are currently three implementations known to the authors. One has been developed at the Open Group Research Institute at Grenoble, France, and another one at SNMP Research International in Knoxville, TN, USA.

The implementation used for the experiments described in this paper has been developed jointly by the NEC C&C Research Laboratories in Berlin, Germany, and the Technical University of Braunschweig, Germany.[5]

---

[5] see http://www.ibr.cs.tu-bs.de/projects/jasmin/

This implementation supports SNMPv3 security and uses the Java virtual machine [9] as script language. It separates the SNMP agent functionality from the runtime engine for executing Java byte code. The agent controls one or more runtime engines via the Script MIB eXtensibility protocol (SMX) which is defined by RFC 2593 [10].

SMX facilitates adding new script languages to the agent implementation. A runtime engine for a new language can be built independent of the agent. The only change required for the agent is adding a new entry to the language table. It is planned to extend the current implementation by a real scripting language, such as Tcl, Perl, or Python.

## 3   The General Switch Management Protocol

The General Switch Management Protocol (GSMP) has been suggested by Ipsilon Networks Inc. in 1996. The first version 1.1 published as experimental RFC 1987 [3] defined a communication protocol between an ATM switch and a switch controller, with the controller acting as master and the switch as slave. It is available available on several commercial ATM switches.

GSMP 1.1 allows the controller to

- configure the switch,
- configure ports,
- establish and remove virtual point-to-point connections,
- establish and remove virtual point-to-multipoint connections,
- request monitoring information,
- request event notifications.

The switch acknowledges all received control messages. Monitoring requests are acknowledged by sending port statistics or connection statistics. If event notification has been requested by the controller, the switch notifies the controller on events such as *port* up and *port down* by GSMP messages which have to be acknowledged by the controller.

Messages between switch and controller are sent over a reserved ATM connection which must be established in advance. This allows the control process to be executed on the switch, as well as on a device connected to a port of the switch.

The abstract switch model of GSMP 1.1 just considered plain connections without further properties for Quality of Service (QoS). This drawback was one of the major motivations for developing GSMP 2.0 published as experimental RFC 2297 [4] in 1998. However, the suggested solution for QoS support was not accepted as widely as the original GSMP 1.1.

In February 1999 the new IETF GSMP working group has started to refine the QoS support of the abstract switch model and adapt GSMP also to non-ATM switching technologies.

# 4 IP Switching with IPSOFACTO

IPSOFACTO maps IP flows to connections in ATM networks [6]. The ATM switch controllers run an IP routing protocol and perform IP forwarding. ATM signaling is not used. Figure 3 shows components of an IPSOFACTO network. An IPSOFACTO network consists of ATM switches (IPSOFACTO routers), ATM hosts running the IP protocol stack (IPSOFACTO clients), and IPSOFACTO gateways to other data link layer technologies, e.g. Ethernet. IP packets are transferred over ATM connections. In the initial state, a switch forwards all packets coming in from other routers or from hosts to the IPSOFACTO controller. In this state we call all connection identifiers *unused*.

If an IP packet arrives with an *unused* incoming connection identifier, it is passed to the controller. The controller performs IP routing in order to decide to which outgoing port the packet must be forwarded. Then the controller selects an *unused* outgoing connection identifier of this port and sends the packet.

In a further step, the controller creates a connection by establishing a short-cut from the incoming connection identifier of this packet to the outgoing one. Thereby, the incoming connection becomes *used*. Now, all subsequent packets arriving via this connection are switched directly to the same outgoing connec-

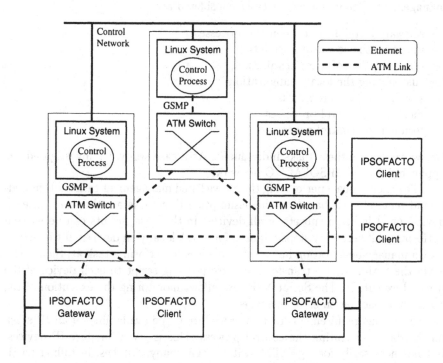

**Fig. 3.** An IPSOFACTO network containing three routers, two gateways to Ethernet, and three IPSOFACTO clients. An IPSOFACTO router consists of an ATM switch, and a Linux system running a GSMP control process.

tion without executing the IP protocol stack. For multicast IPSOFACTO may replicate packets and forward them to several several outgoing connections.

Recently, the IPSOFACTO approach has been accepted by the IETF as the multicast extension of Multi Protocol Label Switching (MPLS) [7]. So far MPLS only supports unicast. As multicast extension, the IPSOFACTO approach would be used for multicast only, unicast would be handled by MPLS itself. This version of IPSOFACTO will not anymore be restricted to ATM. Like MPLS it can be applied to several switching technologies.

The current implementation of IPSOFACTO has been developed by the NEC C&C Research Laboratories in Princeton. This implementation and also the upcoming implementation as multicast extension for MPLS use external control processes connected to the switch via GSMP 1.1. Control processes run on Linux machines connected directly to the controlled switch by an ATM link (see Figure 3). The devices hosting the control processes are accessible via an IP control network.

## 5 Managing Control Processes

The main topic of this paper is automated and remote management of control processes with the Script MIB, which is part of network and service configuration management. The management tasks considered are

- software installation for control processes,
- updating the software installation,
- removing the software installation,
- customizing the local configuration,
- starting control processes,
- monitoring control processes,
- terminating control processes.

Below we discuss these tasks individually. As a case study, we investigated the applicability to an IPSOFACTO network.

The general idea – performing the above listed management tasks automatedly and remotely – is based on the assumption that tasks are the same on each device, or at least on subsets of all devices. In this case, scripts can be written performing all necessary steps required for a task locally on devices. If we assume that a management station has a list of devices to perform a task at, then it can – via the Script MIB – transfer the corresponding script to each device of the list and execute it. The Script MIB also allows monitoring the execution of the script and reacting on error messages.

An obvious requirement for this procedure is the availability of an IP stack on the device executing the control process. This is given for pure IP devices, but not necessarily for e.g. ATM switches. On many switches, installing an IP stack is just a matter of a local pre-installation, on some it might be impossible to get one. For the IPSOFACTO control processes this problem did not occur, because the control processes were running on Linux machines.

## 5.1 Installing Network Control Software

In case of a software installation task, the installation script has to transfer the network control software from a repository to the device, and install it properly. For the transfer, ftp or http are recommendable protocols, because they can easily be used within scripts.

After the transferred files have been put in place, it might be necessary to edit the configuration of the device which is stored in some configuration storage, such as files or non-volatile RAM. This may cause problems, because the current state of the file or other storage to be edited might depend on the history of the device, i.e. the required steps of editing might depend on what has been installed before. This is a typical problem of automated software installation and it cannot be avoided in some cases.

When installing IPSOFACTO, we ran into another problem. The software to be installed included a new operating system kernel. So after installation the device had to be rebooted. Similarly, editing the configuration as described above may only becomes effective after a reboot.

A reboot interrupts the management of the device for some time and since we do not consider persistent scripts, actions to be performed before and after the reboot have to be part of different scripts. Furthermore, it is not recommendable to call a reboot at the end of the installation script, because an error message which might have been generated during installation might get lost. Therefore, after finishing the installation successfully, the manager should start a separate script which reboots the system.

Unfortunately, the Script MIB does not support the installation of scripts which are executed automatically after a reboot, i.e. when the SNMP agent is restarted. Hence, the manager has to poll the device until it becomes operational again after reboot. Then further steps, e.g. starting the installed control process, can be performed.

## 5.2 Removing and Updating Software

Requirements for software removal scripts are similar to those for the installation scripts. The major difference is that usually no transfer of the network control software is required. Editing of configuration storage has to be reverted, and instead of installing files, files are being removed.

In case of the removal of IPSOFACTO software, the old kernel has to be restored, which requires again a transfer of software, if the old one is stored on the device itself. As for the installation, a reboot is required after removal.

Software can be updated by removing the old version and installing the new version. In many cases this procedure can be abbreviated, because only few files need to be replaced, and editing of the configuration storage might not be necessary. In this case, it is more efficient to use update scripts performing only this reduced number of steps.

## 5.3 Customizing the Local Configuration

While the steps performed for software installation often are the same for all devices, network control processes might require local configuration which is specific to each device. The process can obtain the local configuration information from configuration storage or from the arguments passed to it when it is started. Providing the local configuration information might require manual steps and therefore inhibits the automation of this task.

E.g. the IPSOFACTO control process needs to be informed about the number of ports of the controlled switches, the IP addresses assigned to these ports, and the IP addresses of the adjacent switches or hosts. To solve the problem we manually created a configuration file for each switch. The files were put into the software repository and named according to the device they were to be used for.[6]

After this preparation, the script for installing the local configuration was no longer device specific.

## 5.4 Starting and Terminating Control Processes

Scripts for starting and terminating control processes are rather simple. The starting script just has to start one or more processes using the software installed previously. The terminating script must be able to identify the processes to be terminated. This can be done by scanning the process table, or with support of the starting script which then needs to store the process identifiers of processes it started.

If the starting script passes local configuration information to the control processes, a manual preparation of each device might be necessary.

For IPSOFACTO, the starting script containing just three simple steps worked well. However, the terminating script, scanning the process table and terminating the IPSOFACTO processes, could not bring the device to a consistent state from where IPSOFACTO or some other control process could be started subsequently. The reason is that the current IPSOFACTO implementation does not contain code for a clean termination – automated management was not considered during design of the software. Consequently, after terminating IPSOFACTO, the device had to be rebooted in order to bring it into a state allowing further operation (cf. section 5.1).

We also tested termination and restarting of control processes without rebooting, with a simple GSMP control process which just established and removed a single ATM connection.

---

[6] It is also possible to automate this task by generating the individual files from a single description of the entire network.

## 5.5 Monitoring Control Processes

How a control process is monitored may vary significantly. It depends on the runtime environment of the control process, and on the output produced by the process. We identified two typical monitoring actions: scanning the process table to find out whether the process is still running and what resources it consumes, and parsing log files. Parsing log files includes checking output sent to the standard output, since the standard output can be redirected to a file.

For both monitoring actions, two kinds of scripts can be useful: scripts running permanently and repeating their actions with a given frequency, and scripts performing a monitoring action only once. The permanently running scripts are preferable if a fault condition should be detected quickly. These scripts can notify the manager when they detect such a condition. The other kind of scripts is useful if the manager wants to obtain monitoring information on a non-regular basis.

## 5.6 Complexity of the Management Procedure

In this section we analyze the complexity of the management procedure described above. The following section discusses a possibility of reducing it.

The procedure requires the development of a script for each management task. In order to execute the whole procedure, for each script and for each device on which the script is run, several steps have to be performed: the script must be installed at the script table, a launch entry with proper script arguments must be created, the script must be started and controlled via the run table, and after successful execution, the created entries in the launch table and in the script table should be removed.

Each of these steps requires several SNMP requests to be sent to the device. However, the steps are identical or very similar for each script and a management application can use a common subroutine for each of them. Consequently, the management application is rather simple, once these subroutines are available as a library for accessing the Script MIB.

The major effort and complexity reside in the creation of the scripts themselves. However, this complexity is unavoidable, because most of the steps are definitely required for managing these control processes. Hence, the additional complexity of the presented procedure is small, while the advantage of managing a set of devices automated-ly and remotely might be quiet high.

## 5.7 Possible Simplification of the Management Procedure

There is a possible simplification of the procedure. Instead of transferring scripts to the managed device which in turn install software and run it, it is possible to implement a GSMP control process as a script directly managed via the Script MIB. In this case, management steps, such as installing the software, starting it, and terminating it, are performed by only a few SNMP requests. The effort required for the whole management procedure is then comparable to the effort required for a single task of the procedure described above.

Unfortunately, this simplification has some restrictions. The control process has to be written in a language supported by the used Script MIB implementation. This might require porting existing control software to another language which might be not preferable to use for other reasons. Preferred languages for control processes on network devices are C and C++, because these languages can easily interface with operating systems and communication stacks usually being written in C. However, C or C++ are currently not supported by any Script MIB implementation, because their portability is restricted.

Furthermore, the simplification is only efficient if configuration files and log files can be avoided, because otherwise further scripts are required for installing or reading them, respectively. Hence, the configuration information should be passed within the list of arguments, and the output is restricted to the means of the Script MIB, i.e. producing intermediate results and notifications. Here, the final script result is not of much interest, since the control process is intended to run until it is terminated explicitly.

Hence, the simplification can only be applied to control processes for which these restrictions are acceptable. In our opinion this hold only for a small set of network control processes.

# 6  Conclusions and Future Work

Our case study with GSMP control processes showed that it is possible and efficient to manage control processes for programmable networks with the SNMP Script MIB as part of configuration management. This includes installing, configuring, starting, updating, terminating, and de-installing control processes.

The main effort for these management tasks is caused by writing scripts. But since most of the steps contained in the scripts are required anyway for managing the control processes, the generated overhead is very small. On the other hand, the reduction of work introduced by an automated remote management of network control processes on a set of devices can be quiet significant.

We showed that the suggested management procedure is even applicable for control processes which are hard to manage, particularly which require a customized kernel and which do not leave the device in a proper state after termination.

For simple control processes, the procedure can be simplified by managing the control process directly via the Script MIB without using additional scripts.

Since we did not have to consider GSMP specific issues, we assume that we can apply this way of managing control processes also to other kinds of programmable networks. Particularly, we are interested in studying the applicability to the IEEE PIN standard, as soon as an implementations is available.

# Acknowledgments

The authors would like to thank Jürgen Schönwälder at the Technical University of Braunschweig who is one of the authors of the Script MIB and who designed and developed – together with Matthias Bolz and Sven Mertens – the Script MIB agent used for this paper.

Further contributions came from the NEC C&C Research Laboratories in Heidelberg, Germany, where Jürgen Röthig, Sibylle Schaller and Frédéric Griffoul installed, supported, and enhanced the used IPSOFACTO system.

# References

1. J. Boyle, R. Cohen, D. Durham, S. Herzog, R. Rajan and A. Sastry. *The COPS (Common Open Policy Service) Protocol.* internet draft, draft-ietf-rap-cops-06.txt, February 1999.
2. D. Tennenhouse, J. Smith, W. Sincoskie, D. Wetherall and G. Minden. *A Survey of Active Network Research.* IEEE Communications Magazine 35(1):80-86, January 1997.
3. P. Newman, W. Edwards, R. Hinden, E. Hoffman, F. Ching Liaw, T. Lyon and G. Minshall. Ipsilon's General Switch Management Protocol Specification Version 1.1. RFC 1987, Ipsilon Networks, Inc., Sprint, August 1996.
4. P. Newman, W. Edwards, R. Hinden, E. Hoffman, F. Ching Liaw, T. Lyon and G. Minshall. Ipsilon's General Switch Management Protocol Specification Version 2.0. RFC 2297, Nokia, Sprint, Fiberlane Communications, March 1998.
5. D. B. Levi and J. Schönwälder. Definitions of Managed Objects for the Delegation of Management Scripts. RFC 2592, SNMP Research, TU Braunschweig, May 1999.
6. A. Acharya, R. Dighe and F. Ansari. A Framework for IP switching over fast ATM cell transport (IPSOFACTO). In *Proc. SPIE Voice Video and Data Communications, Broadband Networking Technologies,* pp. 20-28, November 1997.
7. D. Ooms, W. Livens, B. Sales, M. Ramalho, A. Acharya, F. Griffoul and F. Ansari. *Framework for IP Multicast in MPLS.* internet draft, draft-ietf-mpls-multicast-00.txt, Alcatel, NEC, Bell Labs, June 1999.
8. J. Schönwälder and J. Quittek. Secure Management By Delegation within the Internet Management Framework. In *Proc. 6th International Symposium on Integrated Network Management,* Boston, May 1999. (to appear).
9. T. Lindholm and F. Yellin. *The Java Virtual Machine Specification.* Addison Wesley, 1997.
10. J. Schönwälder, and J. Quittek. *SMX - Script MIB Extensibility Protocol Version 1.0.* RFC 2593, TU Braunschweig, NEC Europe Ltd., May 1999.

# Integrating SNMP into
# a Mobile Agent Infrastructure

Paulo Simões, Luis Moura Silva, and Fernando Boavida Fernandes

University of Coimbra, CISUC - Dep. Eng. Informática
Pólo II, Pinhal de Marrocos
P-3030 Coimbra, Portugal
{psimoes,luis,boavida}@dei.uc.pt

**Abstract.** Mobile Code is an emerging paradigm that is gaining momentum in several fields of application. Network Management is a potential area for the use of this technology, provided it will be able to interoperate with well established solutions for Network Management. This paper presents the integration a classic NM protocol, like SNMP, into a platform of Mobile Agents. Our platform, called JAMES, has been developed in the context of an Eureka Project ($\Sigma!1921$) where the project partners are University of Coimbra, Siemens SA and Siemens AG. Since the main target of the platform is network management, it includes a set of SNMP services allowing mobile agents to easily interface with SNMP agents, as well as with legacy SNMP-based management applications. In the paper we present a brief overview of the general architecture of the platform and we describe in some detail the framework we used to provide for integration between mobile agent applications and SNMP.

## 1 Introduction

Typically, existing Network Management (NM) applications are based on one of two protocols established almost a decade ago to address the problem of interoperability in heterogeneous environments: SNMP [1], for data networks, and CMIP [2], for telecommunication networks. These protocols are based on static and centralized client/server solutions, where every element of the network sends all the data to a central location that processes the whole data and provides the interface to the user operator. By this reason, the management applications are not flexible, have problems of scalability and produce too much traffic in the network.

It is now widely recognized that the use of decentralization in this kind of applications potentially solves most of the problems that exist in centralized client/server solutions [3, 4]. The applications can be more scalable, more robust, can be easily upgraded or customized and they reduce the traffic in the network.

Several approaches have been followed in this quest for decentralized management, starting with early work on Management by Delegation [5] and including Active Networks [6], management environments based on CORBA [7], Web-based network management [8], Intelligent Agents [4] and Mobile Agents

[9]. For an extensive typology of distributed network management paradigms, please refer to [10].

Of these approaches, Mobile Agent technology is one of the most promising but still requires some detailed study. A Mobile Agent corresponds to a small program that is able to migrate to some remote machine, where it can execute some function or collect some relevant data and then migrate to other machines in order to accomplish some other tasks. The basic idea of this paradigm is to distribute the processing throughout the network: that is, send the code to the data instead of bringing the data to the code.

In the last few years the use of Mobile Agent technology has received an extraordinary attention from several Universities and research institutes and a notable investment from leading companies, including IBM, Oracle, Digital and Microsoft [11]. Mobile agents have been applied in several areas, like mobile computing, electronic commerce, Internet applications, information retrieval, workflow and cooperative work, network management and telecommunications [12–14].

Several commercial implementations of mobile agents have been presented in the market, including Aglets from IBM [15], Concordia from Mitsubishi [16], Odyssey from General Magic [17], Voyager from ObjectSpace [18] and Jumping Beans from AdAstra [19]. However, although these software products have some interesting features, we believe they are too much general-purpose for most NM applications.

In the JAMES project [20], we are developing from scratch a new Mobile Agent infrastructure that is being tuned and customized for the applications we have in mind in the area of telecommunications and network management. Although the discussion of the issues we take into account is beyond the scope of this paper, we can point to aspects like efficient code migration; fault-tolerance and robustness; flexible code distribution and easy upgrading; mechanisms for resource control; disconnected operation; portability; and interoperability with existing management technologies.

This issue of interoperability with existing management technologies, like SNMP, CORBA and CMIP, is crucial for the success of mobile agents in the network management area. In order to insure the deployment of applications for the management of large and heterogeneous systems, mobile agent systems need to provide interoperability. The reasons are twofold.

First, those technologies provide access to management information and services. Mobile agents are a very attractive approach to incorporate mobile code into the existing local management services, in order to perform intelligent tasks closer to management data. However, they will not entirely replace the protocols used by classic management applications to interface with management services in heterogeneous environments. Instead, they will complement them with powerful programming constructs allowing more efficient solutions for network management. Nevertheless, some management protocols are still necessary to retrieve and process the management information. This is the case when some of the managed Network Elements (NEs) are unable to host mobile agents, when the management services of NEs are not directly available to the hosted mobile agents or when the direct interfaces with management services are non-standardized.

Second, management applications based on mobile agents often need to coexist with legacy management systems. Mobile agents are particularly well suited to develop and deploy new network management services, but it seems much more attractive to use these services from installed management applications than to develop separate specialized applications. If these services provided using mobile agents include SNMP or CORBA interfaces, for instance, they may integrate into the legacy management systems at use. In this way, mobile agents can be introduced, in an incremental and integrated fashion, to solve specific problems for larger management frameworks still based on classic paradigms.

CORBA has been one of the first technologies to be addressed by mobile agent systems, which is not surprising given its usefulness in a wide variety of application fields. The most visible initiative in this area is the MASIF standard (Mobile Agent System Interoperability Specification [21]). Although MASIF is mainly a CORBA interface for interoperability between agent systems, its concepts that can also be used for interoperability with CORBA-based management applications and CORBA services. Right now only Grasshopper [22], from IKV++, claims to be MASIF compliant, but other platforms that already provide CORBA access to and from external objects are expected to follow soon.

Integration between mobile agents and classic NM paradigms, like SNMP, was not given the same level of attention. Few platforms provide some degree of support for their usage, and even fewer include a well-defined framework for interoperability with classic management architectures.

One can argue that integration of classic management protocols with mobile agents can be relegated to the applications developer, eventually using the same general-purpose libraries used by static management systems. However, code mobility, security constraints and resource usage control imposed on mobile agents applications seriously limit the usage of these protocols without explicit support from the underlying infrastructure. This is why JAMES includes explicit support for interoperability with SNMP devices and applications.

The SNMP support that is offered by the JAMES platform might be used whenever it is necessary to interact with SNMP agents (local or remote) or to provide SNMP services to legacy applications. It includes support for agent mobility and it can be dynamically installed or removed from the platform. Furthermore, it is transparent to SNMP devices and SNMP Managers, not requiring any kind of specific adaptation from them.

In this paper, we will describe how we have done the integration of SNMP into our system of mobile agents, in order to provide this support for interoperability. The rest of the paper is organized as follows: Section 2 discusses related work and some of the design premises that lead to the JAMES design. Section 3 presents a brief overview of the JAMES Platform and Section 4 describes the design and functionality of the SNMP modules of JAMES. Section 5 concludes the paper.

# 2 Related Work

SNMP is not directly supported by any of the commercial implementations of mobile agents. However, there are a few ongoing research projects mixing SNMP with mobile agents.

The INCA Architecture [23], from NEC CCRLE-Berlin, provides access to SNMP devices based on a common Java SNMP library. Unfortunately, the lack of available documentation restricted us from an accurate analysis of this proposal.

The Discovery Platform [24], from the University of Maryland, proposes the use of the SNMP information model to represent the internal knowledge base of the platform. In this way, the host management information and the platform management information are unified in a single MIB tree, accessible directly from the mobile agents platform. This approach claims a few advantages: the agent information base and the host management information can be accessed using the same mechanisms and it is possible to add any object with arbitrary complexity to the tree. However, it requires specific support from the native SNMP agent residing at the local host and assumes that SNMP is always the most adequate protocol to access local management information. It also ties the agent management information with the SNMP functional limitations. Furthermore, it does not address the problem of accessing external SNMP agents, which continues to require a separate SNMP engine.

The Astrolog/MAGENTA platform [25], from IRISA, employs mobile agents to support the mobility of the network operator. However, the core NM system is based on a hierarchy of stationary agents. The mobile agents execution environments, designated as *lieus*, include a built-in SNMP agent available directly to local mobile agents as well as to the remote applications that use SNMP. Apparently, these SNMP agents do not support dynamic expansion, which means offered services are monolithic. This approach also affects the system portability: since SNMP agents are internal to *lieus*, it is necessary to adapt the *lieu* implementation for each type of managed NE, reproducing functionality that was, quite probably, already provided by native SNMP agents.

The Perpetuum Mobile Procura (PMP) Project [26, 27], from the Carleton University, proposes the use of DPI (SNMP Distributed Protocol Interface [28]) as a means to talk with local SNMP agents whenever there is not a more sophisticated interface with local resources. DPI is also used to extend SNMP agents through the download of Java classes. This is one of the few projects where SNMP is used both to access local management services and to interface with legacy management applications. However, the need for DPI support from the native SNMP agent affects the system portability.

All these projects provide interesting features. However, none of them is completely satisfactory. INCA doesnt seem to address interoperability with SNMP applications. Discovery and Astrolog do provide higher levels of interoperability but their design is too committed with SNMP and requires explicit support from SNMP devices, which affects portability. The PMP architecture is more independent (SNMP is seen as an optional feature) but usage of SNMP depends on DPI, which also affects portability.

In the JAMES project we considered a novel approach for SNMP support, with three key goals in mind.

First, we also want to provide operability with both SNMP devices and applications, in order to keep a large set of potential application fields.

Second, we see SNMP just as another tool to be added to the Swiss Army knife that mobile agents may use to solve management problems. Some problems require SNMP, others need to use CORBA or proprietary interfaces to interface with NEs, while for others it is sufficient to access relational databases (using JDBC) or even raw text files. This means that solutions where SNMP would affect the platform portability or functionality were not acceptable.

Third, we want SNMP support to be transparent to existing SNMP devices and applications. Any requirement of changes to SNMP devices or applications would jeopardize one of the main reasons to use SNMP: the fact that it is immediately available almost anywhere.

These premises led to the design of a new framework for SNMP integration that:

- provides maximum interoperability, covering three different service ranges: interaction with local and remote SNMP-agents; interaction between SNMP-managers and mobile agents; and infrastructure management using SNMP,
- supports agents mobility - usage of SNMP does not restrict the migration of mobile agents,
- is an optional feature of JAMES, not imposing additional overheads to the platform when turned-off,
- is non-intrusive to the SNMP architecture, in the sense that no intervention is required on existing SNMP devices and SNMP Managers. This preserves the overall portability.

## 3  The General Architecture of the JAMES Platform

The JAMES Platform provides the running environment for mobile agents. There is a distinction between the software environment that runs in the manager host and the software that executes in the NEs: the central host executes the JAMES Manager while the nodes in the network run a JAMES Agency. The agents are written by application programmers and will execute on top of that platform. The JAMES system provides a programming interface that allows the full manipulation of Mobile Agents. Fig. 1 shows a global snapshot of the system, with a special description of a possible scenario where mobile agents will be used.

Every NE runs a Java Virtual Machine and executes a JAMES Agency that enables the execution of mobile agents. JAMES agents will migrate through these machines in the network to access some data, execute some tasks and produce reports that will be sent back to the JAMES Manager. There is a mechanism for authentication in the JAMES Agencies, to control the execution of agents and to avoid the intrusion of non-official agents. The communication between the different machines is done through stream sockets. A special protocol was

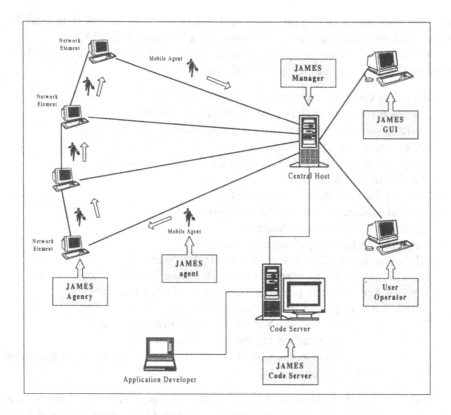

**Fig. 1.** An Overview of the JAMES Platform

developed to transfer the agents across the machines in a robust way and is atomic to the occurrence of failures.

The application developer writes the applications that are based on a set of mobile agents. These applications are written in Java and should use the JAMES API for the control of mobility. After writing an application, the programmer should create a JAR (Java Archive) with all the classes that make part of the mobile agent. This JAR file is placed in a JAMES Code Server. This server can be a different machine or in the same machine where the JAMES Manager is executing. In both cases, it maintains a code directory with all the JAR files available and the mapping to the corresponding mobile agents. The communication between the client program that is used by the application developer and the Code Server is done by the HTTP protocol. The Code Server interacts with the JAMES Manager through a dedicated stream socket.

The host machine that runs the JAMES manager is responsible for the whole management of the mobile agent system. It provides the interface to the end-user, together with a Graphical User for the remote control and monitoring of agents, places and applications. Management applications using mobile agents can bypass this end-user interface using a Remote API. This interface includes tools to manage all the Agents and Agencies in the system, and it is available in two different communication methods: Java RMI and CORBA.

The JAMES platform is still in its first version but the main features of the platform can be summarized in the following list:

- Kernel of the JAMES Manager and JAMES Agency,
- Service for remote updating of Agents and Agencies,
- Flexible code distribution (caching and prefetching schemes),
- Atomic migration protocol,
- Support for fault-tolerance through checkpoint-and-restart,
- Reconfigurable itinerary,
- Support for disconnected computing,
- Watchdog scheme and system monitoring,
- Mechanisms for resource control,
- Logging and profiling of agent activity,
- GUI interface to allow the remote control of agents,
- Remote Access to the platform through a Java RMI interface,
- Remote Access to the platform through a CORBA interface,
- CORBA access to and from external objects,
- Integration of Java-based SNMP services into the platform,
- Inter-agent communication (through JavaSpaces [29]),
- Multi-paradigms for agent execution (simple agent, migratory agents and Master/Worker model).

The explanation of all these mechanisms is out of scope of this paper, but we will give some emphasis to a few of the issues considered important for our domain of applications: remote software upgrading, reliability and robustness.

## 3.1 Remote Software Upgrading

The JAMES platform provides a flexible mechanism for the remote upgrading of mobile agents as well as Agencies. Each Agency is seen as a stationary agent: it cannot move around the network once installed in a machine but it should be easy to upgrade, customize and install by a central host.

Two modules compose the JAMES Agency: a small rexec daemon and the Agency itself. The rexec daemon is a static piece of software: once installed it does not need to be constantly upgraded. The Agency itself is a more dynamic module, since it can be changed whenever required.

The Java rexec daemon (JREXEC) implements an instance of the *Class Loader* and receives some network commands regarding the installation and control of the JAMES Agency. This daemon will be instantiated every time the machine is booted. The daemon can receive a JAR file containing a JAMES Agency and it will perform its local installation. After this first step, the JAMES Manager can send some remote commands to the JREXEC Daemon:

- Refresh the local memory by calling the Java garbage collector.
- Kill the local Agency.

- Install a new Agency on the local machine.
- Upgrade the local Agency with a new set of classes.

This scheme will be useful in dynamic environments since it provides a flexible way to upgrade remote software.

## 3.2 Fault-Tolerance

The JAMES platform has some special support for fault-tolerance. The first version includes a checkpoint-and-restart mechanism, a failure detection scheme, an atomic migration protocol and some support for fault-management. The platform is able to tolerate any failure of a mobile agent, a JAMES Agency or the JAMES Manager.

**Fault-Tolerance at the Agencies.** Periodically, the internal state of the JAMES Manager and Agencies will be saved as a checkpoint in persistent storage. The internal state consists of all the internal objects that keep all the relevant state about the platform and the execution of the agents. If any of the servers (Agency or Manager) fails or is simply shut down the system has enough information to recover the server to a previous consistent state. This state is retrieved from persistent storage and all the internal state can be reconstructed. The checkpointing mechanism will make use of the Java object serialization facility and is completely transparent to the application programmer.

**Fault-Tolerance at the Mobile Agents.** If there is a communication or node failure that affects the execution of the agent, the system insures a forward progress of the mobile agent. This is also achieved through a checkpointing mechanism. When a mobile agent finishes a task in a JAMES Agency its internal state is saved to stable storage before being transmitted to the next destination. The agent is migrated to another host but its data will remain in stable storage until it has been successfully restarted in the next Agency. When it is restarted in the new place the system takes a new checkpoint of the agent and the previous place is informed. The previous checkpoint of the agent can then be removed from stable storage. This checkpointing mechanism is transparent to the application developer and is incorporated in the migration protocol to assure the atomicity of the agent transfer. This means that either the agent is completely migrated to its destination or whenever is a failure the agent is not lost and the system is able to recover the agent in the previous Agency. We have used a conventional two-phase commit protocol to achieve the exactly-once property in the migration of the agents.

When there is a failure in a migration protocol or one of the Agencies in the itinerary is not available, the agent can execute one of the three following procedures:

1. go back to the JAMES Manager,

2. jump to the next available Agency in the itinerary,

3. or just wait until the destination Agency is up and running.

The procedure to follow by a mobile agent in the occurrence of a failure can be customized by the application programmer.

### 3.3 Resource Control

One important feature in a platform of mobile agents is a good set of mechanisms for resource control. In the JAMES platform we have included some schemes to control the use of some important resources of the underlying operating system, namely: the use of threads, sockets, memory, disk space and CPU load.

These schemes have proved to be very effective when we were doing some stress testing. In some situations when the Agencies are running almost out of any of those resources it was still possible to maintain the platform up and running. Without such mechanisms the Agencies would normally hang up. With resource control the platform has become clearly more robust and this is a crucial step if we want to use it in production codes.

## 4  Integration of SNMP into the JAMES Platform

JAMES includes a framework of full-fledged SNMP services already integrated and available to the NM-application developer, resulting in broader application fields and reduced development costs. In order to preserve the platform portability, these services have been written in Java. As represented in Fig. 2, three basic SNMP services are considered:

- a service allowing mobile agents to interact with SNMP-agents, acting as SNMP-managers,
- support for communication between SNMP-managers and mobile (or stationary[1]) agents,
- a management service allowing legacy management platforms to administer the JAMES infrastructure itself using SNMP.

These services provide the following features:

- management of NEs not supporting JAMES Agencies but equipped with SNMP-agents,
- management of NEs supporting JAMES Agencies but restricting direct access to management information for security or architecture reasons,
- management of the JAMES infrastructure itself as an SNMP-service,
- usage of mobile agents to deploy intermediary management services layered between NEs (SNMP capable or not) and legacy SNMP-managers. These could be new services or just management information processing closer to the NEs,
- usage of mobile or stationary agents for fast development and deployment of SNMP services.

---

[1] JAMES supports "stationary agents" in the sense that agents can make little or no use at all of their migration capability.

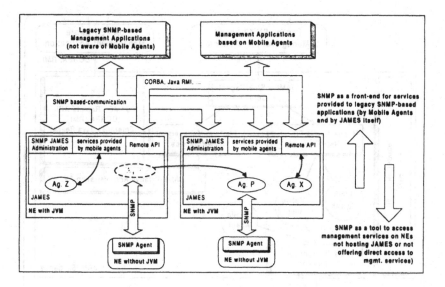

**Fig. 2.** Proposed Integration Framework

## 4.1 Design of SNMP Services

SNMP Since SNMP is just one of several protocols to be used by NM applications, the following design constraints were considered:

- SNMP support must be optional, not increasing resource usage when turned-off.
- SNMP support may not increase the complexity of the platform.
- The design of SNMP support may not compromise the platform scalability and functionality.
- SNMP support must be portable across different hosts without conflicting with SNMP services already installed in the hosts, like native SNMP agents.

These issues resulted in a modular design (Fig. 3) where SNMP services are placed outside the platform core and can be dynamically installed and removed, without imposing a permanent overhead in the JAMES infrastructure. Most services consist themselves of mobile agents (the Service Agents, granted with exceptional permissions to access necessary resources) providing services to common agents through inter-agent communication. The Agency offers a directory service where common mobile agents can locate the Service Agents (or implicitly require their installation). This solution provides an elegant lightweight framework to support specific services. In the future, new kinds of services can be easily integrated in the JAMES platform.

## 4.2 SNMP Data Handling Services

These services include all the tools needed to handle SNMP data and SNMP Protocol Data Units. These tools are available as a set of Java classes for high level

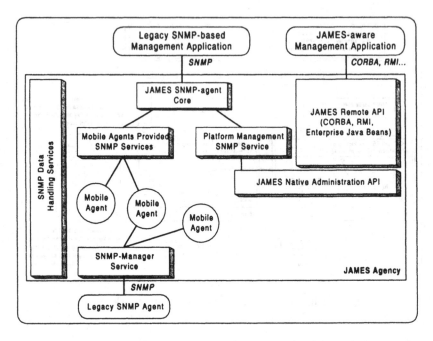

**Fig. 3.** High-Level Structure of SNMP Services of JAMES

representation of SNMP data types and PDUs. A set of Java-based ASN.1/BER [30] encoding methods is also available to be used by other SNMP Services. Mobile agents impose no particular requirements to this service, meaning general-purpose Java-based SNMP tools, like [31], could have been used without prior adaptation.

Presentation of the internal information of the platform, as suggested by [24], was not considered because the SNMP information model was considered too poor for that purpose.

### 4.3 SNMP Manager Service

This service allows mobile agents to interact with SNMP Agents using a manager-API, to query SNMP-agents, and a Trap Listener that receives SNMP Traps and redirects them to the interested mobile agents. When compared with similar Services integrated in classical management applications, this Service presents two key differences: support for mobility - mobile agents receive SNMP Traps independently of their present location and migrate without abandoning ongoing SNMP queries - and the service location within the platform - based on the already mentioned Service Agents.

The SNMP Manager-API is based on the traditional concepts found in most high-level SNMP stacks (sessions or contexts, request operations and event handlers), with protocol details being transparently handled. This Service, located

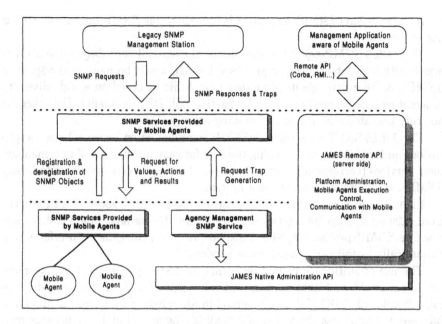

**Fig. 4.** JAMES Services for Integration with Management Applications

in Service Agents, might be replaced with a third-party classic SNMP stack integrated in the Agents code, trading-off mobility support.

This possible trade-off is based on the assumption that JAMES mobile agents can delay migration whenever completion of on-going SNMP transactions is crucial, since they implicitly control their migration. This degrades performance and affects the programming model (agent migration has to become aware of SNMP transactions) but still allows for some mobility.

The Trap Listener also uses traditional concepts found on other Trap Multiplexers. Mobile agents register their interest on the reception of certain SNMP Traps. Registrations may be valid just while the agent remains at the Agency, for a pre-defined period of time or for the agents entire lifetime (in the last two options, the Trap Listener may have to forward the Trap Arrival Notification to the new location of the agent). The arriving SNMP Traps produce Trap Arrival Notifications.

## 4.4 Services for Interoperability with Legacy SNMP Managers

While the Service described in the previous section covers communication between mobile agents and SNMP agents, there are three other services providing interoperability with legacy SNMP Managers (Fig. 4). The SNMP-agent Core maintains an SNMP-agent with data being supplied by the two underlying services. The present interface used to register new variables or groups at the MIB-table, to issue Traps and to reply to SNMP requests is proprietary, although future adaptation of standard protocols for expansible SNMP agents like DPI is not excluded.

The JAMES SNMP-agent is independent of eventually existing native SNMP-agents although integration, as proposed by [32], would be more in the spirit of SNMP[2]. Since native agents are either monolithic or based on a wide diversity of agent-expansion mechanisms, like SMUX [33], DPI or AgentX [34], there is no truly portable and non-intrusive integration method.

The JAMES SNMP-agent allows SNMP communication between legacy applications and mobile agents, opening the way for easy installation of new management services (corresponding to one or several mobile agents) available to legacy SNMP-based network management systems.

In such a scenario mobile agents can be used to pre-process data gathered from existing management services (thus offering higher level functionality), operate as SNMP proxies for NEs using proprietary management interfaces and dynamically install new management services.

The use of stationary or mobile agents for fast deployment of management services available to legacy applications is not new. The Java Dynamic Management Toolkit (JDMK) [35], a commercial product from Sun, is not based on mobile agents but shares the vision of a flexible scheme to build new management services. JDMK is meant for fast development and deployment of Java-based management services, including a complete set of tools to create and remotely install these services using Java and push/pull techniques[3]. It provides a sophisticated set of development tools and includes support for SNMP, CORBA (IIOP), HTTP and Java RMI. The PMP Project presents a framework where mobile agents use DPI to provide services to SNMP Managers.

The JAMES approach consists of a Service Agent where mobile agents interested on providing an SNMP interface must register their SNMP objects. Later on, SNMP requests from outside applications result in events passed to mobile agents. These events will then trigger predefined management actions resulting in SNMP responses.

The JAMES SNMP agent also allows SNMP-based management of the JAMES platform itself. Although a richer interface is available to dedicated applications using Java RMI and CORBA, a subset of management functions has been translated into an SNMP MIB that provides monitoring, fault-management and performance management. This is implemented using a Service Agent (the Agency SNMP Management Service) that acts as a translator between the SNMP-agent Core and the internal JAMES administration API (Figure 4). The intention is not to use SNMP to fully administer JAMES but to provide a basic set of SNMP-based management services.

It should be stressed that the option of separating the SNMP services provided by the JAMES mobile agents from the native SNMP-agents, although jus-

---

[2] i.e., it is preferred to maintain two separate agents answering in different ports than to try integration of both agents into a single one

[3] This means JDMK management services do not have support for full mobility across different hosts.

tified for sake of portability, imposes a small constraint when compared to more integrated solutions, like the one of the PMP project. It is not possible, for instance, to extend a MIB of the native SNMP-agent. This is not problematic since the most usual use of mobile agents, in this context, will be the provision of new services and not a very localized expansion of existing SNMP Services. That is considered outside our scope and more appropriate for products like JDMK.

## 5 Conclusions

The JAMES Project exploits the paradigm of mobile agents in the field of network management. We are developing a Java-based platform of mobile agents and we have some important goals in mind, like: high-performance, flexible code distribution, remote software upgrading, reliability, robustness, and support for CORBA and SNMP. Within this project we expect to show that Mobile Agents can overcome some of the problems that exist with traditional Client/Server solutions.

During this project, the platform will be used in software products in the area of network management. Our industrial partners (Siemens S.A.) have been developing prototype applications in the area of performance management that use our platform of mobile agents. These prototypes are already finished and we are now conducting a benchmarking study to compare the use of mobile agents over traditional client/server solutions to see if we corroborate some of the advantages of this new paradigm in the field of distributed computing.

In this paper we discussed the provision of explicit SNMP support for management applications based on mobile agents. This kind of support is important whenever SNMP is the only available interface to access management information. Another reason to provide SNMP support is the possibility of using mobile agent technology to develop new management services to be used by legacy management applications. However, integration of SNMP into mobile agent systems has not received as much attention as CORBA-based interoperability and the number of mobile agent platforms providing such integration is still very reduced.

The framework in the JAMES project for the integration of SNMP differs from previous work because a great deal of attention is given to keep it transparent for SNMP devices and applications. Another distinctive issue of our approach is the fact that SNMP support is dynamically installable and removable, not affecting the platforms functionality or complexity when not being used.

## Acknowledgements

This project was accepted in the European Eureka Program ($\Sigma$!1921) and it is partially supported by ADI (*Agência de Inovacão*) and FCT (*Fundacão para a Ciência e Tecnologia*). Special thanks to Rodrigo Reis, for the help in the development of several SNMP services, and to the rest of the project team from University of Coimbra and Siemens.

# References

1. Rose M.: The Simple Book - An Introduction to Management of TCP/IP-based Internets, 2nd Edition. Prentice-Hall International Inc. (1994)
2. ISO/IEC: ISO/IEC 9595: Information technology - Open Systems Interconnection - Common Management Information Service Definition. International Organization for Standardization, International Electrotechnical Commission (1990)
3. Goldszmidt, G., Yemini, Y.: Decentralizing Control and Intelligence in Network Management. Proceedings of the 4 th International Symposium on Integrated Network Management, Santa Barbara (1995)
4. Magedanz, T., Rothermel, K., Krause, S.: Intelligent Agents: An Emerging Technology for Next Generation Telecommunications. Proceedings of INFOCOM96, San Francisco, CA (1996)
5. Yemini, Y., Goldszmidt, G., Yemini, S.: Network Management by Delegation. Proceedings of IFIP 2 nd International Symposium on Integrated Network Management, Washington (1991)
6. Tennenhouse, D., Smith, J., Sincoskie, W., Wetherall, D., Minden, G.: A Survey of Active Network Research. IEEE Communications Magazine (1997)
7. OMG: The Common Object Request Broker Architecture and Specification. (1995)
8. Wellens, C., Auerbach, K.: Towards Useful Management. The Simple Times, Volume 4, Number 3 (1996)
9. Bieszcad, A., Pagurek, B., White, T.: Mobile Agents for Network Management. IEEE Communications Surveys, 4Q (1998)
10. Martin-Flatin, J., Znaty, S.: Annotated Typology of Distributed Network Management Paradigms. Technical Report SSC/1997/008, cole Polytechnique Fdrale de Lausanne (1997)
11. Agent Product and Research Activities. http://www.agent.org/pub/activity.html
12. Intelligent Agents. Communications of the ACM, Vol. 37, No. 7 (1994)
13. Hermans, B.: Intelligent Software Agents on the Internet. http://www.hermans.org/agents/index.html
14. Pham, V., Karmouch. A.: Mobile Software Agents: An Overview. IEEE Communications Magazine, pp. 26-37 July (1998)
15. IBM Aglets Workbench. http://www.trl.ibm.co.jp/aglets/
16. Concordia. http://www.meitca.com/HSL/Projects/Concordia/
17. General Magic Odyssey. http://www.genmagic.com/agents/
18. Voyager. http://www.objectspace.com/voyager/
19. Jumping Beans. http://www.JumpingBeans.com/
20. Silva, L., Simes, P., Soares, G., Martins, P., Batista, V., Renato, C., Almeida, L., Stohr, N.: JAMES: A Platform of Mobile Agents for the Management of Telecommunication Networks. Proceedings of IATA'99 (3rd International Workshop on Intelligent Agents for Telecommunication Applications), Stockholm (1999)
21. Mobile Agent System Interoperability Facilities Specification. OMG TC Document orbos/97-10-05 (1998)
22. Grasshopper. http://www.ikv.de/products/grasshopper/
23. Nicklish, J., Quittek, J., Kind, A., Arao, S.: INCA: an Agent-based Network Control Architecture. Proceedings of IATA'98 (2nd International Workshop on Intelligent Agents for Telecommunication Applications), Paris (1998)
24. Lazar, S., Sidhu, D.: Discovery, A Mobile Agent Framework for Distributed Application Development. Technical Report, Maryland Center for Telecommunications Research, University of Maryland Baltimore County (1997)

25. Sahai, A., Morin, C.: Enabling a Mobile Network manager (MNM) Through Mobile Agents. Proceedings of Mobile Agents, Second International Workshop MA98, Stuttgart, Germany (1998)
26. Perpetuum Mobile Procura Project. Carlton University, http://www.sce.carleton.ca/netmanage/perpetum.shtml
27. Bieszczad, A.: Advanced Network Management in the Network Management Perpetuum Mobile Procura Project. Technical Report SCE-97-07, Systems and Computer Engineering, Carleton University (1997)
28. Wijnen, B., Carpenter, G., Curran, K., Sehgal A., Waters, G.: Simple Network Management Protocol Distributed Protocol Interface Version 2.0, RFC 1592 (1994)
29. JavaSpaces. http://java.sun.com/products/javaspaces
30. Information Processing, Open Systems Interconnection: Specification of Basic Encoding Rules for Abstract Syntax Notation One. ISO (1987)
31. AdventNet SNMP. http://www.adventnet.com/products/snmpbeans
32. Susilo, G., Bieszczad, A. and Pagurek, B.: Infrastructure for Advanced Network Management based on Mobile Code. Proceedings of the IEEE/IFIP Network Operations and Management Symposium NOMS'98, New Orleans (1998)
33. Rose, M.: SNMP MUX protocol and MIB. RFC 1227 (1991)
34. Daniele, M., Wijnen, B., Francisco, D.: Agent Extensibility (AgentX) Protocol Version 1, RFC 2257 (1998)
35. Java Dynamic Management Kit. http//www.sun.com/software/java-dynamic

# JAMAP: A Web-Based Management Platform for IP Networks

Jean-Philippe Martin-Flatin, Laurent Bovet and Jean-Pierre Hubaux

Institute for computer Communications and Applications (ICA)
Swiss Federal Institute of Technology, Lausanne (EPFL)
1015 Lausanne, Switzerland
**martin-flatin@epfl.ch**
**http://icawww.epfl.ch**

**Abstract.** In this paper, we describe JAMAP, a prototype of a Web-based management platform for IP networks. It is written entirely in Java. It implements the push model to perform regular management (i.e. permanent network monitoring and data collection) and *ad hoc* management (i.e. temporary network monitoring and troubleshooting). The communication between agents and managers relies on HTTP transfers between Java applets and servlets over persistent TCP connections. The SNMP MIB data is encapsulated in serialized Java objects that are transmitted as MIME parts via HTTP. The manager consists of two parts: the management server, a static machine that runs the servlets, and the management station, which can be any desktop running a Web browser. The MIB data is transparently compressed with gzip, which saves network bandwidth without increasing latency too significantly.

## 1  Introduction

Web technologies have proved very attractive to Network and Systems Management (N&SM) for several years. In July 1996, a special issue of *The Simple Times* summarized the different ways of integrating HTTP, HTML and applets with standard IP network management platforms. Whereas most of the industry, as far as a customer could see, and most of the press then limited Web-based management to the sole use of Web browsers to display Graphical User Interfaces (GUIs), this collection of articles had the merit of widely advertising the wide range of possibilities opened up by Web technologies in N&SM. The most radical approach came from Wellens and Auerbach, who suggested to embed not only HTTP servers but also applets in network equipment, and who based the communication between managers and agents on HTTP instead of SNMP [16]. The common belief, then, as exposed by Bruins [3], was that HTTP was useful to initiate the interactive dialog between the administrator and the agent, but that further interactions should be based on SNMP.

Since then, the industry has trumpeted its adoption of Web technologies very loud, but the real achievements that we can see on the market today are more modest. HTTP servers are now routinely embedded by many router vendors, but management applets are not. Configuration management has probably been the main beneficiary so far of the recent adoption of Web technologies: several management platforms now enable administrators to run Java applications on the manager (the cheap alternative to downloading an applet from an agent) in order to configure agents. But to the best of our knowledge, all the main players in the IP systems and network management market (HP Openview, IBM/Tivoli Netview, Cabletron Spectrum...) still use SNMP for communication between managers and agents once the configuration phase is accomplished. We have attended demonstrations by several vendors of Java applications that included an SNMP stack in order to perform standard SNMP polling behind the Web interface, which proves that the full potential of Web technologies in N&SM has still not spread across the entire industry.

Despite this slow pace of the industry, the research community has been very active in the meantime, leading to a growing understanding of the issues and challenges at stake. If we ignore the revolutionary approaches that depart entirely from traditional SNMP-based management (e.g., Java-based mobile agents and multi-agent systems), we still have a lot of literature witnessing that we have gained experience in the integration of Web technologies with traditional N&SM. At the end of 1996, Deri [5] described possible mappings between URLs and command line interfaces, and Harrison et al. proposed the HTTP Manageable MIB [7]. In 1997, Maston [11] described the basics of network element management with HTML, while Kasteleijn [8], Barillaud et al. [2] and Reed et al. [13] reported their experiences with building management prototypes respectively for ATM backbone networks, local-area networks and PC systems. More references will be presented in Section 7.

In 1998, we proposed an architecture that goes beyond Wellens and Auerbach's [9, 10]. In addition to embedding HTTP servers and management applets in all managed devices, and to using solely HTTP to communicate between managers and agents, we suggested to push management data from agents to managers and to rewrite the managers entirely in Java, thereby leveraging on the simplicity of servlet programming. In this paper, we present the low-level design of this architecture, we indicate the design decisions which were made among all the candidates listed in [10], and we report progress on the building of a prototype called JAMAP (JAva MAnagement Platform). In particular, we describe how data is structured and encoded inside HTTP messages (Wellens and Auerbach only gave a high-level description of HTTP-based management data transfers).

In the IP world, the advantages of our architecture over the classic SNMP management frameworks (v1, v2c and v3) are fourfold. First, by going from a pull to a push model, we decrease significantly the network overhead of management data, because the manager no longer has to keep requesting the same OIDs (Object IDentifiers) to the same agents at every polling cycle. This almost halves the network overhead, because the description of the OIDs takes a lot more space than their values. Second, by grouping all the MIB data of a push cycle together and by compressing them with gzip, we reduce even more the network overhead without increasing latency too significantly, which has a positive effect on the scalability of the N&SM system. Third, by adopting Java, we free vendors from the burden of porting add-ons like CiscoWorks from one management platform to another (HP OpenView, Cabletron Spectrum, etc.) and from one operating system to another (Windows x.y, Solaris u.v, Linux a.b, etc.). Fourth, by using only well-known and pervasive Web technologies instead of SNMP technologies, we prove that N&SM need not rely on domain-specific skills (SNMPv1, SNMPv2c, SNMPv3, SMIv1, SMIv2, BER...). N&SM applications are just another case of distributed applications, and can rely on standard distributed technology. Therefore N&SM platforms can be maintained by less expensive and easier-to-find Java programmers, and can reuse components developed for other application domains. By combining these advantages with the "write once, run anywhere" claim of Java, the price of N&SM platforms can be driven down significantly, and site-specific developments can be rendered much easier for administrators.

The remainder of this paper is organized as follows. In Section 2, we present an overview of the architecture of JAMAP. In Section 3, we introduce three advanced technologies used in JAMAP. In Sections 4, 5 and 6, we describe the different applets and servlets run by the agent and the two constituents of the manager: the management station and the management server. In Section 7, we present some related work. Finally, we conclude in Section 8 with some perspectives for future work.

## 2 Architecture of JAMAP

Our architecture integrates push and pull communication models to manage IP networks [9, 10]. For regular management, i.e. when tasks are repetitive and performed identically at each time step, we use the push model and the publish-subscribe paradigm. Initially, managers subscribe to some MIB data published by the agents. Later, the agents push this data at regular time intervals, without the manager requesting anything else. For *ad hoc* management, i.e. when tasks are performed over a short time period (e.g. troubleshooting), we use the pull model for one-shot retrievals, and the push model otherwise (e.g. short-term monitoring).

For the information model, we keep SNMP MIBs unchanged in the agents because we believe that they constitute the main achievement of SNMP. It took years for the industry to define and deploy these MIBs in all sorts of network devices and systems, and it would not make sense to change them. Their main limitation is that, due to the SNMP management frameworks, most (all?) of them are confined today to the instrumentation level, that is, offer low-level semantics. But there is no reason why we should not see higher level MIBs appear in the future. From standard SNMP-based management, we also borrowed the organizational model, with managers and agents, but we changed the SNMP 2-tier architecture into a 3-tier architecture.

The main novelty demonstrated by JAMAP is that it uses a push model to transfer management data (i.e., data extracted from SNMP MIBs at the agent) from the agent to the manager. Fig. 1 depicts push-based monitoring and data collection, while the handling of notifications is represented on Fig. 2. The push model, also known as the publish-subscribe paradigm, involves three phases:

- *publication*: each agent announces the MIBs that it manages and the notifications that it may send to a manager;

- *subscription*: agent by agent, the administrator (the person) subscribes the manager (the program) to different MIB variables and notifications via subscription applets; the push frequency is specified for each MIB variable;

– *distribution*: at each push cycle, the push scheduler of each agent triggers the transfer of MIB data from the agent to the manager; unlike what happens with traditional polling, the manager does not have to request this data at each push cycle; the transfer of notifications is triggered by the health monitor; notifications and MIB data use independently the same communication path.

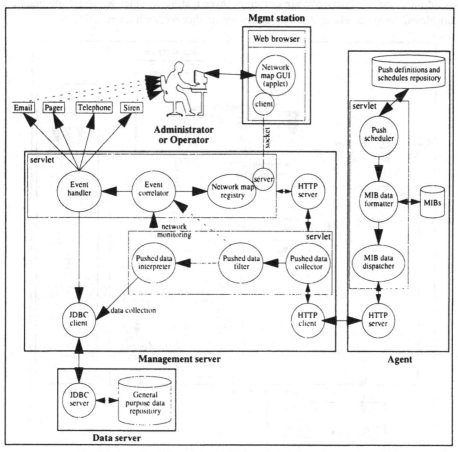

**Fig. 1.** Push-based monitoring and data collection

Our main motivation for developing of JAMAP was to prove the feasibility and relative simplicity of our design innovations. The core of JAMAP, that is, the push engine and the communication between the agent and the manager, was implemented in only two weeks, thereby demonstrating that our design was simple to implement. The different servlets and applets depicted in Fig. 1 and Fig. 2 took a lot longer to write and debug, as expected, and we had to make a number of simplifications to finish the first version of JAMAP in time to demonstrate it internally in March 1999. First, the persistence of data (MIB data, log of events, agents' configuration files, network topology, etc.) currently relies on flat files. Eventually, it will be ensured by a public-domain RDBMS (Relational DataBase Management System, e.g. msql) accessed via JDBC (Java DataBase Connectivity), as represented on the figures. Second, we have not yet written a network map GUI applet. Instead, as illustrated by Fig. 3, we use an event notification applet that simply displays incoming events, line by line, in a window. For the future, we plan to generate automatically a network map from a file describing the network topology, and to change the color of the icons according to the events received. Third, our event correlator is still very simple, with many rules hard-coded on an *ad hoc* basis. We are currently investigating whether we could integrate a full-blown event correlator written in Java by another research team.

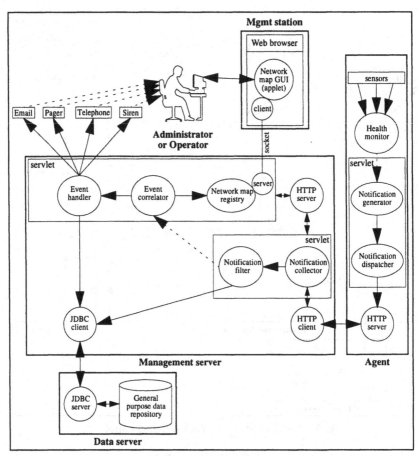

**Fig. 2.** Push-based notification handling

Fig. 3 and Fig. 4 are synthetic views of the communication between the different Java applets and servlets running on the agent and the manager. They both illustrate our 3-tier architecture with the management station, the management server and the agent. The push arrow between the MIB data dispatcher servlet and the MIB data subscription applet represents the path followed by MIB data retrieved for *ad hoc* management. The other push arrows depict regular management. The dotted arrows represent the applet-to-servlet dialogs that take place at the subscription phase. These figures will be explained in detail in Sections 4, 5 and 6.

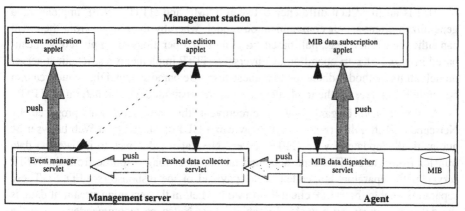

**Fig. 3.** Communication between Java applets and servlets:
monitoring and data collection

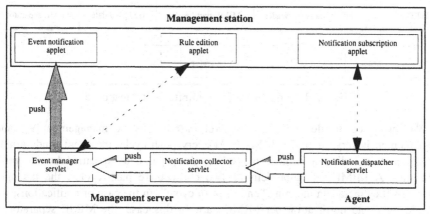

**Fig. 4.** Communication between Java applets and servlets: notifications

## 3 Advanced Technologies Used in JAMAP

In this section, we describe three advanced technologies used in JAMAP: MIME-based
push, Java servlets and Jàva serialization.

### 3.1 MIME multipart and MIME-based push

Unlike other distributed application technologies such as sockets and Java Remote
Method Invocation (RMI), HTTP offers no native support for bidirectional persistent
connections [9]. With HTTP, a connection is always oriented: it is not possible to
create a persistent connection in one direction (from the client to the server) and to
send data afterward in the opposite direction (from the server to the client). Before an
HTTP server can send data to a client, it must have received a request from this client.
In other words, an HTTP server cannot send unsolicited messages to an HTTP client.

This is an important difference between SNMP and HTTP. SNMP implements a generalized client-server communication model, whereby the request from the client can either be explicit (e.g., pull-based get and set operations) or implicit (e.g., push-based snmpv2-trap operation). Conversely, HTTP implements a strict client-server model: all its methods adhere to the request-response paradigm, and the request cannot be implicit. As a result, the implementation of the push model is not natural in HTTP.

A simple and elegant way to circumvent this limitation was proposed by Netscape [12] in a different context: How can a GUI displayed by a Web browser be automatically updated by an HTTP server? Netscape's idea was to initiate the data transfer from the HTTP client, and send an infinitely long response from the HTTP server, with separators embedded in the payload of the response (see Fig. 5). These separators enable the HTTP client to work out what, in the incoming stream of data, is the data for a given push cycle. To achieve this, Netscape recommended to use the multipart type of MIME (Multipurpose Internet Mail Extensions [6]).

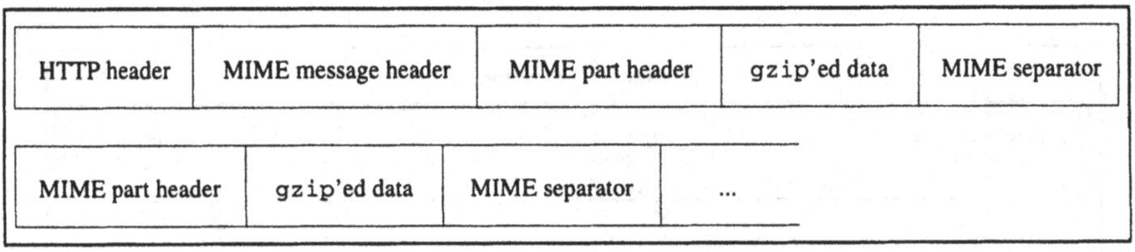

| HTTP header | MIME message header | MIME part header | gzip'ed data | MIME separator |
|---|---|---|---|---|
| MIME part header | gzip'ed data | MIME separator | ... | |

**Fig. 5.** TCP payload of the infinite HTTP response

We proposed to do the same in Web-based network management [9], and implemented it very simply in JAMAP. At every push cycle, the agent sends a new MIME part including a number of {OID, value} pairs, as specified by the push scheduler. A MIME separator delimits two consecutive push cycles; the manager interprets it as metadata meaning "end of push cycle". In the case of notifications, we encode only one notification per MIME part. In this case, the MIME separator is considered by the manager as metadata meaning "end of notification".

MIME parts transferring MIB data are compressed with gzip (MIME content transfer encoding). This saves a lot of network bandwidth when the manager subscribes to many MIB variables, and does not increase latency too significantly. MIME parts carrying notifications are not compressed because the compression ratio would be poor for so little data, and the increased latency would not be worth the meager savings in network overhead.

## 3.2 Java servlets

JAMAP relies heavily on HTTP-based communication between Java applets and servlets. Servlets [4] only recently appeared on the Web; they are an improvement over the well-known CGI (Common Gateway Interface) scripts. Unlike the CGI scripts that are typically written in a scripting language like Perl or Tcl/Tk, servlets are Java classes loaded in a Java Virtual Machine (JVM) via an HTTP server. The HTTP server must be configured to use servlets and associate a URL with each loaded servlet. At startup time, one servlet object is instantiated for each configured servlet. When a request is performed on a servlet URL, the HTTP server invokes a method of the servlet depending on the HTTP method used by the request. All servlets implement one method per HTTP method. For instance, the doGet() method is invoked when an HTTP GET request comes in for the corresponding URL.

Modern operating systems generally support multithreading. As a result, most HTTP servers now support concurrent accesses. Several HTTP clients may therefore invoke concurrently the same method of the same servlet. This allows the sharing of the same servlet by multiple persistent connections. We used this feature extensively in JAMAP when we tested it with several agents. Like any URLs, Java servlets can also leverage on the general-purpose features of HTTP servers (e.g. access control).

As we write this paper, servlet environments are still in constant evolution. During our work, Sun's specification of the servlets changed from version 2.0 to version 2.1, but public-domain implementations remained at 2.0. For JAMAP, we first used the Apache HTTP server version 1.3.4 and the Apache servlet engine Jserv 0.8. But we had problems because Jserv 0.8 did not support concurrent accesses to servlets and the response stream was buffered (both problems were later corrected in Jserv 1.0). In the meantime, we switched to another HTTP server, Jigsaw 2.0.1, which offered good support for servlets.

### 3.3 Java serialization

Serialization is a feature of Java that allows the translation of an arbitrarily complex object into a byte stream. In JAMAP, we used it for ensuring the persistence of the state of an object and for transferring objects over the network. Objects containing references to other objects are processed recursively until all necessary objects are serialized. The keyword transient can be added to the declaration of an attribute (e.g. an object reference) to prevent its serialization.

For network transfers, instead of defining a protocol, one can use serializable classes dedicated to communication. Such classes offer a writeObject() method on one side, and a readObject() method on the other. For persistence, serialization proved very useful to store rules and agents configurations.

In the next three sections, we will describe the different applets and servlets running on the different machines of the management system (see Fig. 3 and Fig. 4): the management station, the management server and the agent.

## 4 Management Station

The management station is the desktop of the administrator or operator. It can be any machine (a Linux PC, a Windows PC, a Mac, a Unix workstation, etc.) as long as it runs a Web browser and supports Java. Unlike the management server, it is not static: the administrator can work on different machines at different times of the day. In the subscription phase of the push model, he/she configures the agent via the MIB data subscription applet and the notification subscription applet. The rules used by the pushed data collector and the event manager servlets can be modified at any time via the rule edition applet. Events are displayed by the event notification applet.

## 4.1 MIB data subscription applet

The MIB data subscription applet communicates directly with the agent. It provides the subscription system for regular management. It is also used to perform push-based and pull-based *ad hoc* management. Its main tasks are the following:

- browse MIBs graphically;
- select MIB variables or SNMP tables and retrieve their values once (pull model);
- select MIB variables and monitor them for a while (text fields, time graphs or tables);
- monitor some computed values (e.g. interface utilization); and
- subscribe to MIB variables or SNMP tables and specify a push frequency (per MIB variable).

Computed values are typically the results of equations parameterized by multiple MIB variables. We implemented a sort of multiplexer to support them. This kind of simple preprocessing could be delegated to the agent in the future.

## 4.2 Notification subscription applet

Similarly, the notification subscription applet also communicates directly with the agent. It enables the administrator to set up a filter for notifications at the agent level. Notifications that have not been subscribed to by the manager are silently discarded by the agent.

## 4.3 Rule edition applet

The rule edition applet controls the behavior of two objects:

- the pushed data interpreter object living in the pushed data collector servlet; and
- the event correlator object living in the event manager servlet.

The administrator can write rules in Java via the applet, or can edit them separately and apply them via the applet. (Java is used here as a universal scripting language.) For instance, an event can be generated by the pushed data interpreter if the value of a MIB variable exceeds a given threshold. A typical rule for the event correlator would be that if a system is believed to be down, then all applications running on it should also be down, so events reporting that NFS (Network File System) is not working or that an RDBMS is not working should be discarded.

More complex rules can easily be written. For instance, the pushed data interpreter can check if the average value of a given MIB variable increased by 10% or more over the last two hundred push cycles. In fact, these rules can be arbitrarily complex, as there is no clear-cut distinction between what is in the realm of offline data mining and what should be performed immediately, in pseudo real-time. The trade-off is that the pushed data interpreter should not be slowed down too much by an excessive amount of rules, otherwise it might not be able to apply all the relevant rules to incoming data between two consecutive push cycles.

## 4.4 Event notification applet

The event notification applet is connected to the management server to receive events. We use it as a debugger, as we do not manage a production network with our platform. This applet displays a simple list of events and manages a blinking light and sound system to grab the operator's attention in case of incoming events. It is intended to remain permanently in a corner of the administrator's and operator's desktop screens. Eventually, it will be complemented by the network map GUI applet.

## 5 Management Server

The management server runs three servlets: the pushed data collector, the notification collector and the event manager. In principle, this management server could easily be distributed over multiple machines if need be (e.g. for scalability reasons), as the communication between servlets relies on HTTP, and the data server is already a separate machine. For instance, we could run the three servlets on three different machines, and data mining on a fourth. But so far, we have only tested our software with a single management server.

### 5.1 Pushed data collector servlet

The pushed data collector servlet consists of three core objects (see Fig. 1), plus a number of instrumentation objects not represented on that figure. The pushed data collector object connects to the agent upon startup, and enters an infinite loop where it listens to the socket for incoming data and passes on this data "as is" to the pushed data filter object. If the connection to the agent is lost, e.g. due to a reboot of the agent, the pushed data collector immediately reconnects to it so as to ensure a persistent connection [9].

The pushed data filter object controls the flow of incoming data. If it detects that too much traffic is coming in from a given agent (that is, from a given socket), it tells the pushed data collector object to close permanently the connection to that agent (that is, the collector should not attempt to reconnect to the agent until the administrator explicitly tells it to do so). The rationale here is that a misbehaving agent is either misconfigured, bogus, or under the control of an intruder pursuing a denial of service attack, and that the good health of the management system should be protected against this misbehaving agent. When this happens, the administrator is informed via email.

If the pushed data filter object is happy with the incoming data, it passes it on "as is" to the pushed data interpreter object. The latter unmarshalls the data and checks, MIB variable by MIB variable, whether it was subscribed to for monitoring, data collection or both.

In the case of data collection, the MIB variable is not processed immediately. Instead, it is stored in a persistent repository (an NFS-mounted file system currently, an RDBMS in the future) via a logger object. We assume that an external process will process it afterward to perform some kind of data mining (e.g., it could look for a trend in the variations of the CPU load of an IP router to be able to anticipate when it should be upgraded).

In the case of monitoring, the MIB variable is processed immediately. The pushed data interpreter object applies the rules relevant to that agent and that MIB variable. If it notices something important (e.g., a heartbeat is received from an IP router which was considered down), the pushed data interpreter object generates an urgent event and sends it via HTTP to the event correlator object living in the event manager servlet. We took special care for the case where the same MIB variable is used for both monitoring and data collection. The data is then duplicated by the pushed data interpreter.

A nice feature of our rule system is that rules may be dynamically compiled and loaded in by the servlet. Dynamic class loading is a feature of the Java language. The core API provides a method to instantiate objects from a class by giving its name in the form of a string. The class loader of the JVM searches the class file in the file system, and loads it into the JVM's memory. This enables the servlet to load a class at runtime without knowing its name in advance. Once a class is loaded, it behaves just as any other class. We are limited only by the fact that a class cannot be modified at runtime. This means that if a rule is already registered under a certain class name and that rule is modified by the administrator, another class name must be used for that new version of the rule.

To solve this problem, we implemented a simple technique that consists in postfixing the class name with a release number and incrementing this release number automatically. As a result, the administrator can create, modify and debug rules dynamically. The drawback is that the memory used by loaded classes (especially those corresponding to the "old" rules) is freed only when the JVM is restarted. The administrator should therefore be careful not to fill up the memory in the rule debugging phase. Clearly, this feature should be used with special care on a production system; but it proved to be particularly useful for debugging rules.

## 5.2 Notification collector servlet

As depicted in Fig. 2, the notification collector servlet consists in principle of two core objects, the notification collector and the notification filter. Contrary to pushed data, we do not need an interpreter for notifications because we know already what happened: we do not have to work it out.

The notification collector object works exactly as the pushed data collector object. The notification filter object also works as the pushed data filter object. In fact, in the current version of JAMAP, the notification collector servlet and the pushed data collector servlet are just one single servlet. This enables us to use a single persistent connection between the agent and the manager for transferring MIB data and notifications. (Note that this would not be the case if we were to distribute the servlets over several machines.) Notifications received by the pushed data interpreter object are currently passed on "as is" to the event correlator object living in the event manager servlet, without any further processing.

## 5.3 Event manager servlet

The event manager servlet connects to one or more pushed data collector servlets (one, in the case depicted in Fig. 3 and Fig. 4) and waits for incoming events. Events are processed by the event correlator object. This object performs a simple correlation with regard to the network topology, in order to discard masked events. For instance, if a router is down, all machines accessed across it will appear to be down to the pushed data interpreter. Based on its knowledge of the network topology (which is hardcoded in the current version of JAMAP), the event correlator is able to keep only those events that cannot be ascribed to the failure of other equipment.

When an event is not discarded by the event correlator object, it is transmitted to the event handler object corresponding to its level of emergency (this level of emergency is encapsulated inside the event). Each event handler is coded to interface with a specific notification system (e.g., an email system, a pager, a telephone, a siren, etc.). In our prototype, we only implemented an email-based notification system.

## 6  Agent

The agent runs a lightweight JVM [9] and two servlets: the MIB data dispatcher and the notification dispatcher.

### 6.1  MIB data dispatcher servlet

The MIB data dispatcher servlet consists of three core objects (the push scheduler, the MIB data formatter and the MIB data dispatcher) plus a number of instrumentation objects not represented on Fig. 1. During the subscription phase, the push scheduler object stores locally the subscription sent by the MIB data subscription applet (we call it the agent's configuration). Later, during the distribution phase, the push scheduler object uses this configuration to trigger the push cycles. It tells the MIB data formatter object what MIB variables should be sent at a given time step. The MIB data formatter object accesses the in-memory data structures of the MIBs via some proprietary, tailor-made mechanism, formats the MIB data as a series of {OID, value} pairs, and sends it to the MIB data dispatcher object. The latter compresses the data with gzip, assembles the data in the form of a MIME part, pushes the MIME part through and sends a MIME separator afterward to indicate that the push cycle is over.

In the future, the MIB data dispatcher servlet will be able to retrieve the agent's configuration from the data server via the management server. Thus, the agent will not necessarily have to store its configuration in nonvolatile memory, a useful feature for bottom-of-the-range equipment.

### 6.2  Notification dispatcher servlet

The notification dispatcher servlet consists of two core objects (the notification generator and the notification dispatcher) plus a number of instrumentation objects not represented on Fig. 2. During the subscription phase, the notification generator object stores locally the subscription sent by the notification subscription applet. In other words, it sets up a filter for notifications coming in from the health monitor. During the distribution phase, the health monitor checks continuously the health of the agent based on input from sensors. When a problem is detected, the health monitor asynchronously fires an alarm to the notification generator object in the servlet via some proprietary mechanism. The notification generator object checks with the filter if this alarm should be discarded. If it was not subscribed to by the manager, the alarm is silently dropped. If it was, the notification generator object formats it as an SNMPv2 notification and sends it to the notification dispatcher object, which, in turn, wraps it in the form of a MIME part, pushes it to the management server via HTTP, and sends a MIME separator afterward to indicate that this is the end of the notification.

As we do not manage a real-life network with JAMAP, the notifications that are generated by the health monitor are all simulated. Instead of using real sensors, we fire, from time to time, one notification taken in a pool of predefined notifications; the selection of this notification is based on a random number generator. As with the previous servlet, the notification dispatcher servlet will eventually be able to retrieve the agent's notification filter from the data server via the management server.

## 7 Related Work

In the recent past, two very promising contributions came from industrial research: the Web-Based Enterprise Management (WBEM) initiative and Marvel.

WBEM came to life in 1996, by making sensational marketing announcements that it would unify (at last) N&SM by defining a new information model and a new communication model. By obsoleting all existing technologies and management frameworks, it did not gain much credibility. In1997, the WBEM Consortium became more realistic: it adopted HTTP as its transfer protocol, selected the Extensible Markup Language (XML) to structure management data, and delivered the specifications for a new information model: the Common Information Model (CIM) [15]. Then, the WBEM initiative was taken over by the Distributed Management Task Force (DMTF) and integrated into its more global work plan—a guarantee of its independence toward any particular vendor. A lot of work is currently under way, split across 14 Technical Committees. Apart from CIM, whose specifications were updated several times already and are now fairly stable, most of the technical specifications are still ongoing work, e.g. the definition of CIM operations over HTTP. Several of our proposals could fit into this framework, such as the use of push rather than pull technologies and the encapsulation of XML into MIME parts.

The most interesting prototype freely available to date is probably Marvel by Anerousis [1]. The main difference with JAMAP is that Marvel relies on RMI for manager-agent communication, and builds on it to offer a distributed object-oriented N&SM platform. This enables a very elegant architecture and a clean design, but is exposed to a well-known criticism: can we reasonably expect all managed devices to support RMI in the future? For the Jini camp [14], which advocates universal plug-and-play based on Java, the answer is clearly *yes*. We have doubts about it: bottom-of-the-range devices are very price sensitive, and despite the decreasing prices of CPU and memory, the extra cost of embedding Java software still makes a difference today—enough to win or lose customers. For top-of-the-range devices, the support for Java RMI makes perfect sense. But if we want to have a unified N&SM framework for all devices, we should be careful not to have too stringent requirements—otherwise, our proposals will simply be rejected by the industry. Our requirement that a lightweight JVM be embedded in all devices seems to be the farthest we can reasonably go for the next couple of years. It should be noted that Sun's EmbeddedJava technology might bring an answer to this question in the future.

# 8   Conclusion

We have presented JAMAP, a prototype of N&SM platform written entirely in Java. It implements the push model to perform regular management (i.e. permanent monitoring and data collection for offline analysis) and *ad hoc* management (i.e. temporary monitoring and troubleshooting). The communication between agents and managers relies on HTTP transfers between Java applets and servlets over persistent TCP connections. The SNMP MIB data is encapsulated in serialized Java objects that are transmitted as MIME parts via HTTP. The manager consists of two parts: the management server, a static machine that runs the servlets, and the management station, which can be any desktop running a Web browser. The MIB data is transparently compressed with `gzip`, which saves network bandwidth without increasing latency too significantly.

Our approach offers many advantages over traditional SNMP-based management: it reduces the network overhead of management data transfers; it delegates part of the processing overhead from the manager to the agents; it reduces the development costs of management software for both equipment and N&SM platform vendors (and consequently the cost of the N&SM platform for the customers); and it makes it easier to find engineers with the expertise necessary for customizing a management platform to specific sites. Other advantages not developed in this paper include the better potential for distributing management with mobile code, the simplicity to implement low-level security, the potential for high-level semantics, and the usual advantages of 3-tier over 2-tier architectures. The main disadvantage is the slow speed of execution of Java code, especially JDBC, which may cause scalability problems. More work is necessary to assess if we can work around these difficulties, or if we have to resort to alternatives to manage large production systems and networks.

For future research, we plan to investigate different schemes to structure and encode management data, instead of serializing Java objects that encapsulate SNMP MIB data. Our objective is to get a higher level of semantics while keeping both network overhead and end-to-end latency reasonably low. In particular, we want to study the pros and cons of going from a string-based to an XML-based representation of MIB data, and to measure the effects of `gzip` compression in both cases. It would also be useful to perform a detailed performance analysis of these different structuring and encoding schemes, and to compare them with SNMP.

## Acknowledgments

This research was partially funded by the Swiss National Science Foundation (FNRS) under grant SPP-ICS 5003-45311. We wish to thank H. Cogliati for proofreading this paper. We are also grateful to AdventNet, IBM and R. Tschalär for making useful Java classes freely available to academic researchers.

# References

1. N. Anerousis. "Scalable Management Services Using Java and the World Wide Web". In A.S. Sethi (Ed.), *Proc. 9th IFIP/IEEE Int. Workshop on Distributed Systems: Operations & Management (DSOM'98), Newark, DE, USA, October 1998*, pp. 79–90.

2. F. Barillaud, L. Deri and M. Feridun. "Network Management using Internet Technologies". In A. Lazar, R. Saracco and R. Stadler (Eds.), *Integrated Network Management V, Proc. 5th IFIP/IEEE Int. Symp. on Integrated Network Management (IM'97), San Diego, CA, USA, May 1997*, pp. 61–70. Chapman & Hall, London, UK, 1997.

3. B. Bruins. "Some Experiences with Emerging Management Technologies". *The Simple Times*, 4(3):6–8, 1996.

4. J.D. Davidson and S. Ahmed. *Java Servlet API Specification. Version 2.1a.* Sun Microsystems, November 1998.

5. L. Deri. *HTTP-based SNMP and CMIP Network Management.* Internet draft <draft-deri-http-mgmt-00.txt> (now expired). IETF, November 1996.

6. N. Freed and N. Borenstein (Eds.). *RFC 2046. Multipurpose Internet Mail Extensions (MIME). Part Two: Media Types.* IETF, November 1996.

7. B. Harrison, P.E. Mellquist and A. Pell. *Web Based System and Network Management.* Internet draft <draft-mellquist-web-sys-01.txt> (now expired). IETF, November 1996.

8. W. Kasteleijn. *Web-Based Management.* M.Sc. thesis, University of Twente, Enschede, The Netherlands, April 1997.

9. J.P. Martin-Flatin. *The Push Model in Web-Based Network Management.* Technical Report SSC/1998/023, version 3, SSC, EPFL, Lausanne, Switzerland, November 1998.

10. J.P. Martin-Flatin. "Push vs. Pull in Web-Based Network Management". In *Proc. 6th IFIP/IEEE International Symposium on Integrated Network Management (IM'99), Boston, MA, USA, May 1999*, pp. 3–18. IEEE Press, 1999.

11. M.C. Maston. "Using the World Wide Web and Java for Network Service Management". In A. Lazar, R. Saracco and R. Stadler (Eds.), *Integrated Network Management V, Proc. 5th IFIP/IEEE Int. Symp. on Integrated Network Management (IM'97), San Diego, CA, USA, May 1997*, pp. 71–84. Chapman & Hall, London, UK, 1997.

12. Netscape. *An Exploration of Dynamic Documents.* 1995. Available at <http://home.mcom.com/assist/net_sites/pushpull.html>.

13. B. Reed, M. Peercy and E. Robinson. "Distributed Systems Management on the Web". In A. Lazar, R. Saracco and R. Stadler (Eds.), *Integrated Network Management V, Proc. 5th IFIP/IEEE Int. Symp. on Integrated Network Management (IM'97), San Diego, CA, USA, May 1997*, pp. 85–95. Chapman & Hall, London, UK, 1997.

14. Sun Microsystems. *Jini.* Available at <http://www.sun.com/jini/>.

15. J.P. Thompson. "Web-Based Enterprise Management Architecture". *IEEE Communications Magazine*, 36(3):80–86, 1998.

16. C. Wellens and K. Auerbach. "Towards Useful Management". *The Simple Times*, 4(3):1–6, 1996.

# Session 5

# Management of Programmable and Active Networks

*Chair: Raouf Boutaba*
*University of Toronto, Canada*

# Service Configuration and Management in Adaptable Networks *

Livio Ricciulli

Computer Science Laboratory, SRI International
333 Ravenswood Avenue
Menlo Park, CA 94025, US
livio@csl.sri.com
http://www.csl.sri.com/ancors

**Abstract.** We describe ANCORS, an architecture for the design, configuration, and management of adaptable networks. We describe the primary components of the architecture and their common system management infrastructure. We describe alternative techniques that can be used for the management of adaptable networks and discuss their relative strengths. We then propose an open and extensible management framework for adapting the management infrastructure to newly deployed network services. We exemplify the use of this framework by outlining four different representative management applications.

## 1 Introduction

Current networking systems are very static and are a result of years of standardization efforts that allow different vendors and software developers to interact through a set of well-defined protocols. Active networking is motivated by the notion that the improvement and evolution of current networking software is greatly hindered by slow and expensive standardization processes. Several active networking research projects [1, 4, 5, 12–14, 11] try to accommodate changes to network software by facilitating the safe and efficient dynamic reconfiguration of the network. Adaptive networks may be seen as the composition of the two main orthogonal approaches to active network design discussed in [13].

- In the *discrete approach* administrators issue explicit commands that load, modify, or remove networking software. With this approach a network is active in the sense that it can be dynamically changed administratively.
- In the *integrated approach* the network is modified by the data packets that travel through it. When packets travel through the network, they automatically cause required software resources to be loaded on demand. This approach is being followed today by most active networking research and allows a much finer-grain dynamism.

---

* The work presented in this paper is currently funded by the Information Technology Office of the Defense Advanced Research Projects Agency, under contract number DABT63-97-C0040.

Adaptable networks result in much more flexibility in designing and using networks, but pose several challenging technical problems. One of these problems is how to provide a unifying paradigm for the management of active networks. As new active network software is developed and deployed, both its static characteristics and runtime behavior should be made known. It should be possible to allow newly developed system-level software to reuse existing system/network management paradigms and delegate its management and monitoring functions to them. Thus, a major challenge that must be met for managing dynamic and ever-evolving networks is to extend the adaptability of the network services to their management. Statically defined network management (NM) databases of the style of SNMP Management Information Bases (MIBs) can no longer be used to specify the management of evolving systems because this would require constant updates to the MIBs and NM tools to reflect the additions of new entities.

We are exploring new ways by which network management can be dynamically updated to include new services in its control and monitoring scope. Our NM paradigm focuses on supporting services that are relatively permanent and long-lived and that can benefit from having a specialized monitoring and configuration infrastructure. Examples of these kinds of services are the execution environments (EEs) produced by current active networking research groups, engineering and prototyping tools such as the one described in [10], and network monitoring tools like RMON and intrusion detection engines from the EMERALD project [7].

## 2 Overall Picture (ANCORS)

The ideas in this paper are derived from the ANCORS (Adaptable Network COntrol and Reporting System) project. ANCORS is intended to streamline and, at the same time, enrich the management and monitoring of adaptable networks, while adding new support to the NM paradigm to assist network designers.

ANCORS targets an active network environment, where powerful design and assessment capabilities are required to coordinate the high degree of dynamism in the configuration and availability of services and protocols. To this end, we have formulated an architecture of a network management and engineering system that, while inheriting some components from current NM technology, introduces distributed simulation as an additional tool for design and performance assessment. Some components of the ANCORS architecture map very well to already existing technology. Recognizing this, the architecture has been explicitly designed to accommodate other NM engineering solutions.

The ANCORS architecture is divided into data, assessment, and control layers, as illustrated in Figure 1. The data layer operates at the data packet level and offers a set of services for the manipulation of network data. The assessment layer performs analytical reviews of network behavior to extract relevant semantic information from it. The control layer performs higher-order functions

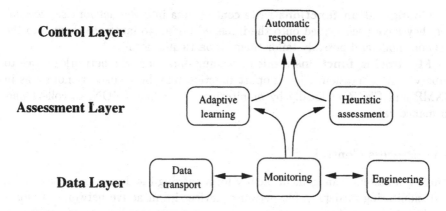

**Fig. 1.** The ANCORS Architecture

based on expert knowledge. All the components constituting these logical layers may be independently deployed throughout the network, using common system management support. ANCORS may distribute data-layer services across domains[1], but deploys assessment-and control-layer services to the specific domain they manage. Depending on the amount of resource sharing resulting from the deployment of active networking services, the assessment layer may also be distributed across multiple domains. Because the control layer must possess a significant amount of authority to perform changes in the network, it should be deployed only within a single domain. Several control services may then cooperate at the inter-domain level to exchange information for making better control decisions about their respective domains.[2]

## 3  Deployment and Management Infrastructure

Active network services require similar support functions from network or system management. The support functions can be broadly characterized as those achieving (1) process control, (2) configuration, or (3) monitoring.

**Process control functions** allow the loading and unloading of network services to and from network nodes. The physical location of the code that implements the network services may be different from the physical location of their deployment. For this reason, a reliable transport protocol such as TCP should be used to transfer the code. We have implemented a software prototype (*Anetd* [9]) that performs these process control functions. The prototype has a very flexible and general-purpose API to deploy and control (1) native executables, (2) Java applications, and (3) ANCORS executables.

---

[1] In this context, a domain consists of a collection of software and hardware objects managed by a single administrative authority.

[2] A discussion about inter-domain information exchange between control service is beyond the scope of this paper.

**Configuration functions** write control data into the network services after they have been loaded onto the intended nodes, to integrate them into the network node and possibly tailor them to particular needs.

**Monitoring functions** result in reading data from the network service to supervise its operation. This support function may be invoked remotely as in SNMP and CMIP, or locally by monitoring agents like RMON, to collect performance data.

## 3.1  Process Control

*Anetd* is a system management facility for managing the deployment, operation, and monitoring of deployable network services in an active network. *Anetd* is specifically targeted for the secure management and coordination of active networking research over the Internet. *Anetd* follows the discrete active networking approach, providing code mobility to legacy network software (e.g., SNMP agents) and system management support for new active networking applications. *Anetd* support focuses on services that are fairly permanent and long-lived, that can benefit from having a separate system management infrastructure, and that are fairly encapsulated (i.e., they do not rely on large numbers of shared libraries that may not be commonly available). *Anetd* also facilitates the deployment of auxiliary resources needed by the applications to ease the porting of existing software. However, *anetd* is not intended to deploy a large number of libraries or require large installation directories.[3]

From a system management perspective, *anetd* views all services within the ANCORS architecture (Figure 1) as equivalent. *Anetd* handles process control requests coming from the management stations or automatic response services to either load new services or terminate existing ones. Its placement in the AN-CORS layered architecture [11] is illustrated in Figure 2.

The assessment layer interprets monitoring results from the data layer, and the control layer reacts to significant conditions as they are reported by the assessment layer. The automatic response services may reconfigure both the assessment services and the data-layer services in response to changes in the network behavior. Note from Figure 2 that this architecture allows the traditional but nonscalable approach of having the management station directly monitor and control the data layer. This aspect of our architecture can be very useful when simple network management technologies are employed that do not require ad-hoc distributed monitoring functions (e.g., when using legacy SNMP-based polling mechanisms).

## 3.2  Configuration and Monitoring (Network Management)

Because in most cases the configuration and monitoring functions are intimately tied to the semantics of a network service, in active networks, these functions

---

[3] In these cases, we advise standard manual installation techniques or (as in the case of Java) bundle the required resources with *anetd* in advance.

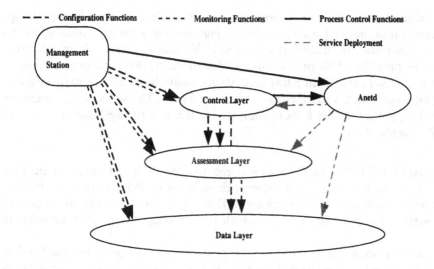

**Fig. 2.** ANCORS's Management Architecture

cannot be generally known in advance by the NM tools. As new services are deployed, the NM tools should adapt to the newly introduced functionalities. Two possible approaches can be followed in providing the management of active networks. We believe that both approaches should be allowed and should be integrated in a common management framework that can make best use of their respective advantages.

**Active Management** One strength of active networking concepts is that the network can be adapted at runtime by network operators. Within this framework, when a new network service is deployed, all necessary management agents and control software can also be deployed by the network operators in parallel. For example, as a new admission control protocol is deployed on the routers of an IP network, its corresponding MIB and SNMP agent may also be dynamically deployed. Such adaptation can also be achieved at a finer granularity by just adding methods to an existing agent that can access the new deployed service (as suggested in [2]).

**Knowledge-Based Management** Knowledge-based management (KBM) tries to integrate new network services much more closely into the NM system to provide greater software reuse and composition. In this paradigm when a new network service is deployed, it only exports an interface without requiring the deployment of specific NM code. In this context the NM management software should be able to correctly interpret the exported interface and directly integrate the new service in a pre-existing semantic framework. For example, when a new service is deployed it may export several alarms indicating failures and/or methods through which the service could be monitored or configured. The methods and alarms would then be interpreted and categorized by an existing NM application into specific predefined classes. For example, a service providing access control and bandwidth allocation such as RSVP may export an alarm indicating that the provisioned bit rate is not available to the service or there is an unusual number of bad packets. In KBM such alarms would be correctly interpreted and perhaps correlated with alarms originating from other services. In summary, KBM supports a higher level of composition through the dynamic extensibility of NM application.

**Discussion** KBM is hard because it requires the design of predetermined semantic contexts that are general enough to be extensible but that are not too general to be impractical to implement. However, it provides a logical framework through which one could achieve a high level of integration and more software reuse.

Active management is conceptually simpler and perhaps more practical but lacks the ability to support composition. When a new service and its corresponding management code are deployed, they could be (and in some cases should be) completely isolated from the rest of the NM system. For instance, in the above example, when an alarm is generated as a result of unavailable bit rate, it must be interpreted by a human and manually relayed to the service provider in the form of a complaint.

It is not clear which approach is preferable. In general, active management may be preferable for active applications that do not have much interaction with the system or other active components, while KBM will provide support for composition of services having a high degree of interdependencies. We believe that the management of programmable networks should allow both approaches and should be designed in an open fashion.

In the next sections we describe a design of a powerful and extensible common management framework (CMF) that tries to merge these two concepts through the reuse of Web-based tools. We will further exemplify KMB in Section 3.2.

## 4 CMF

An infrastructure to manage and support active networks must be open, simple, and flexible, and therefore we do not intend to have a unique format for the information exchanges between network services and management stations.

To support multiple management frameworks, we introduce a discovery mechanism to probe newly deployed services. The idea is quite simple and is somewhat similar to the approach followed today on the Web. Each network service listens on a port known to *Anetd*. After deployment, the services respond to a predefined and universally agreed-upon *Anetd* command **INIT** (the equivalent of GET / in HTTP). The **INIT** command will cause the network services subscribing to CMF to respond with a MIME-encapsulated reply. In general, the reply contains information to be used for the configuration and monitoring of the service itself and the configuration of other related services. In other words, as the result of an **INIT** command, the services export the interfaces necessary for their operation.

Using MIME encapsulation as three main advantages:

1. It allows the reuse of existing powerful tools, such as HTML browsers, that can be extended to handle user-defined application types and that conveniently integrate into current Web-based technology.
2. By breaking down a potentially very large application domain for managing active networks, it makes the problem more tractable. In particular, it allows the design of domain-specific semantic interpretation of the exported interfaces without the need of extremely general and potentially ambiguous specifications.
3. The MIME dereferencing mechanism naturally supports extensibility.

In the simplest scenario, the service replies with an encapsulated message in HTML format. This reply format allows the administrator to use standard HTML forms to configure and later interactively monitor the service through HTML forms.

## 5   CMF Applications

We will describe the design of four different management APIs that are being developed as part of an ongoing effort in realizing a worldwide testbed for active networks (ABONE [8]). These examples show how we intend to use our CMF design in enabling active networking software to be included at runtime into an active network management infrastructure. We refer to network management, in this case, as the ability to monitor and control aspects of the active networking software that go beyond the process control functions of *Anetd* and allow much finer grain resolution within a deployed service.

### 5.1   The Text/Ancors MIME

Within the *Anetd* implementation of CMF, we have developed a specific MIME environment (*text/ancors*) that assists in the deployment, monitoring, and control of active networking software. This MIME, can be used to (1) generate GUIs through HTML forms or (2) to build, in command-line mode, ad-hoc management front ends based on standard Unix string processing tools like *Perl* or *Awk*, or to operate from terminals that do not support graphics.

Each of the lines returned by a deployed network service can be either a simple text line or a GUI line. Text lines and GUI lines are differentiated by the fact that a GUI line starts with tags LOAD, QUERY, INIT, CONF, GET, PUT, KILL, GETACL, or GETWEB (that correspond to *Anetd*'s commands), while text lines do not. GUI lines serve the dual purpose of specifying an interface and offering a convenient way to automatically issue *Anetd* commands.

GUI lines have the following format:

```
<Anetd_command>&[submit!<submit_label>]&[new]&[add]&<any>{!|?}<port>&<any>{?|!}<host>[&any{!|?}<arg>]+
```

where:

- $<$ *Anetd_command* $>$ is one of the possible *Anetd* commands (LOAD, QUERY, INIT, CONF, GET, PUT, KILL, GETACL, GETWEB) to be invoked. This field determines which *Anetd* command will be issued upon activation of this GUI line.
- The optional *submit!* $<$ *submit_label* $>$ argument pair specifies that a clickable button with the label $<$ *submit_label* $>$ should appear to the user. When this button is pressed, one or more *Anetd* commands are executed.
- The optional *new* keyword specifies that, when the submit button is pressed, a new window is created by the GUI to display the results. If *new* is missing, results overwrite the current window.
- The optional *add* keyword specifies that this command should be automatically executed after the execution of the command specified in the previous GUI line.
- !|? separates an argument tag from its default value. ! specifies that the argument should be hidden to the user, and ? means that a value should appear in an input field and should be editable by the user. When the argument is editable, the tag is used to describe the input field.
- $<$ *any* $>$ !|? $<$ *port* $>$ is a required argument pair that directs the *Anetd* command to an appropriate port.
- $<$ *any* $>$ ?|! $<$ *host* $>$ is a required argument pair that directs the *Anetd* command to an appropriate host.
- [*any*!|? $<$ *arg* $>$]+ is a list of tag/value pairs that are used to complete the specification of the command. $<$ *any* $>$ is any character string.

When GUI lines are returned, they are interpreted by a local client's script to generate HTML forms. GUI lines of the *text/ancors* MIME can therefore indirectly also issue any *Anetd* command. For example, the following GUI line

GET&new&submit!Get&port!3322&hostname?grumpy.csl.sri.com&file!file.out

would automatically produce the HTML form of figure 3

```
<FORM ACTION=file:exec.ax method=get TARGET=new>
<INPUT TYPE=SUBMIT VALUE=LOAD>
<INPUT NAME=exec VALUE=LOAD TYPE=HIDDEN>
<INPUT NAME=port VALUE=3322 TYPE=HIDDEN>
<INPUT NAME=host VALUE=grumpy.csl.sri.com TYPE=text>
<INPUT NAME=file VALUE="file.out" TYPE=text>
</FORM>
```

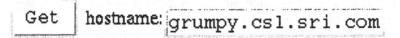

**Fig. 3.** GUI Example

This form would not be correctly interpreted and executed by a standard HTML browser, and it is therefore necessary to process it with the ANCORS front end. Notice that the action is the local file *exec.ax*; this local script is responsible for parsing the form arguments and issuing the LOAD command. When the user presses the clickable button, the *Anetd* command

```
GET 3322 grumpy.csl.sri.com file.out
```

is executed, and the returning output is displayed in a newly created window.

The ancors GUI front end was developed specifically to facilitate the use of *Anetd* and its related deployment capabilities and is fully integrated with the ANCORS executable specifications to properly handle *text/ancors*, simple *text/text*, and standard *text/html* MIME types. The ANCORS GUI front end was derived from the public-domain HTML browser called "Plume" written in TCL [6]. The browser was modified to invoke local scripts as well as remote scripts through the CGI protocol. The local scripts denoted with the extension *ax* are responsible for invoking various *Anetd* commands triggered by the clickable buttons.

## 5.2  SNMPV2 MIME Type

This example shows how our framework can be used to build a bridge with traditional non-active NM approaches. It is important to keep backward compatibility so that one can leverage legacy applications in solving problems that do not require innovation. For this reason, we show how an SNMP MIME type and its corresponding applications are capable of dynamically deploying and configuring SNMP agents. A deployed service wanting to use SNMP replies with information encapsulated in an SNMP-specific MIME type (application/SNMPV2). The reply might be similar to the following:

```
content-type application/SNMPV2

<SNMP>
<AGENT=http://www.abone.org/SNMP/snmpd>
<PORT=8000>
<MIB=http://www.abone.org/SNMP/mib.txt>
<ACL=http://www.abone.org/SNMP/acl.conf>
<PARTY=http://www.abone.org/SNMP/snmpd/party.conf>
<VIEW=http://www.abone.org/SNMP/snmpd/view.conf>
<CONTEXT=http://www.abone.org/SNMP/snmpd/context.conf>
<ENVIRONMENT VAR=MIBFILE VAL=mib.txt>
</SNMP>
```

This reply specifies the URL of the SNMP agent, the associated MIB, and access control information to be loaded with the service. It causes the management station to use *Anetd* to load the requested SNMP agent and MIB and to either spawn an SNMP browser to access the deployed service or update an existing SNMP management application.

## 5.3  Java_nm MIME Type

This example shows how CMF can be used to implement active NM mechanisms. In this approach the service replies by providing Java applications or applets that can then be embedded either in the central management stations or in a distributed monitoring agent, perhaps in a scheme similar to the one proposed in [2]. A reply using this MIME type might be something like

```
content-type application/java_nm

<JAVA>
<AGENT APPLICATION=http://www.abone.org/java/agent PARAM=<parameters>>  or
<AGENT APPLET=http://www.abone.org/java/agent_appl PARAM=<parameters>>
<AGENT FILES=http://www.abone.org/java/mib.txt FILES=http://www.activate.org/java/acl>
<AGENT_ENVIRONMENT VAR=MIBFILE VAL=mib.txt>

<MANAGER APPLICATION=http://www.abone.org/java/manager PARAM=<parameters>>  or
<MANAGER APPLET=http://www.abone.org/java/manager_appl PARAM=<parameters>>
<MANAGER FILES=http://www.abone.org/java/mib.txt FILES=http://www.activate.org/java/acl>
<MANAGER_ENVIRONMENT VAR=MIBFILE VAL=mib.txt>
</JAVA>
```

Notice that the MIME can either specify an application or an applet for both the agent side and the manager side. The application would not require special support other than an interprocess communication mechanism with the EE and the NM station, respectively. In this mode one only exploits the portability of Java to implement ad-hoc management protocols, and the solution may not be functionally different from what is provided by SNMP. With the specification of an applet, one can instead provide a mechanism that exploits active networking concepts. In this case the applet is assimilated by either a management or an agent EE, thus effectively extending the NM system at runtime. To support this latter mode of operation, it is possible to reuse existing active network software prototypes (such as ANTS [13]).

## 5.4   Active Management Information Base MIME

This example shoes how KBM can be used within the CMF design. KBM focuses on the fact that the data formats of standard NM frameworks (SNMP, CMIP) do not provide semantic interpretation of the MIB data. This limits their applicability to static and ad-hoc management where human intervention is necessary to interpret the meaning of specific management information and manually configure the management infrastructure. In dynamically changing networks, it will be necessary to (1) dynamically extend MIBs to include new management entities that come into existence and (2) automate the task of recognizing the semantic meaning of new or modified management primitives, to avoid frequent and costly human management operations.

In our design, an active network MIB is defined using multiple dimensions. The first dimension is analogous to the current MIB specification in which management information is organized in a tree structure reflecting the logical decomposition of the information. Figure 4 details how we plan to initially hierarchically organize active object definitions. This structure is deliberately very general because it is intended to be extended at runtime with new kinds of objects that are brought into existence with the deployment of new network services.

Active NM objects will also be defined by a vector of attributes, each of which is chosen from a discrete set of values and characterizes the objects in other dimensions. As an example, the following attributes may introduce useful additional dimensionality.

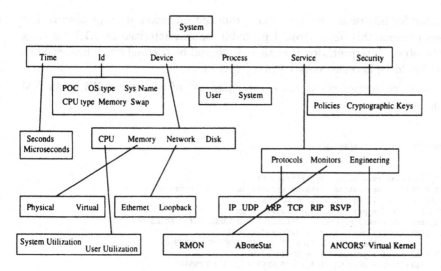

**Fig. 4.** Example Top-level MIB definition

- Criticality. This attribute specifies to what extent the value of the object is critical for the correct operation of the system. For example, (0) would mean that the value of the object does not affect operations, (1) would mean that the value of the object has significance at the local level, and (2) would mean that the value of the object has significance at the system level.
- Frequency of Change. This attribute tells the NM system how often the value(s) of the object is expected to change. For example, (0) would mean that the value(s) of the object does not change, (1) would mean that the value(s) of the object changes with the frequency of human interactions (every seconds to minutes), and (2) would mean that the value(s) of the object changes with the frequency of system interactions (less than every second).
- Accessibility. This attribute regulates who can access or affect the objects. For example, (0) would mean that the object is public and anyone can access it, (1) would mean that the object is accessible by authorized users and that access control should be enforced, and (2) would mean that the object should be accessible only by the super-user.

These attributes facilitate the runtime inclusion of new objects into an NM infrastructure. For example, if a new monitoring service is added to an active network node to perform a specialized monitoring function, this service may introduce new objects in the hierarchy upon deployment and classify them according to their significance. Depending on what the monitor is doing it would associate different values to its attributes. For example, if the monitor produced an object that estimated CPU utilization, its attributes would probably be set to 0,1,0 to indicate that this object has a noncritical significance, it changes every few seconds, and it should be widely accessible. On the other hand, consider a monitor for intrusion detection that produced intrusion attempt alarms. For obvious reasons, this object would probably be characterized as 2,1,1 meaning that the object interpretation is critical, it should be checked every few seconds, and it should be accessed only by privileged users.

A deployed service could cause the extension of an active MIB in an NM station as follows:

```
content-type application/anetm

<AMIB>
<EXTEND MIB=http://www.abone.org/amib/mib.txt>
<OBJECT NAME=service.protocol.rsvp.Encapsulation RPC=get_version()
MODE=READ  CRITICALITY=0 FREQUENCY=0 ACCESS=0>
<OBJECT NAME=service.protocol.rsvp.Encapsulation
RPC=get_encapsulation() MODE=READ  CRITICALITY=0 FREQUENCY=0 ACCESS=0>
<OBJECT NAME=service.protocol.rsvp.RefreshInterval
RPC=get_refresh() MODE=READ  CRITICALITY=0 FREQUENCY=0 ACCESS=0>
<OBJECT NAME=service.protocol.rsvp.SessionTable
RPC=get_table() MODE=READ CRITICALITY=0 FREQUENCY=1 ACCESS=0>
<OBJECT NAME=service.protocol.rsvp.BadPackets
RPC=get_badpackets MODE=READ CRITICALITY=1 FREQUENCY=1 ACCESS=0>
</AMIB>
```

The above reply might be returned by an activated RSVP service such as ARP [3]. This reply exports management operations and indicates that these operations should be used to extend a base active MIB located on an ABONE code server. The object name specifications will be automatically added to the ABONE active MIB, thus actively extending it at runtime. Analogously executing the **INIT** probe on other EEs may further extend the local active MIB with other functions particular to that EE[4].

This NM paradigm requires the development of a special-purpose NM application capable of correctly interpreting the information returned by the service. This application, after querying the EE with the **INIT** probe, will automatically add the remote procedure stubs in appropriate threads. The threads in the NM application will in turn reflect the values of the attributes exported by the deployed service, thus providing different types of polling modalities, access control mechanisms, and priority. Each time a remote procedure is called (whether the initial **INIT** call or subsequent remote procedure calls), it will respond with a MIME-encapsulated reply that will be recursively interpreted by the NM application. Leaf calls (procedures that only return data objects) may replay either with simple text MIMEs (which will simply display textual information), HTML formatted text, or special-purpose MIMEs designed to decode a particular binary encoding. The remote procedure stubs will also be classified, in the traditional manner, according to their structural role. They will be grouped into tree structures to facilitate the observation and control of the services from a process-oriented perspective.

---

[4] Collisions may occur when two different services choose the same name for an object. The colliding objects will be renamed using appropriate informative formats.

# 6 Conclusion

The dynamism of adaptable networks will require novel management and assessment techniques and tools to aid in the design, deployment and operation of network services. The integration of these different management aspects in a unified paradigm such as the one proposed in ANCORS requires a very flexible and open management framework that can be used in different ways. We have proposed a simple, open mechanism to support a plurality of management paradigms while observing a consistent architectural view. We have also outlined four different management approaches, from simple HTML based to more complex knowledge based, that show the generality of our open management framework and that will be used as case studies in the management of the ABONE.

# References

1. D. Scott Alexander, Marianne Shaw, Scott M. Nettles, and Jonathan M. Smith. Active bridging. *Proceedings of the ACM SIGCOMM'97 Conference*, Cannes, France, September 1997.
2. F. Barillaud, L. Deri, and M. Feredun. Network management using internet technologies. *Integrated Network Management V*, San Diego, 1997.
3. R. Braden. Active signaling: the arp project. *In OPENSIG Workshop, University of Toronto*, Toronto, CA, October 1998.
4. J. Hartman, U. Manber, L. Peterson, and T. Proebsting. Liquid software: A new paradigm for networked systems. Technical Report 96-11, University of Arizona, 1996.
5. U. Legedza, D. J. Wetherall, and J. V. Guttag. Improving the performance of distributed applications using active networks. *Submitted to IEEE INFOCOM'98*, 1998.
6. J. K. Ousterhout. *Tcl and the Tk Toolkit*. Addison-Wesley, 1994.
7. P.A. Porras and P.G. Neumann. EMERALD: Event monitoring enabling responses to anomalous live disturbances. *Proceedings of the National Information Systems Security Conference*, Baltimore, October 1997.
8. Livio Ricciulli. ABONE: Active network back bone. *http://www.csl.sri.com/ancors/abone*, 1998.
9. Livio Ricciulli. ANETD: Active NETwork Daemon. Technical report, Computer Science Laboratory, SRI International, 1998.
10. Livio Ricciulli. High-fidelity distributed simulation of local area networks. *Proceedings of the 31st Annual Simulation Symposium*, Boston, April 1998.
11. Livio Ricciulli and Phillip A. Porras. ANCORS: An adaptable network control and reporting system. *Integrated Network Management V*, Boston, 1999.
12. Jonathan Smith, David Farber, Carl A. Gunter, Scott Nettle, Mark Segal, William D. Sincoskie, David Feldmeier, and Scott Alexander. Switchware: Towards a 21st century network infrastructure. *http://www.cis.upenn.edu/ switchware/papers/sware.ps*, 1997.
13. D. J. Wetherall, J. V. Guttag, and D. L. Tennenhouse. ANTS: A toolkit for building and dynamically deploying network protocols. *Submitted to IEEE OPENARCH'98*, 1998.

14. Y. Yemini and S. da Silva. Towards programmable networks. *IFIP/IEEE International Workshop on Distributed Systems: Operations and Management*, L'Aquila, Italy, October 1996.

# Virtual Active Networks – Safe and Flexible Environments for Customer-Managed Services

Marcus Brunner[1] and Rolf Stadler[2]

[1]Computer Engineering and Networks Laboratory, TIK
Swiss Federal Institute of Technology Zurich (ETH)
Gloriastr. 35, CH-8092 Zurich, Switzerland
E-Mail: brunner@tik.ee.ethz.ch

[2]Center for Telecommunications Research (CTR)
and Department of Electrical Engineering
Columbia University, New York, NY 10027-6699
E-Mail: stadler@ctr.columbia.edu

**Abstract.** Recent research has demonstrated the benefits of active networks: customized network services can easily be built and modified, packet streams can be processed inside the network, etc. This paper addresses the question how the benefits of active networking can be exploited in a telecom environment, where a large number of customers must share a common network infrastructure. We introduce a framework that allows customers to deploy and manage their own active services in a provider domain. The key concept in this framework is the *Virtual Active Network (VAN)*. A VAN is a generic service, offered by the provider to the customer. From the customer's point of view, a VAN represents an environment on which the customer can install, run and manage active network services, without further interaction with the provider. From the provider's perspective, the VAN serves as the entity for partitioning the provider's resources and isolating customers from one another in virtual environments. We describe how the VAN concept, VAN management, and customer service management is realized on ANET, an active networking testbed.

**Keywords.** Management of Active Networks, Service Provisioning, Service Management, Active Network Testbeds

## 1 Introduction

In today's telecom environments, customers and service providers typically interact via two interfaces--the management interface and the service interface. The management interface, based on standardized management protocols, is generally used for service provisioning and service management. The customer accesses the service through the service interface. Both interfaces are service specific; a provider has to support different service and management interfaces for each service offered, which makes the introduction of new services dependent on standardization, and therefore time consuming and expensive.

The introduction of active networking technology in telecom environments, characterized by the use of active networking nodes as network elements, will change the role of these interfaces in two ways. First, using active networking nodes enables the definition of a generic service interface for network services, based on the concept of *active packets* (see Section 2). In addition, this service interface can be used by the customer for service management interactions, i.e., for operations related to the installation, supervision, upgrading and removal of a specific service. Therefore, service management operations can be performed by a customer without interaction with the provider's management system. Second, the management interface, i.e., the interface through which the customer and the provider management systems cooperate, can be restricted to the task of service provisioning. Similar to the service interface, the management interface can be kept generic; it relates to a generic service abstraction that allows for installing and running a large class of network services.

The introduction of active networking technology, where network nodes perform customized processing of packets, will change both types of interactions described above. The granularity of a service abstraction and its related control capabilities can be chosen, ranging from a very limited, constrained service model to a very detailed one. The key concept that provides this capability is the *Virtual Active Network (VAN)*, which is the focus of this paper. In the same way as an active network can be understood as a generalization of a traditional network, a VAN can be seen as a generalization of a traditional Virtual Private Network (VPN). Similar to a VPN, a VAN can be used by a customer to run active networking services, using a provider's networking resources. In contrast to a traditional VPN, however, a VAN gives a customer a much higher degree of controllability. Further, the VAN concept supports rapid installation and upgrade of customer-specific active network services in a telecom environment.

The paper is organized as follows. Section 2 briefly reviews the concept of active networking. Section 3 outlines our framework for customer-provider interaction in an active telecom environment, i.e., an environment that is based on active networking technology. Section 4 introduces the VAN concept, and Section 5 gives aspects of VAN provisioning. Section 6 describes an active networking platform we have built for experimenting with active networking concepts and shows how VAN provisioning and customer-controlled service management is realized on our platform. Section 7 surveys current efforts on active technologies for network management. Section 8 summarizes the contributions of this paper and gives an outlook on further work.

## 2 The Concept of an Active Network

The processing of packets (or cells) inside traditional networks is limited to operations on the packet headers, primarily for routing purposes. Active networks break with this tradition by letting the network perform customized computation on entire packets, including their payloads. As a consequence, the active network approach opens up the possibilities of (1) computation on user data inside the network and (2) tailoring of the packet processing functions in network nodes according to service-specific requirements.

Active networks transport *active packets* [1] (also called capsules [2]). Active packets carry programs, in addition to data. A network node executes such a program, which possibly modifies the nodes' state and possibly generates further active packets to be sent over the outgoing links. Specifically, an active packet can include a program that modifies or replaces the nodes' packet processing function.

Similar to traditional networks, an active network consists of active network nodes, which are connected via links. In addition to transmission bandwidth, the key resources of an active network node include memory and CPU resources for processing active packets.

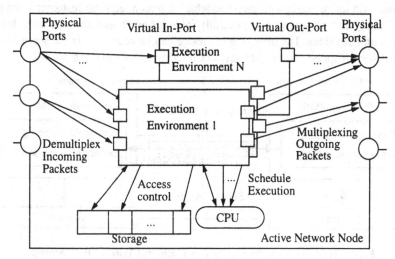

**Figure 1:** Active Node Architecture

Figure 1 gives a model of an active network node. The basic functions of such a node are (1) the control of the incoming packets, (2) the control of the outgoing packets, (3) packet processing, and (4) memory access. An active network node runs several Execution Environment in parallel. Each active packet arriving at a physical port contains an identifier of the Execution Environment that will process this packet.

Figure 1 also illustrates that an active network node can be seen as a generalization of traditional network node, such as an IP router. An IP router is limited in the sense that there is only one Execution Environment and a single set of pre-installed functions for packet processing.

A different view of an active network node is given in Figure 5, which stresses operating system aspects. This figure is specialized for a provider-customer environment where each customer service is run in a separate Execution Environment.

# 3 Customer-Provider Interactions in Active Telecom Environments

## 3.1 Interactions in Traditional Environments

Figure 2 shows the interaction taking place between a customer domain and a provider domain for the purpose of service provisioning, service delivery, and service management. Depending on the type of service, customers and providers interact in two fundamentally different ways. The first way is characterized by a provider offering functionality in its domain through a service interface. A typical example of such a service is a virtual network, e.g., a Virtual Path (VP)-based service, which is purchased by a customer with geographically separated premises networks in order to construct a company-wide enterprise network. In the provisioning phase, the customer negotiates the connectivity and resources of the service, i.e., the virtual network topology and the quality of service (QoS) requirements. (A customer may request a set of constant bit rate (CBR) VPs of a certain bandwidth with delay and loss bounds.) This interaction takes place via the management interface, which interconnects the customer's and provider's management systems, and generally includes communication between human operators on both sides. The provisioned service can be accessed via the service interface, which corresponds to the user-network interface (UNI) in our example.

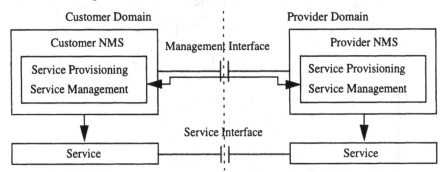

**Figure 2:** Management Interaction in a Traditional Telecom Environment

The second way of interaction shown in Figure 2 relates to the case where a customer outsources control and management of a specific service to a provider, which installs and runs the service in the customer domain. In this case, the customer gives the provider access to its networking elements via management interfaces. The customer is not involved in service installation, upgrade, and management, but can concentrate on its core business instead. The provider customizes the service according to the customer's requirements.

### 3.2 Our Framework for Active Telecom Environments

In an active networking environment, the above described two ways of interactions between a customer and a provider can be realized in a much more flexible way with respect to service abstractions and control capabilities for the customer in the provider's domain and vice versa. In the following, we outline our framework for interaction in an active networking environment, which we have first proposed in [3].

Figure 3 shows the interaction between a customer domain and a provider domain for service provisioning, service delivery and service management in our framework. When comparing Figure 3 with Figure 2, the key differences between a traditional environment and an active telecom environment that follows our approach become clear. We propose that the provisioning of a specific (active) network service X is split into two different operations--a) the *provisioning of a generic service*, which we call the VAN service, is performed via the cooperative VAN provisioning interface; and b) the *installation of the specific service* X is performed via the generic service interface, without further interaction with the provider. The same interface is used by the customer for managing service X during its lifetime.

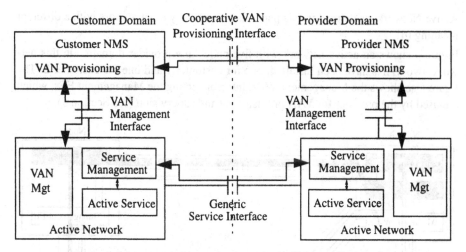

**Figure 3:** Management Interaction in an Active Telecom Environment
that follows the VAN concept

The *generic service interface* for accessing network services is enabled through the concept of active packets. It is used for data transport, as well as for all operations related to the installation, supervision, upgrading and removal of a specific service X. (See Section 6.2 for an example of service installation and supervision through this interface).

The *cooperative VAN provisioning interface*, i.e., the interface through which the customer and the provider management systems cooperate, is restricted to the task of VAN provisioning. VAN provisioning includes negotiating the Virtual Active Network topology and the resources allocated to the VAN.

Within a domain, a VAN is created, changed, and monitored by the VAN provisioning system, which interacts via the *VAN management interface* with the active networking platform. This interface can be realized using management protocols, such as SNMP or CMIP, or--by exploiting active networking technology--it can be realized using a similar interface as the generic service interface. In the latter case, VAN provisioning via the VAN management interface uses the same techniques as service provisioning via the generic service interface. (See Section 6.1 for a specific example.) The (local) VAN management interface for an active network node is given in Section 6.

## 4 The Virtual Active Network (VAN)

A *Virtual Active Network (VAN)* can be described as a graph of virtual active nodes interconnected by Virtual Links. Virtual active nodes are also called *Execution Environments (EEs)*, following the terminology of the AN working group [1]. A virtual active node has resources attached to it in form of processing and memory resources, provided by the underlying active networking platform. Similarly, a virtual active link has bandwidth allocated to it. We envision that a single (physical) active node can run several virtual active nodes belonging to different VANs, and a single (physical) network link can support several Virtual Links for different VANs. (The term Virtual

Active Network, as defined in this paper, is also used by other authors with a different meaning [4].)

Figure 4 shows an active network with five nodes in a provider domain. On this network, two VANs have been installed, one for customer 1 and one for customer 2. The figure also shows the Management VAN, interconnecting the Management EEs, which are used by the provider for VAN provisioning and supervision (see Section 5).

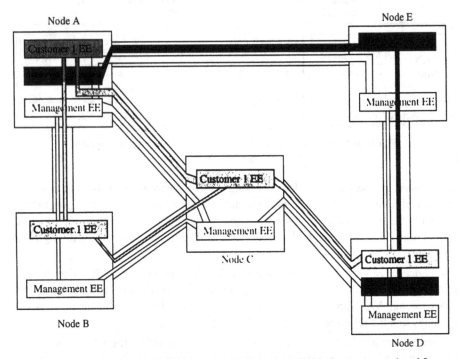

**Figure 4:** An active network with nodes A-E, on which VANs for customers 1 and 2 have been installed.

What problem exactly does the VAN concept address and what are its benefits? First, the VAN provides a *generic service abstraction* for an active telecom environment. From a provider's point of view, the VAN is the entity according to which active network resources are partitioned and according to which the customers, using the provider's infrastructure, must be isolated from one another. The VAN is further the (only) object that is shared between provider and customer, and it is the object of negotiation between the two parties. Specifically, the provider is not concerned about which specific service(s) a customer is running on its VAN. The task of the provider is solely to monitor and police the use of resources on the VAN level and to ensure that the QoS, as agreed upon between customer and provider, can be guaranteed.

Second, from a customer's perspective, the VAN concept allows for installation and *management of active network services, without interaction with the provider.* (As mentioned above, all interactions between customer and provider relate strictly to the VAN.) The customer can run a large variety of active network services on the VAN.

These services are only restricted by the specific Execution Environment(s) the VAN supports. (Developing Execution Environments for active networks is currently subject of intensive research. In our work, we base on the current state of the AN working group [8]). Note that the high degree of customer control over services running in a provider's domain, which a VAN provides, is virtually impossible to realize with today's "traditional" networking technology.

Third, --exploiting a general benefit of active networking-- the VAN concept enables *rapid deployment of new network services.* Deploying and upgrading network services is difficult and time consuming in today's networks, due to the closed, integrated architecture of network nodes. With the concept of a VAN, which divides the active network resources into partitions for different customers, the installation of any customer-specific service becomes feasible, and, as explained before, it can be accomplished by the customer alone, without interaction with the VAN provider.

Lastly, customers can run a mix of different network services on a single VAN. This allows customers to perform *dynamic re-allocation of VAN resources* to the various services, according to their own control objectives and traffic characteristics--again, without interaction with the VAN provider.

As mentioned before, the VAN concept can be compared to that of a Virtual Path (VP)-based Virtual Private Network (VPN). Similar to a VAN, a VP-based VPN provides customers with a service abstraction, on which they can run their own services, such an IP-based data or real-time services. Since a VP is a simple abstraction, a customer's ability to control traffic inside the provider's domain is very limited. (See [19] for a discussion of this point.) A VAN, on the other hand, is a much more complex abstraction than a VP, and, consequently, gives customers extensive control capabilities inside the provider's domain. In a similar way as dynamic bandwidth provisioning can be performed in a VP-based VPN [19], we envision that VAN resources can be re-negotiated during the life-time of a particular VAN via the VAN management interface shown in Figure 3.

## 5 VAN Provisioning and Supervision

Figure 5 gives an operating system point of view of an active network node in the provider's environment. A node operating system layer configures and provides access to the node's resources, such as links, processing and memory resources. This layer runs the Execution Environments, separates them from each other, and polices the use of the resources consumed by each Execution Environment.

Figure 5 specifically shows the case where a provider offers Virtual Active Networks to several customers (Customer 1, Customer 2, ..., Customer N). Each customer runs its service in a separate Execution Environment, which corresponds to a Virtual Node of the VAN.

A privileged Execution Environment, the *Management EE,* runs the provider's VAN management system, which creates the customer EEs and is able to modify, monitor and terminate them. The Management EE is accessed by the provider's VAN provisioning system via the local VAN management interface, which is described in Section 6.

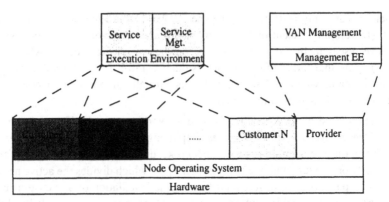

**Figure 5:** Architecture of an Active Network Node in a Telecom Environment

At the beginning of the VAN provisioning phase, the customer and the provider negotiate the topology and the resource requirements for the customer's VAN. The provider's VAN provisioning system then maps the VAN topology onto its active networking platform and interacts with some of the active nodes via the VAN management interface to create this VAN. By accessing the Management EEs on the active nodes, the provider sets up EEs for the customer and interconnects them via virtual links, according to the VAN topology that has been negotiated with this particular customer.

Note that the design given in Figure 5 is compliant with the architecture of an active network node developed by the AN Working Group [1]. The difference between Figure 5 and [8] is that we explicitly assign each Execution Environment to a particular VAN, i.e., to a particular customer.

## 6 Realizing VAN Provisioning and Management on the ANET Platform

We have built an active networking platform, in order to test, evaluate and demonstrate active networking services and management concepts. The core of this platform consists of a cluster of Ultra-SPARCs, interconnected via an Ethernet and an ATM LAN. Each active network node runs on a separate workstation. On top of this infrastructure, we have implemented traffic generators, traffic monitors, a VAN management system, and a service management system.

All software components of our platform are written in Java. We chose Java because of its strengths as a prototyping language for networking environments, and because Java directly supports the realization of active packets through the concept of mobile code. Additional Java features which we take advantage of include object serialization, thread support, and safe memory access achieved by the type-safety of the language. In our implementation, an active network node is implemented entirely in software, which gives us the flexibility of experimenting with different designs. Achieving high performance, such as realizing a high throughput of packets on a network node, is not the focus of our work on the ANET platform. (Instead, we plan to realize the VAN concept, once it has been fully studied on the ANET platform, on a high-performance active node, which is currently under development in our lab at ETH Zurich [5].)

The complexity of the software we have built to date--active network node, provider management system, and service management system--is in the order of 400 Java classes with 30'000 lines of code.

In the following, we describe the realization of an active network node, as outlined in Figure 5, on ANET. The in-bound ports of the active node deliver the incoming packets to the appropriate Execution Environments, identified by a multiplexing identifier in the packet header or in underlying protocol headers. The node operating system schedules the Execution Environments, taking into account the processing resources allocated to each of the Execution Environments. Packet schedulers on the outgoing ports multiplex and transmit packets produced by the Execution Environments to neighboring nodes.

The provider VAN management system, which performs VAN provisioning and supervision, interacts with customers over the cooperate VAN provisioning interface, and with the active network nodes via the VAN management interface. On ANET, we have implemented the VAN provisioning system on a VAN management station. This management station performs VAN management operations by sending active packets via the Management VAN to particular Management EEs in the network. These active packets, which are executed in the Management EEs, perform the management operations on the active nodes via the local VAN management interface.

Table 1 lists the most important functions of the *local VAN management interface* as implemented in the ANET prototype. The functions are described using a Java-like notation with input parameters in brackets and return values in front of the function name.

| |
|---|
| `vin_portid install_Virtual_InPort (in_portid, eeid, inmid);` |
| `vout_portid install_Virtual_OutPort (out_portid, eeid, outmid, bandwidth);` |
| `void remove_VirtualPort (vportid);` |
| `eeid install_EE (ee, cpu_resource, memory);` |
| `void remove_EE (eeid);` |
| `cut_through_id install_ThroughLink`<br>`(in_portid,inmid,out_portid,outmid,qlen,bandwidth)` |
| `void remove_ThroughLink(cut_through_id);` |

**Table 1:** Local VAN Management Interface of an ANET active node

The *install_Virtual_InPort* function creates a *Virtual In-Port* for the Execution Environment identified by *eeid*. It further configures a physical port identified by the *in_portid* to dispatch incoming packets with multiplexing identifier *inmid* to the just created Virtual In-Port.

The *install_Virtual_OutPort* function creates a *Virtual Out-Port* for the Execution Environment identified by *eeid*, and multiplexes outgoing packets leaving the Execution Environment over the just created Virtual Out-Port with multiplexing identifier *outmid*. The outgoing stream of packets is constrained by the amount of *bandwidth* reserved with this function. Any virtual port can be removed in case the VAN topology changes.

The *install_EE* function installs a new Execution Environment given in the parameter *ee*. The node operating system is configured to give the Execution Environment a portion of *cpu_resource* and *memory* and to police it to not overconsume the reserved resources. An Execution Environment identifier is returned for further use.

The *install_ThroughLink* function installs a cut-through path from the physical port with identifier *in_portid* to the physical port identified by *out_portid*. Packets arriving at *in_portid* tagged by the multiplexing identifier *inmid* travel along the cut-through path and are not executed in an Execution Environment. They are switched to the specified outgoing link, where they are sent with multiplexing identifier *outmid*. The node operating system has to know what amount of *bandwidth* is expected along the cut-through path to configure the packet scheduler accordingly. Further, a buffer with length *qlen* is created to store the packets in case they have to wait some time until the packet scheduler serves them.

The local VAN management interface includes functions that are not shown in Table 1. Most of them relate to monitoring operations, such as gathering statistics about the state of the node operating system, the resource consumption by the customer Execution Environments, virtual ports, and cut-through links.

Similar to the VAN management station, we have implemented the (customer-operated) service management system on a service management station. The service management station sends active packets into the VAN to perform management operations, such as the installation of a particular service and the supervision of the service.

In the following, we illustrate some of the design principles and capabilities of the ANET platform, by describing a series of demonstrations we can perform.

### 6.1 Demonstrating VAN Provisioning and Supervision

Figure 6 shows the situation at the start of the demonstration. The provider network

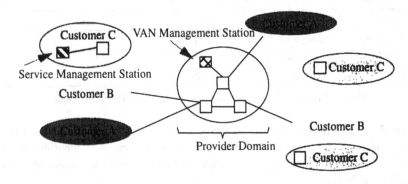

**Figure 6:** Situation at the Start of the Demonstration

consists of three active network nodes. The provider VAN management station is connected to one of these nodes. Three customers are involved in the scenario. Customer A and B have two (active) customer premises networks each, and customer C has three. The Virtual Active Networks for customer A and customer B have been set up by the VAN management system. The view of the provider VAN management station at this point in the demonstration is displayed in Figure 7a. It shows the VANs for customers A and B and the management VAN. Further, customer premises networks are represented by a star labeled customer A, B, and C.

The VAN provisioning capability is demonstrated by setting up a new VAN for customer C. The process of provisioning a VAN includes the installation of Execution Environments on all three nodes, connecting the Execution Environments by setting up Virtual Links between them and connecting one end of a Virtual Link to the customer premises. The view of the provider management system after the VAN for customer C has been provisioned is shown in Figure 7b.

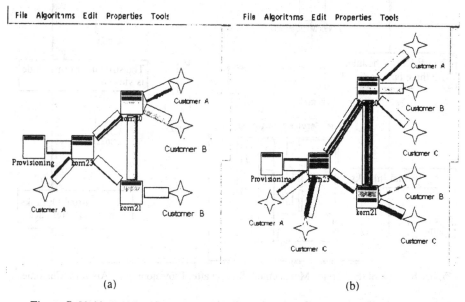

(a)                                            (b)

**Figure 7:** VAN provisioning as displayed on the provider's VAN management station: **before** (a) and **after** (b) provisioning a new VAN.

The service management system in the domain of customer C has now the view of a VAN spanning over the provider domain and all domains of customer C. Figure 8 shows this view, which includes seven nodes. Three of them are in the provider domain and four in the domain of customer C. Note that, on this level of abstraction, nodes in the customer domain do not differ from those in the provider domain in terms of service management capabilities. The service management system has the view of a single active network, on which services can now be installed and supervised.

Figure 8 shows a window from the service management station of customer C. It includes a snapshot of the Execution Environment of a VAN node. In our current implementation, the service management system can display the configuration and the state of Execution Environments in VAN nodes. The figure shows the buffers of the CPU scheduler, the memory, the in-bound, and the out-bound links. Three buffers are associated with the CPU scheduler: the default buffer for (active) packets, a second buffer for packets that belong to service management functions (e.g., filters for detecting specific events), and a third buffer for packets of a mechanism that routes the packets of the service management system. This is the basic configuration of an active network node, after the VAN has been set up by the provider and the service management system has been initialized by the customer. At this point, the service management system is ready to install specific network services and service management functions on the VAN.

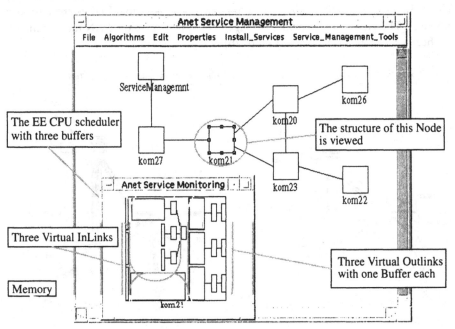

**Figure 8:** View of the Service Management Station after Provisioning a VAN for a Customer

## 6.2 Customer-Controlled Service Installation, Upgrade, and Supervision

On the ANET platform, we can demonstrate the installation, upgrade, and supervision of an IP service. Installing an IP service on a active network node is achieved by configuring a virtual router inside the node's Execution Environment. The service management system sends a sequence of active packets to the Execution Environment. Processing these packets results in installing an IP routing table, creating output buffers for the virtual out-bound links, setting up packet schedulers that operate on these buffers, installing function code for routing and management operations, configuring service-specific control parameters and management parameters, etc. After that, the IP service is initialized, which includes starting the routing protocol.

Upgrading the IP service to an IP service supporting several traffic classes with different QoS requirements is accomplished in our system by reconfiguring the virtual routers inside the Execution Environments. The service management system sends an active packet to each Execution Environment of the VAN. The processing of this packet results in upgrading the packet classifier (to detect the class of a packet), setting up buffers for each traffic class, and substituting the packet scheduler with a scheduler for multi-class traffic.

Figure 9 shows the structure of the Execution Environment after installing an IP service and upgrading it to a multi-class IP service. Compared to Figure 8, the structure of the output-buffers has changed to contain two buffer partitions, and the CPU scheduler part has grown by two additional components, one for the IP routing protocol and one for the management of the multi-class IP service.

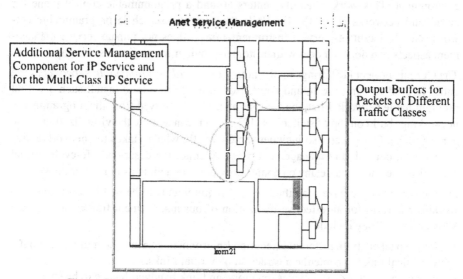

**Figure 9:** Node Structure after Installing an IP Service and Upgrading to a Multi-Class IP Service

In our implementation, the service management system can change the partitioning of the output buffers, by sending active packets to the virtual routers installed on the ANET platform. Further, it can monitor the buffer usage, by configuring the active management component to send packets back to the service management station in regular time intervals. This way, we can perform service management operations the same way as a customer would do while managing its IP service on its own premises.

## 7 Related Work

The networking community is currently putting substantial efforts into investigating the active networking approach. Additional motivation for this work and ongoing projects can be found in [2]. Two areas of current research are (1) designing Execution Environments for active network nodes ([6], [7], [4]), and (2) extracting application-specific functionality to be integrated into the network layer, such as, application-specific packet filtering functions and application-specific packet routing ([8], [9], [10]). An architectural framework for active networks is being developed by the AN Working Group [1].

One part of the Netscript project [11][4] deals with management of active networks. In that project, a platform for programming network services is being built. These services can be automatically instrumented for management purposes, and corresponding MIBs can be generated. During operation, services can be managed through those MIBs. Contrary to the Netscript project, our work leaves open the question of service instrumentation in an active network environment, but it focuses on a flexible framework for supporting interactions between customers and providers.

Research approaches in the area of *programmable networks* focus on developing interfaces that facilitate flexible service creation and resource partitioning in a telecom environment. This work generally centers around a programmable control plane for broadband networks [12][13][14]. While the current research in programmable networks clearly facilitates service instrumentation, it does not pursue service management aspects and does not deal with customer-provider interaction, as this paper does.

The Genesis project [15] brings up the notion of *virtual programmable networks* as the entity to bind resources to it, and they describe the life-cycle to install such a virtual programmable network. First, the Genesis approach is derived from the programmable networking (build on top of switchlets [12]), which concentrate the virtualization to the control plane. Our paper also includes the data path, which makes the network active on the data, control, and management plane. Second, the described life-cycle virtual networks, does not include any customer-provider interaction, as our paper does.

During our work we have identified several requirements to be met by an active networking platform for an effective realization of our management framework and the VAN concept. They include:

* Active packets from different Execution Environments have to be multiplexed onto a physical link to enable the abstraction of Virtual Links.
* Resources, such as CPU-cycles, memory, and link bandwidth have to be shared among different Execution Environments.
* An active network node has to prevent a customer from consuming more resources as he is entitled to.
* Access to memory has to be protected against unauthorized read and write.

High-performance platforms under development today lack at least one of these requirements. The ANN project [5] follows the approach of trusted code. The installation of code into a network node is performed by loading code from a trusted code server, which prohibits a customer from introducing any code into the node. Further, the CPU-cycles and link bandwidth are equally shared between different classes of flows, which restricts customizable resource allocation. Finally, multiplexing is achieved by using ATM on the physical link, which relieves the node operating system to perform the multiplexing.

The Switchware project [16] takes a language based approach. The memory access is controlled via a type-checked Programming Language for Active Networks (PLAN) [17]. Switchware does not support resource partitioning. Multiplexing is implicitly build into the active packet carrying the code to evaluate on intermediate active nodes. The executing code calls in a controlled way previously installed routines on the network node.

## 8 Discussion and Further Work

Rapid deployment of new services on an network infrastructure is the main driving force behind active networking research. In this work, we specifically focused on service provisioning and management in an active telecom environment and we showed the promising potential that active networking opens up in this area.

We identified the concept of a Virtual Active Network as the key abstraction in our framework. The VAN

- defines the object and level of customer-provider interaction,
- provides a basis for the provider to manage the resource consumption of customers in a safe way, and
- allows a customer to install, upgrade, and supervise a customer-specific service in a VAN spanning both the customer and provider domains.

We illustrated the above properties of a VAN by describing a series of demonstrations conducted on the ANET active networking platform.

We believe that our work opens up the way for further research. Obviously, efficient and flexible resource partitioning mechanisms need to be developed for sharing of CPU, memory, and link bandwidth in an active networking environment. Also worth pursuing are toolkits to support the design and implementation of active services. We have experienced that service management functionality is often similar for different active services. This similarity lets us conclude that a set of generic components can be build that will facilitate the realization of active services and their management applications.

## References

1. AN Architecture Working Group, "Architectural Framework for Active Networks," K. Calvert (editor), 1998.
2. D. Tennenhouse, J. Smith, W. Sincoskie, D. Weatherall, G. Minden, "A Survey of Active Network Research," IEEE Communications Magazine, Vol. 35(1), 1997.
3. M. Brunner, R. Stadler, "The impact of active networking technology on service management in a telecom environment," IFIP/IEEE International Symposium on Integrated Network Management (IM '99), Boston, MA, May 10-14, 1999.
4. S. Da Silva, Y. Yemini, D. Florissi, "The Netscript Project," ICC Workshop on Active Networking and Programmable Networks, Atlanta, 1998.
5. D. Decasper, G. Parulkar, S. Choi, J. DeHart, T. Wolf, B. Plattner, "A Scalable, High Performance Active Network Node," IEEE Network, Vol. 13(1), 1999.
6. D. Weatherall, J. Guttag, D. Tennenhouse, "ANTS: A Toolkit for Building and Dynamically Deploying Network Protocols," IEEE Conference on Open Architecture and Network Programming (OPENARCH'98), San Francisco, USA, April 1998.
7. J. Smith, D. Farber, C. Gunter, S. Nettles, D. Feldmeier, W. Sincoskie, "SwitchWare: Accelerating Network Evolution," Technical Report MC-CIS-96-38, CIS Department, University of Pennsylvania, May 1996.
8. S. Bhattacharjee, K. Calvert, E. Zegura, "An Architecture for Active Networking," Proceedings of High Performance Networking (HPN'97), 1997.

9. U. Legedza, J. Guttag, "Using Network-level Support to Improve Cache Routing," 3rd International WWW Caching Workshop, Manchester, England, June 1998.

10. S. Bhattacharjee, K. Calvert, E. Zegura, "Self-organizing wide-area network caches," IEEE INFOCOM, 1998.

11. Y. Yemini, S. da Silva, "Towards Programmable Networks," IFIP/IEEE International Workshop on Distributed Systems: Operations and Management (DSOM'96), L'Aquila, Italy, 1996.

12. J. van der Merwe, I. Leslie, "Switchlets a Dynamic Virtual ATM Networks," Fifth IFIP/IEEE International Symposium on Integrated Network Management (IM'97), San Diego, California, U.S.A., May, 1997, pp. 355-368.

13. A. Lazar, K. Lim, F. Marconcini, "Realizing a Foundation for Programmability of ATM Networks with the Binding Architecture," IEEE Journal of Selected Areas in Communications, Vol. 14(7), September 1996.

14. J. Biswas, A. Lazar, J. Huard, K. Lim, S. Mahjoub, L. Pau, M. Suzuki, S. Torstensson, W. Wang, S. Weinstein, "The IEEE P1520 Standards Initiative for Programmable Network Interfaces," IEEE Communications Magazine, Vol. 36(10), 1998.

15. A. Campbell, M. Kounavis, D. Villela, H. De Meer, K. Miki, J. Vicente, "The Genesis Kernel: A Virtual Network Operating System for Spawning Network Architectures," IEEE Conference on Open Architecture and Network Programming, (OPENARCH'99), 1999.

16. S. Alexander, W. Arbaugh, M. Hicks, P. Kakkar, A. Keromytis, J. Moore, C. Gunter, S. Nettles, J. Smith, "The Switchware Active Network Architecture," IEEE Network, Vol. 12(3), May/June 1998.

17. M. Hicks, P. Kakkar, J. Moore, C. Gunter, S. Nettles, "Network Programming with PLAN," IEEE Workshop on Internet Programming Languages, May 1998.

# Accelerating Code Deployment on Active Networks

Tôru Egashira and Yoshiaki Kiriha

C&C Media Research Laboratories, NEC Corporation
4-1-1, Miyazaki, Miyamae-ku, Kawasaki 216-8555, Japan
Tel: +81-44-856-2314, Fax: +81-44-856-2229
{egashira,kiriha}@ccm.CL.nec.co.jp

**Abstract.** Active networks enable their users to specify how each packet is processed on network nodes. One of the essential techniques for active networks is the programmable node approach, which enables network nodes to evolve their packet processing functions by loading new software components into the nodes. Possible component loading strategies include demand loading. It reduces the usage of node resources and localizes possible problems, although the component loading time defers packet processing. This paper discusses the component loading time of the demand loading strategy, and proposes a scheme to shorten the loading time by masking the propagation delay of components. We have implemented the scheme *pre-supplying* on a Java-based system and have evaluated its effectiveness. The result shows that the proposed scheme shortens the loading time of a test component by as much as 70%.

**Keywords.** Management of active networks, Mobile code, Demand loading, Code server, Prefetching

## 1. Introduction

As mobile code technology including mobile agents and applets has been improved and widely accepted, applying it to the underlying network system has been explored. Active networks [1] are ideal examples as they stand on mobile code technology. The use of mobile code in active networks is split into two approaches: *programmable node* and *capsule*. The former enables network nodes to evolve their functions including routing, modifying and forwarding of the received packets by loading new software components into the nodes. The latter approach embeds a piece of program code in each packet, or "capsule" in this context, so that the behavior of each packet on nodes is self-described. These approaches complement each other; the programmable node approach can define a large set of packet handling functions that cannot fit into a single capsule, while capsules can define the handling of individual packets by choosing which handling functions to use and making minor additions to them.

Since a capsule may decide its next hop during its journey, predetermining which nodes should have software components for the capsule is difficult. Therefore, the possible deployment strategies of software components are limited as follows:

- Broadcasting, i.e. distributing the components to *all* nodes in advance
- Accompanying, i.e. letting the components accompany the capsule
- Demand loading, i.e. nodes load the components when the capsule arrives

None of these alone are suitable for every purpose because each of them has its own advantages and disadvantages. The demand loading strategy, on which this paper focuses, limits the deployment of components to where they are needed, thus reducing node resource usage and localizing possible problems, e.g. the emergence of undetected bugs and compatibility problems among the new and existing components. However, the packet processing must be deferred during the component loading time.

This paper discusses the component loading time of the demand loading strategy, and proposes a scheme to shorten the loading time by masking the propagation delay of components. We have implemented the scheme *pre-supplying* on a Java-based system and have evaluated its effectiveness.

## 2. System Model

Before discussing loading time, we define a simplified model of a demand loading system. Our system model includes three types of entities: *module, supplier,* and *consumer* (Figure 1).

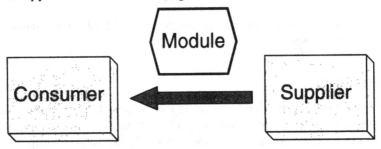

**Figure 1: System model.**

### 2.1. Module

A module is the unit of a software program. All software components are composed of modules. Modules are atomic; i.e. they have no substructures. In other words, no module contains any other modules. It is also the unit of program transmission; components are transmitted from a supplier to a consumer module-by-module.

Programs can be split into two types: binary codes and human-readable, also known as scripts. A module may be either type and the difference is observed only as initialization overhead. Each module must be initialized in order to be ready to run. The initialization includes the compilation and linkage processes. For example, a script typically needs to be compiled to an intermediate language or a binary code before running. Compared with scripts, binary codes generally need less initialization overhead. We assume the initialization of a module cannot be done concurrently with its execution. Consequently, initialization must be finished before the module is used.

## 2.2. Supplier

A supplier is a subsystem that provides consumers with modules. A supplier is assumed to store all modules that consumers potentially need. Each module that a supplier stores has a unique name. A consumer requests a supplier for a module by its name. The supplier then transmits the module specified to the consumer.

## 2.3. Consumer

A consumer is a subsystem that executes components that are composed of modules. It may execute many components concurrently. It requests a supplier to send modules that are required to continue the component execution. Upon receiving a module, a consumer compiles it, links it, and/or does on it any other required initialization tasks to make it as the part of the running component. Some of the modules that compose a component may be left unrequested if the application quits the execution prematurely.

## 2.4. Example

An example that conforms to our system model is the Java applet system. In this example, a Java class file is a module. Java class files compose applets, which correspond to components. An HTTP server and a web browser correspond to a supplier and a consumer respectively.

# 3. Module Granularity

In this section, we consider the effect of module granularity on the component loading time. In this paper, the granularity of a module is defined by its size in bytes. Moreover, we define component loading time as the elapsed time between the date a consumer starts loading a component and the date the component becomes ready.

An example of the effect of the module granularity can be observed on Java applet systems that support packaged class files. A large Java applet which is composed of a number of class files takes considerable loading time for a browser to start running the applet if each class file is loaded one-by-one via an HTTP connection. Therefore, newer browsers have the capability to load packaged class files. With packaged class files, a browser can obtain all class files in a package via a single HTTP connection. As the number of request-response roundtrips becomes smaller, the browser can save the applet loading time. Such loading time reduction can be regarded as the result of module granularity tuning.

Concerning the elements of component loading time, they are (Figure 2):

- the module loading time,
- the module initialization time, and
- the component execution time elapsing until the component becomes ready.

The module loading time is further divided into:

- the propagation delay, and
- the module transmission time.

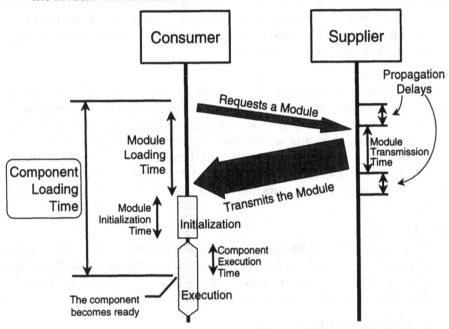

**Figure 2: Component loading time.**

The granularity of a module affects its initialization time and transmission time. Hence, making the module granularity finer will reduce the component loading time (a to b in Figure 3). However, making the module finer than a certain amount will increase the component loading time (c in Figure 3). As an excessively small module cannot carry enough quantity of code, the consumer will have to load another supplemental module, but this will add another propagation delay to the component loading time. It thus follows that to minimize the component loading time, the module granularity chosen must be as small as possible but still enough for a component to become ready by loading a single module. This means that a "kick-start" module must be prepared for each component.

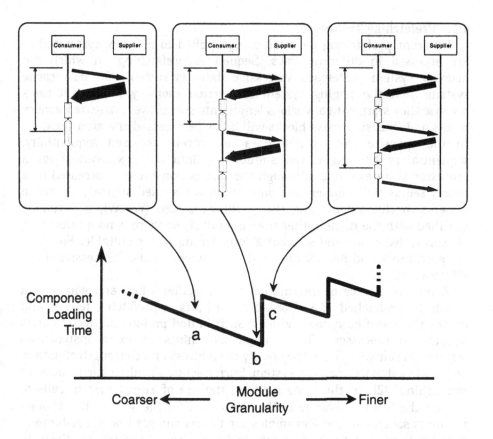

**Figure 3: The influence of module granularity on component loading time.**

However, as such tailored modules cannot be shared among components, more resources and longer loading time may be required than in finer module approaches when the consumer executes many components. Since an active network node is considered to execute many components, we sought another approach.

## 4. Masking of Propagation Delay

As described above, propagation delay accumulation is the main problem of modules with excessively fine granularity. However, if the propagation delay can be properly masked, using finer modules will result in shorter component loading time. A technique that can mask the propagation delay is *prefetching*. It is widely used in the memory systems of computers. In this technique, a memory system attempts to guess which data are likely to be accessed by a processor. Then it moves the data from the high-latency storage into the low-latency cache before the processor actually accesses them. In the rest of this section, we discuss existing prefetching techniques and propose an improved technique.

## 4.1. Prefetching Techniques

Different prefetching techniques are applied to memory systems that are accessed in different ways. Sequential prefetching, in which the memory system prefetches successive data, is suitable for disk cache systems and the paging system for virtual memory implementations because they store data of various length into successive fixed-size memory blocks and thus successive blocks will likely be accessed one after another. In the opposite case, where data are rarely accessed sequentially, sequential prefetching is not suitable. A data cache subsystem for a processor is an example; although the instruction cache is accessed in a nearly sequential manner, the data cache is accessed sparsely. In cache systems for filesystems and the world wide web (WWW), a datum is specified with the name rather than a number, so there is no *a priori* idea of "successive data" and sequential prefetching is not suitable. For such systems, hints and history are used to complement the "successive data" information.

A hint is a piece of information that specifies when and which data should be prefetched. Based on obtained hints, a prefetcher fetches and caches the specified data. A kind of such hinted prefetching technique is adopted in processors. These implement hints as extra instructions inserted in software. Then they notify the address and the length of data to be prefetched to the memory system. Such a scheme is also called "software prefetching" [2]. In the same manner, the use of ioctl system calls to declare the future access to a file is proposed for filesystems [3]. Though the hints sources in these examples are the consumers (consumer-hinted), the suppliers of data or other entities can also be the source. Such an example will be described later.

Here, "history" refers to the existing information about past accesses. By analyzing the history, a prefetcher can discover access patterns, extrapolate them, and then predict which data will likely be accessed. As the implementation of this history scheme is more complicated than the schemes mentioned previously, it is typically applied to software-based systems like disk caches [4], filesystems [5], and WWW [6].

Among these prefetching schemes, hinted prefetching and history-based prefetching can be applied to mask propagation delays of module loading. This paper focuses on the history-based prefetching, and leaves the consumer-hinted prefetching for future study.

## 4.2. Issues of History-Based Prefetching

There are other history-based prefetching issues beyond the implementation complexity described above. For example, since the prefetcher must have sufficient history to predict correctly, it cannot work well for a certain period after being initialized.

A solution to this issue is introduced in a WWW caching system [6], in

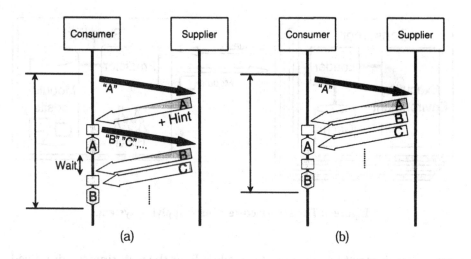

**Figure 4: Example sequences of (a) hinted-prefetching and
(b) pre-supplying.**

which the history is centrally maintained on the server side. The
prefetcher in the client uses hints that the server provides based on the
history. Hence, the system uses both hinted and history-based prefetching.
As the history is maintained by the server, the prefetcher located in the
client side can work well from the beginning, as long as some other clients
have representatively built up enough history by previously accessing the
server.

This solution, however, creates another issue. Because of the propagation delay of hints, it may fail to mask the propagation delay of prefetched
data. Figure 4a describes an example in which we have applied the
history-based hinted prefetching solution to our system model. This
example assumes the supplier has access history of modules A, B, and C in
that order. Therefore, when the consumer requests module A, the supplier
transmits a hint, which tells him that modules B and C will be next. Upon
receiving this advice, the consumer requests modules B and C. Though the
second request is made quickly, the consumer has to wait for some period
since necessary modules are locking at this point. Thus, component loading
time is lengthened. This issue cannot be solved with the prefetching or
"consumer-driven module providing" approaches because they incur hint
propagation delay.

### 4.3. Pre-Supplying

We resolve this issue by making the module providing supplier-driven;
it is mostly the same as history-based hinted prefetching, except that the
supplier transmits modules instead of hints to the consumer. In the case of
the last example, the supplier transmits module A on receiving the request
for it. Then it further transmits modules B and C (Figure 4b). Thus, the

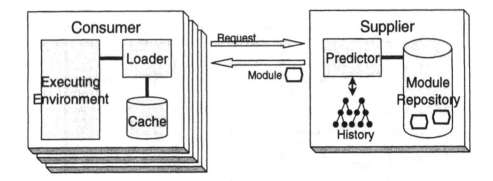

**Figure 5: The architecture of pre-supplying system.**

consumer does not have to wait for module B, or the wait time is minimized. To make this scheme called "pre-supplying" feasible, a consumer must always be ready to receive modules, regardless of whether it has requested them.

## 5. Architecture of Pre-supplying System

In this section, we describe the architecture of the pre-supplying system. The supplier contains two subsystems: a module repository and a predictor (Figure 5). The module repository is a subsystem that provides the predictor with modules on request. The predictor sends modules to consumers on request and on expectation. When it receives a request for a module from a consumer, it loads the requested module from the module repository, transmits it to the consumer, and updates the history data. Additionally, the predictor analyses the history data to predict which module is most likely to be requested next, and transmits the candidate module to the consumer if the module has not been transmitted to the consumer recently. The predictor then repeats the pre-supplying task by transmitting a module that is most likely to be requested after the module that it just pre-supplied. The task is further repeated until the next request from the consumer arrives or when there are no more unsent candidates left.

Figure 6a shows a possible representation of history data. It is a forest of height limited to $h=2$ and thus can model $h$ order Markov processes. Each root node of the forest corresponds to a module, and the subsidiary nodes are modules requested subsequent to the request for the root module. Each edge has weight that is the frequency of the request sequence. For example, when the predictor has observed the sequence of requests shown in Figure 6b, the forest of Figure 6a is made, and it then predicts that module D is the candidate for the next transmission.

Let us return to Figure 5. The consumer contains three subsystems: an executing environment (EE), a loader and a cache. The EE executes

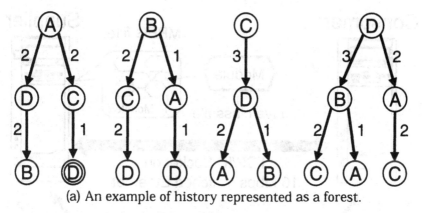

(a) An example of history represented as a forest.

A⇨D⇨B⇨C⇨D⇨A⇨C⇨D⇨B⇨A⇨D⇨B⇨C⇨D⇨A⇨C

(b) The observed sequence of requests.

**Figure 6: An example of history data.**

software components. While executing components, it loads necessary modules from the loader. The loader provides the EE with modules on request. When the EE makes a request for a module, the loader first looks for the module in the cache, which is a cache for modules and is assumed to be empty initially. If the cache already has the requested module, the loader gives it to the EE. Otherwise, the loader makes a request for the module to the supplier. Some time later, it receives the requested module and some pre-supplied modules. It stores them in the cache, and if they include modules for which the EE is asking, it gives the modules to the EE.

## 6. Experiment

We conducted a series of experiments to show the efficiency of the pre-supplying. Figure 7 shows the outline of the test bed system. All the software was developed using Java: the supplier and the consumer were developed as Java applications, and each was deployed on a Java Runtime Environment (JRE) version 1.1.7 virtual machine on a Linux PC. The consumer and the supplier are interconnected with a TCP/IP socket on 10 Mbps switched Ethernet. Using the socket, the consumer requests modules (Java class files) and the supplier transmits them.

We evaluated the loading time of a Java application. The application we used is an MPEG filter, which is an experimental code for programmable nodes in active networks. As shown in Figure 8, it forwards an MPEG stream in RFC 2250 [7] Section 3 format. When the output link is congested and the queue is going to be filled, it selectively drops packets in less-impact-first manner (B pictures first, next P pictures, and finally I

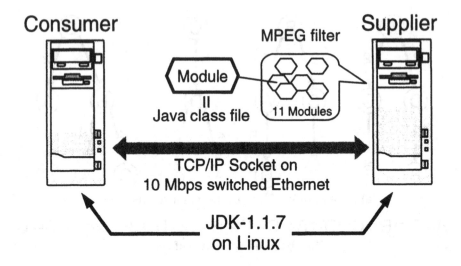

**Figure 7: The test bed system.**

pictures). The loading time is defined as the time between the date the consumer starts loading the application and the date the application indicates it accepts MPEG packets. During the loading time, the supplier transmits 11 modules, the average size of which was about 608 bytes.

We executed the system with pre-supplying (after history data are established) and without pre-supplying (history data are initialized), 20 times for each. The results are shown in Table 1. The results obtained show that pre-supplying reduced the loading time by 74% approximately.

**Table 1: Loading time comparison.**

|  | Loading time [sec] | |
|  | Average | Std. deviation $\sigma$ |
| --- | --- | --- |
| Without pre-supplying | **0.536** | 0.042 |
| Pre-supplying | **0.138** | 0.004 |

The result in Table 1 was the ideal one because it was only a single application that established history and was executed, hence no prediction errors were made. We also evaluated how the performance is degraded according to the prediction errors. There are two types of prediction errors: ordering and missing errors. Suppose that a consumer is going to use modules A, B and C in that order; if the supplier predicts that the order

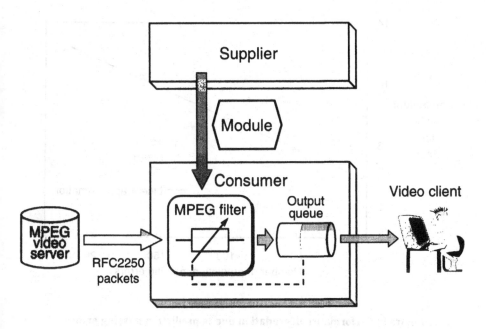

**Figure 8: The experimental active networking system.**

will be A-C-B, it is an ordering error; if the supplier predicts A-C but no B, it is a missing error. In some cases, an ordering error might not be a problem. For example, pre-supplying in order A-C-B will be sufficient for the consumer that uses them each a day. In contrast, a missing error always leads the consumer to make a request for the missed module (provided that the consumer cache did not have the module yet) and thus lengthens the component loading time.

We evaluated the effect of only missing errors because the effect of ordering errors is less directly observed as described above. To see the effect of missing errors, we forced the supplier to make mistakes. We modified it so that it could omit some randomly chosen modules from pre-supplying. Although it predicts correctly and tries to pre-supply candidate modules to the consumer, some of them are not really transmitted. Because the number of modules in the MPEG filter is not enough for this experiment, we used W3C's Jigsaw Proxy Package[†] 2.0.1 instead. In this case, the supplier transmits 216 modules during the loading time; the average size of modules was about 2.80 KB. As shown in Figure 9, the pre-supplying performance dropped linearly from maximum 68% loading-time reduction according to the number of missing errors; i.e. the number of omitted modules.

---

[†] http://www.w3.org/Jigsaw/

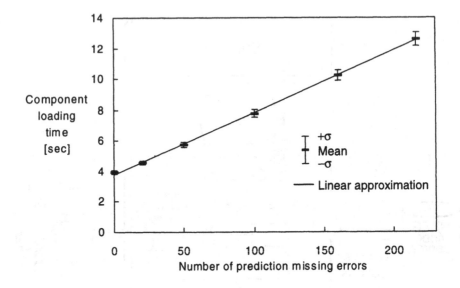

**Figure 9: Performance degradation due to prediction missing errors.**

## 7. Conclusion

In this paper, we have presented a scheme called "pre-supplying" to reduce the loading time of software components for active network nodes. In this scheme, the supplier maintains access history, predicts future accesses, and transmits modules in advance of the requests for them. A series of experiments shows that it reduces the component loading time by approximately 70% and that the reduction will linearly decrease according to the number of prediction errors.

On the test bed system, the information exchanged between the consumer and the supplier was limited to the module requests and the modules themselves. We believe more information including cache usage must be exchanged to make this scheme practical, otherwise the supplier cannot know how many modules can be safely pre-supplied without flooding the consumer's cache.

## References

1. D. L. Tennenhouse, et al., "A Survey of Active Network Research," *IEEE Communications Magazine*, Vol. 35, No. 1, pp. 80-86, January 1997.
2. S. P. VanderWiel and D. J. Lilja, "When Caches Aren't Enough: Data Prefetching Techniques," *IEEE Computer*, Vol. 30, No. 7, pp. 23-30, July 1997.

3. R. H. Patterson et al., "Informed Prefetching and Caching," *Proc. 15th ACM Symp. Operating Systems Principles*, December 3-6, 1995, pp. 79-95.
4. K. Salem, "Adaptive Prefetching for Disk Buffers," NASA Goddard Space Flight Center, CESDIS TR-91-46, January 1991.
5. J. Griffioen and R. Appleton, "The Design, Implementation, and Evaluation of a Predictive Caching File System," Technical Report CS264-96, Univ. Kentucky, June 1996.
6. V. N. Padmanabhan and J. C. Mogul, "Using Predictive Prefetching to Improve World Wide Web Latency," *ACM SIGCOMM Computer Communication Review*, Vol. 26, No. 3, July 1996.
7. D. Hoffman, et al., "RTP Payload Format for MPEG1/MPEG2 Video," RFC 2250, January 1998.

# Panel 2


## Are Programmable Networks Unmanageable?


*Organizer: Morris Sloman*
*Imperial College, London, U.K.*

# Are Programmable Networks Unmanageable?

## Abstract

There is a need to be able to program network components to adapt to application requirements for quality of service, specialized application dependent routing, to increase efficiency, to support mobility and sophisticated management functionality. There are a number of different approaches to providing programmability:

– active networks
– management by delegation
– mobile agents
– intelligent agents
– policy interpretation

However there are a number of questions about the manageability of programmable networks.

- If the network is constantly being reprogrammed is it inherently unmanageable?
- Are these technologies so powerful that they are a security risk?
- Who should be permitted to program the network - users or only managers?
- Who are the 'users'?
- How do we charge 'users' for execution of programs within the network?

The panel will discuss these questions and the panelists will each provide a different view-point on the above issues.

# Session 6

## IT and Enterprise Management

*Chair: James Won-Ki Hong*
*POSTECH, Pohang, Korea*

# Characterization and Measurements of Enterprise Network Traffic with RMON2

Luciano Paschoal Gaspary, Liane Rockenbach Tarouco

Federal University of Rio Grande do Sul
Informatics Institute
Av. Bento Gonçalves, 9500 - Agronomia - CEP 91591-970 - Porto Alegre, Brazil
paschoal@inf.ufrgs.br, liane@penta.ufrgs.br

**Abstract.** The increasing growth of the amount and complexity of applications and protocols executed on computer networks has hindered the work of their administrators. They need to justify the ever-increasing investments accomplished on network equipment acquisition and on communication links leasing. For such, they must: identify who, and with which purpose, most consumes these resources, know if users and resources are located so that the presence of bottlenecks in the network is minimized and detect if some intruder, by means of a high-layer protocol is trying to invade it. An appropriate and current solution capable to answer these subjects is the use of RMON2, MIB that operates above the link layer, providing information needed to monitor client-server applications and end-to-end communications. This work presents the results of a study accomplished on this MIB, aiming at extracting from it means to control the users' activities, to monitor protocols and applications, to optimize the localization of users and resources and to accomplish security management.

## 1 Introduction

The investments accomplished in the expansion and maintenance of computer networks have surprisingly grown in the last years. Their popularization brought about the appearance of a high number of distributed applications and protocols, leading managers and administrators to investigate effective management solutions in order to reduce costs, provide high availability and, at least, maintain the quality of service once noticed.

These objectives were first reached through an immediate adhesion to new technologies. A real example was the recent migration that occurred in many companies, which left the old plane Ethernet standard for technologies such as Gigabit Ethernet and ATM. As most of the time users regard the network as an inexhaustible resource, they incorporate more and more applications and protocols to their daily routine, which for the administrator means the need for constant alterations in the network infrastructure.

These modifications involve costs and, therefore, they need to be justified. This is possible if the administrator can answer simple questions such as: which users or departments use the network? When is it most used? Which applications are executed? What are the activities of a certain user? Do users perceive an appropriate level of service? Are resources correctly allocated?

Answers to these subjects can be obtained with the use of accounting mechanisms. Until recently, the accounting process was precariously accomplished, once manual counting took place. The input and output traffic considering ports, connections and users was acquired by polling each network device. This method presents imprecise results [1], besides being very onerous once it generates a lot of management traffic on the network.

A good alternative to accomplish this task is the use of RMON2, MIB that operates with protocols above the data link layer, providing necessary information to monitor high-layer protocols and distributed applications [2][3]. The information collected by this MIB allows administrators to have a detailed view of the behavior of applications and protocols being executed as well as the resources usage rates and the users who most consume them. With such information, these administrators can redefine network traffic flows aiming at better resources usage. Besides, they can observe who communicates with whom and which applications are being used, which makes possible the establishment of policies to guarantee the appropriate use of the network.

This work presents how the information provided by RMON2 MIB may benefit the maintenance of network control and its usage profile discovery, which is an important task for the company to evaluate if investments on networking technology converge or not for the business interests. The paper is organized as follows. Section 2 presents an overview of RMON and RMON2 [4]. Sections 3,4,5 and 6 present the results of the study. Section 3 describes how to monitor user activities on the network. Section 4 presents how to trace the global usage profile of the network. Section 5 treats of the procedures to be accomplished to determine if users and resources are appropriately positioned. Section 6 describes how to use RMON2 to detect non-authorized users. Finally, in section 7 the final considerations are presented.

## 2    Overview of RMON and RMON2

In recent years the SNMP standard and the specification of MIB-II have been the dominant mechanism for network management. Software agents embedded in network equipment collect information about network traffic and statistics such as the number of input and output frames. With such information a manager knows the amount of traffic that enters and leaves each monitored device, but he is unaware of the behavior of this traffic in the local network as a whole.

The largest contributions to the group of SNMP standards are RMON and RMON2 specifications [5]. Their use has been increasing the efficiency and reducing costs in remote network monitoring and in protocol analysis. While RMON aims at identifying physical problems in the network looking at traffic from router to router, RMON2 monitores network usage patterns, observing the content of the packets of high-layer protocols and applications.

### 2.1    Characteristics and Evolution of RMON

The RMON specification is essentially the definition of a MIB. The efforts for its standardization began in 1990 with the creation of the workgroup RMON by IETF.

The proposed standard, RFC1271, was published in November 1991. The first RFC was specifically projected to Ethernet local networks. Later, in 1993, the workgroup proposed extensions for Token Ring in RFC1513. Due to the growing interest of the market, several manufacturers started to implement solutions considering the future standard. In 1995 the RMON MIB was standardized (RFC1757)[4].

RMON solutions operate in agreement with the client-server paradigm [6]. Client is the application executed in the central management station, which presents the obtained results to the user (administrator of the network). On the other hand, server is the agent software embedded in network devices or dedicated monitoring devices called probes, which collect information defined in RMON MIB and analyze the packets from the network. Agents and management application communicate using the SNMP protocol.

With RMON MIB, administrators can collect information from remote segments of the network in order to monitor its performance and detect possible problems. Figure 1 presents the groups of RMON MIB. It provides:

- traffic statistics for a network segment, for a certain host and for host pairs;
- a versatile mechanism of alarms and events that makes possible the configuration of thresholds and the notification of the administrator on changes of the network behavior;
- mechanisms for packet capture.

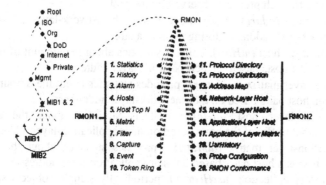

**Fig. 1.** RMON and RMON2 MIB groups

The RMON standard is defined so that the collection of data and its processing are accomplished by the agents (RMON servers). It can collect and store the value of objects defined in any MIB. When the administrator is interested in such information, he polls the agent only once and receives all information stored in *history* group. This decision in RMON standard contributes to the reduction of SNMP traffic and to decrease the processing accomplished by the management station.

RMON solutions have additional advantages. Without leaving the room, a manager can verify the traffic of a local or remote network segment. Therefore, expense of time and resources are almost quite eliminated because, in most cases, it is not necessary to send specialists to remote sites. A specialist in a central site can work in several problems requesting information to several probes located in remote places. Besides, several specialists can cooperate in the resolution of a certain problem requesting information to the same probe.

It is important to highlight that an RMON probe can monitor the whole traffic within the LAN segment to which it is attached. It can capture all the MAC-layer frames and identify their source and destination addresses. Thus, the probe is able to provide detailed information about the amount of frames sent and received by each host of the LAN segment. However, if a router is attached to the LAN, one can neither determine the real source of the traffic that arrives from it nor the real destination of frames leaving the LAN through the router. This restriction is solved by RMON2 standard [6].

## 2.2 High-Layer Protocols Monitoring

The works to extend RMON MIB and include mechanisms to monitor higher-layer protocols began in 1994. This initiative, called RMON2, resulted in the creation of RFC2021 in January 1997 [2]. When monitoring high-layer protocols such as network and application-layer protocols, it is possible to visualize the whole corporate network instead of individual segments. The groups defined in RMON2 MIB are showed in figure 1. Briefly, they are:

- protocol directory (*protocolDir*): repository that indicates all the protocols that the probe is capable to interpret;
- protocol distribution (*protocolDist*): statistics about the amount of traffic generated by each protocol observed by the probe;
- address map (*addressMap*): associates each network-layer address to the respective MAC address, storing them in a table;
- network-layer host (*nlHost*): collects statistics about the amount of input/output traffic of the hosts based on their network-layer addresses;
- network-layer matrix (*nlMatrix*): provides statistics about the amount of traffic between host pairs based on their network-layer addresses;
- application-layer host (*alHost*): collects statistics about the amount of input/output traffic of the hosts based on their application-layer addresses;
- application-layer matrix (*alMatrix*): provides statistics about the amount of traffic between host pairs based on their application-layer addresses;
- user-history collection (*usrHistory*): periodically samples objects specified by the user (manager) and stores the collected information in accordance with parameters also defined by the user;
- probe configuration (*probeConfig*): defines configuration parameters for RMON probes;
- rmon conformance (*rmonConformance*): describes conformity requirements for RMON2 MIB.

# 3  Administration and Statistics on User Activities

If the administrator is interested in tracing the network usage profile it is very important to obtain information about how a certain user or department uses it. What users most use the network? With whom do these users communicate? Which applications and protocols do they execute? Such information enable the administrator to observe users' activities and verify if they fit the company interests.

## 3.1 Volume of Accesses

Information related to the volume of network accesses accomplished by a certain user can be obtained through requests to RMON2 *network-layer host* group. It decodes packets based on their network-layer addresses. Thus, administrators can observe beyond the routers that connect the sub-networks and identify the real hosts that are communicating [7]. The *network-layer host* group is composed of a control table (*hlHostControl*) and a data table (*nlHost*) (see figure 2).

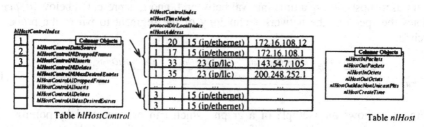

**Table** *hlHostControl*                    **Table** *nlHost*

**Fig. 2.** *nlHost* group tables

The control table has an entry for each interface (sub-network) being monitored. Each entry contains information such as the number of frames received from the interface that the probe decides not to count, number of rows added and removed from the data table and maximum number of data rows (*nlHost* table) acceptable for this interface.

Table *nlHost* provides basic network statistics for each network-layer address seen on a monitored network segment. When a new row is added to table *hlHostControl*, the probe begins to observe packets and to collect network-layer addresses in the respective interface. A new row in table *nlHost* is created for each new discovered address.

Figure 2 shows table *hlHostControl* with three rows. It means that the probe is analyzing packets in three different network segments. As one can observe in table *nlHost*, four hosts were identified in the first segment (first index of the table). The second index (*nlHostTimeMark*) of this table denotes when the row was created or last updated. It allows the management station to retrieve only the updated entries each polling cycle, reducing traffic between this station and the agents. The third index, *protocolDirLocalIndex*, identifies the protocol encapsulation observed. The encapsulations that the probe is able to decode are defined in *protocol directory* group. Finally, the fourth index of this table contains the network-layer address of the monitored device. An example of information retrieved when polling the *nlHost* group is presented in table 1.

**Table 1.** Example of information retrieved from *nlHost* group

| HostAddress | InPkts | OutPkts | InOctets | OutOctets | OutMacNonUnicastPkts |
|---|---|---|---|---|---|
| 172.16.108.12 | 1.000 | 345 | 80.345 | 25.367 | 33 |
| 172.16.108.1 | 2.350 | 733 | 97.334 | 33.292 | 125 |
| 143.54.7.105 | 5.930 | 299 | 112.445 | 5.293 | 0 |
| 200.248.252.1 | 100 | 30 | 49.238 | 3.777 | 12 |

Requests to this group may help administrators to find out which users most use the network and when it occurs. In this context, the *user history* group can be used to store object values in diferent time instants. Thus, if a management station wants to retrieve the value of an object in ten different time instants, only three messages are required: one for configuring the RMON2 probe, one for requesting the report and another for retrieving it (agent response). The savings of this approach are huge when compared to the convencional SNMP MIB, when the same task requires twenty messages (ten requests plus ten responses).

A simple formula to calculate the network usage rate (n.u.r), in percentage, by a certain user (host) during a time interval between $t_1$ and $t_2$ is presented below. *ifSpeed* denotes the speed of the network technology of the segment to where the probe is attached.

$$ n.u.r = \frac{\left( \frac{\left[ (nlHostInOctets_{t_2} + nlHostOutOctets_{t_2}) - (nlHostInOctets_{t_1} + nlHostOutOctets_{t_1}) \right] \bullet 8}{ifSpeed} \right)}{t_2 - t_1} \bullet 100 \tag{1} $$

Figure 3 shows an example of a graph, which can be generated by polling the *nlHost* group and applying the formula just presented. In order to minimize management traffic in the network, one may configure a report in *user history* group and retrieve the *nlHost* object values sampled in different time instants only once. The disadvantage of this approach is that the graph can not be gradually generated and therefore partial views of it are not possible.

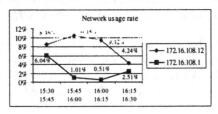

**Fig. 3.** Example of graph depicting the network utilization rate by two hosts

## 3.2 Applications and Protocols Used

Determining user network usage patterns relies on the knowledge of the administrator about the protocols and applications that each user executes as well as when it happens [6]. Such information can be obtained in *application-layer host* group.

The *application-layer host* group comprises a control table (*hlHostControl*), which is the same as the *network-layer host* group, and a data table (*alHost*), as shown in figure 4. Table *alHost* provides the administrator with input/output traffic statistics of hosts, considering application-layer protocols. The term application layer refers to all protocols above the MAC layer.

There is one or more entries in table *alHost* for each application-layer protocol discovered. These entries are also organized according to their network-layer address, so that information such as the HTTP traffic generated from or addressed to a certain host may be easily retrieved. Table *alHost* is indexed by the following objects:

- *hlHostControlIndex:* denotes the segment to where the probe is attached;
- *alHostTimeMark:* time filter;

- *protocolDirLocalIndex:* network-layer protocol identification;
- *nlHostAddress:* network-layer address;
- *protocolDirLocalIndex:* application-layer protocol identification.

Table *hlHostControl*                                                        Table *alHost*

**Fig. 4.** *alHost* group tables

Observe that the object *protocolDirLocalIndex is* used twice to index the table. In fact, two different instances of this object are used: one of them identifies the network-layer protocol and the other consists of an application-layer protocol [7].

Table 2 illustrates an example of data retrieved from *alHost* group. By periodically polling this group or configuring remote reports to store *alHost* group objects in different time instants, the administrator can find out which applications and protocols users most employ and when exactly it occurs.

**Table 2.** Example of information retrieved from *alHost* group

| HostAddress | Protocol | InPkts | OutPkts | InOctets | OutOctets |
|---|---|---|---|---|---|
| 172.16.108.12 | HTTP | 830 | 342 | 45.311 | 42.543 |
| 172.16.108.12 | SMTP | 250 | 24 | 17.900 | 2.406 |
| 172.16.108.12 | FTP | 567 | 158 | 32.193 | 19.765 |
| 172.16.108.5 | HTTP | 2037 | 411 | 209.312 | 56.927 |

The information provided by *alHost* group can be used to draw graphs that indicate both the protocols and applications in use by a certain host and the amount of traffic generated by each of them. Figure 5a shows an example of a chart that can be obtained by polling the probe in two time instants ($t_1$ and $t_2$). It presents the usage rate of each protocol by the host 172.16.108.1 based on the total volume of packets observed coming from and addressed to it during the interval $t_2$-$t_1$. The formula to calculate it follows:

$$a.u.r = \frac{\left(alHostInOctets_{t_2\,prot} + alHostOutOctets_{t_2\,prot}\right) - \left(alHostInOctets_{t_1\,prot} + alHostOutOctets_{t_1\,prot}\right)}{\sum_i \left(alHostInOctets_{t_2\,prot\,i} + alHostOutOctets_{t_2\,prot\,i}\right) - \left(alHostInOctets_{t_1\,prot\,i} + alHostOutOctets_{t_1\,prot\,i}\right)} \cdot 100 \quad (2)$$

Figure 5b shows the protocol usage rate considering four consecutive time intervals. This type of historical graph aids the administrator to determine user access patterns. In this graph, protocol usage rate was calculated based on the speed of the monitored segment. Thus, it is possible to observe the impact that a protocol in use by a certain host is causing to the network. The formula to obtain this information is:

$$a.u.r = \frac{\dfrac{\left[\left(alHostInOctets_{t_2} + alHostOutOctets_{t_2}\right) - \left(alHostInOctets_{t_1} + alHostOutOctets_{t_1}\right)\right] \cdot 8}{ifSpeed}}{t_2 - t_1} \cdot 100 \quad (3)$$

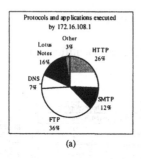 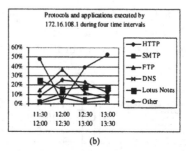

(a)                    (b)

**Fig. 5.** Example of graphs depicting protocol usage rates

## 3.3 Established Communications

It is important to identify who are the local/remote peers of each established communication to further understand the behavior of network users. The *application-layer matrix* group has an important role in this process. It collects traffic statistics between communicating host pairs based on their network-layer addresses. The group consists of several tables. Two of them are depicted in figure 6.

Table *hlMatrixControl*                                      Table *alMatrixSD*

**Fig. 6.** *alMatrix* group tables

The control table (*hlMatrixControl*) is similar to the control tables already presented. The data table (*alMatrixSD*) stores information about the amount of traffic observed between host pairs. It is indexed by the following objects [2]:

- *hlMatrixControlIndex:* denotes the segment to where the probe is attached;
- *alMatrixSDTimeMark:* time filter;
- *protocolDirLocalIndex:* network-layer protocol identification;
- *nlMatrixSDSourceAddress*: source address;
- *nlMatrixSDestAddress*: destination address;
- *protocolDirLocalIndex:* application-layer protocol identification.

Table 3 illustrates an example of data that is retrieved when table *alMatrixSD* is polled. As one can observe, this table counts the traffic from source to destination and vice-versa in two different entries. Through periodic requests to the RMON2 probe or by means of configured reports in *user history* group, it is possible to determine with whom a certain host is communicating, the protocols being used and the amount of traffic generated by them. In table 3, the user on host 172.16.108.12 is currently accessing Alta Vista® and the web site of the own company. Besides, it maintains an FTP connection with Microsoft®.

**Table 3.** Example of information retrieved from table *alMatrixSD*

| SDSourceAddress | SDDestAddress | Protocol | SDPkts | SDOctets |
|---|---|---|---|---|
| 172.16.108.12 | altavista.digital.com | 16 (http/tcp/ip/ethernet) | 15 | 578 |
| altavista.digital.com | 172.16.108.12 | 16 (http/tcp/ip/ethernet) | 237 | 17.900 |
| 172.16.108.12 | ftp.microsoft.com | 17 (ftp/tcp/ip/ethernet) | 29 | 2.193 |
| ftp.microsoft.com | 172.16.108.12 | 17 (ftp/tcp/ip/ethernet) | 12.033 | 409.312 |
| 172.16.108.12 | 172.16.108.1 | 16 (http/tcp/ip/ethernet) | 49 | 5.971 |
| 172.16.108.1 | 172.16.108.12 | 16 (http/tcp/ip/ethernet) | 14.987 | 1.000.329 |

## 4    Network Global Usage Profile

In the previous section, mechanisms to control and to monitor host-based (user) network activities were presented. However, in many situations the administrator must further investigate the network usage profile taking into consideration the whole company or some departments. For instance, such information is essential if the administrator wants to find out the departments that most consume network resources, when the network is overloaded and which users/departments contribute to intensify this problem.

The *protocol distribution* group counts the number of octets and packets monitored by the probe for each supported protocol encapsulation. It consists of two tables: *protocoloDistControl,* which controls the collection of basic statistics, and *protocolDistStats,* which stores the collected data [2]. Each entry of table *protocolDistControl* denotes one network segment and controls a group of entries in table *protocolDistStats,* one for each protocol recognized on this segment (see figure 7).

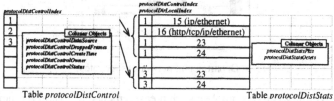

Table *protocolDistControl*                Table *protocolDistStats*

**Fig. 7.** *protocolDist* group tables

Table 4 shows an example of information retrieved from *protocolDist* group. The accomplishment of periodic requests to this group or the retrieval of historical reports from it makes possible the observation on the variation of protocols usage rate during a certain time period (see figure 8).

**Table 4.** Example of information retrieved from *protocolDist* group

| Protocol | protocolDistStatsPkts | protocolDistStatsOctet |
|---|---|---|
| 15 (ip/ethernet) | 3.417 | 1.034.587 |
| 16 (http/tcp/ip/ethernet) | 1.644 | 459.100 |
| 23 (smtp/tcp/ip/ethernet) | 1.290 | 345.923 |
| 24 (ftp/tcp/ip/ethernet) | 483 | 229.564 |

To determine the network usage rate of each department the administrator must know which hosts belong to each department. In this case, the group to be polled is network-layer host. The methodology to be used is the following: the probe counts input/output packets and octets for each identified host. At the end of an accounting interval, the network usage rate is calculated for each host using the formula presented in (1). Afterwards, hosts of each department are grouped and their network usage rates are added.

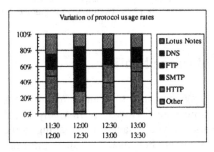

**Fig. 8.** Protocol distribution during a certain period

The graph in figure 9 was drawn based on object values collected in two different time instants. In this case, the resulting information reflects the peculiar situation of the network in that specific interval.

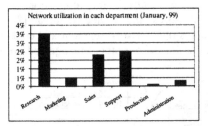

**Fig. 9.** Departmental network usage rates

Another possibility is to accomplish such measurements in several moments of the day, for several days, and to calculate the average of the obtained rates. This methodology provides the administrator with accurate information about network utilization in each department.

The type of information commented above can be decisive in cost allocation, once it helps the administrator to decide where to invest. In this context, the identification of the hosts that accomplish most of the accesses is also important. Such information can be found in *topN* tables from *network-layer matrix* group.

The *topN* tables provide an efficient way for a management station to obtain a ranked list of matrix table entries based on a chosen network statistic [2][7]. Again, a control table (*nlMatrixTopNControl*) and a data table (*nlMatrixTopN*) are used. Each entry in control table refers to a report under construction and has some configurable objects such as classification criterion (packets or octets) and sampling interval (in seconds).

Figure 10 illustrates the two mentioned tables. As one can see, there are two reports under construction. When the administrator requests the generation of a new report, he informs the probe how big it should be using the object *nlMatrixTopNControlRequestedSize*. The probe evaluates its resources (memory, processor) and, if not overloaded, accepts the administrator's solicitation. Otherwise, it arbitrarily informs him the number of entries it will admit (*nlMatrixTopNControlGrantedSize*). In figure 10, the first report has four entries.

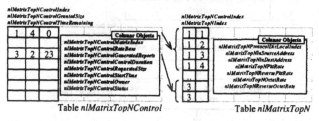

Table *nlMatrixTopNControl*        Table *nlMatrixTopN*

**Fig. 10.** *topN* tables from network-layer matrix group

It is important to highlight that the object *nlMatrixTopNControlTimeRemaining* denotes the time remaining for the next report to be ready. In figure 10, the first report has just been updated (*TimeRemaining=0*). As soon as the report is concluded, the probe automatically begins a new sampling period, whose duration is defined by the object *nlMatrixTopNControlControlDuration*.

Table 5 presents data retrieved from table *nlMatrixTopN*. These data make possible the creation of graphs as in figure 11, which shows the users who most consume network resources.

**Table 5.** Example of information retrieved from table *nlMatrixTopN*

| Protocol | Source Address | Dest Address | TopN PktRate | TopNReverse PktRate | TopN OctetRate | TopNReverse OctetRate |
|----------|----------------|--------------|--------------|---------------------|----------------|------------------------|
| 15 (ip/ethernet) | 172.16.108.12 | 172.16.108.1 | 213 | 32 | 40.065 | 6.023 |
| 15 (ip/ethernet) | 172.16.108.45 | 172.16.108.23 | 156 | 17 | 23.913 | 2.194 |
| 15 (ip/ethernet) | 172.16.106.25 | 200.248.252.1 | 89 | 29 | 12.882 | 6.745 |
| 15 (ip/ethernet) | 172.16.109.7 | 172.16.108.1 | 67 | 13 | 5.294 | 968 |

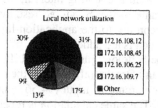

**Fig. 11.** Users who most consume network resources

# 5 Optimization of Users and Resources Distribution

An important contribution of RMON2 is the possibility to verify if users and resources are adequately positioned in the network in order to maximize traffic confinement in each department of the company [1]. The group that provides this information is application-layer matrix, previously presented in section 3.3. The procedure in figure 12 can be applied to optimize the location of users and resources.

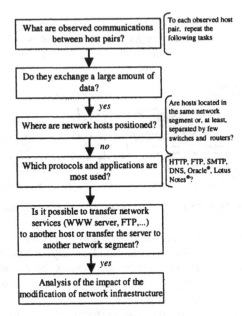

**Fig. 12.** Algorithm for optimization of users' and resources' location

In some cases, users and resources are appropriately positioned, minimizing traffic between different network segments. However, some resources may be overloaded, which affects the response times of protocols and applications. In such cases, load balancing is needed. To do that, the administrator must measure the usage rate of a certain resource. This information is provided by *application-layer matrix* group.

The methodology used to determine the current activities on a certain resource is the following. The probe counts input/output packets and octets for each identified host pair. The monitoring can be accomplished in two time intervals (instants $t_1$ and $t_2$) or periodically. At the end of an accounting interval, all the entries whose source or destination address is the same of the monitored resource are selected. The selected entries are then grouped according to the application-layer protocol. Afterwards, for each group the input/output octets are added.

Table 6 illustrates the methodology just presented. In the monitored resource, one can observe HTTP, SMTP and Oracle traffic. Thus, the rows can be arranged in three groups. In HTTP group, the number of input (34.567) and output (125.954) octets is added in instant $t_1$(160.521). The same calculation is repeated in instant $t_2$ (1.060.521). The amount of HTTP traffic observed on the resource is obtained by subtracting the result of the sum of input/output octets in instants $t_1$ and $t_2$. The same calculation must be accomplished in the other groups.

**Table 6.** Network activities on a certain host

| Source Address | Dest. Address | Protocol | Octets ($t_1$) | | Octets ($t_2$) | | $t_2$-$t_1$ |
|---|---|---|---|---|---|---|---|
| 172.16.108.12 | 172.16.108.1 | HTTP | 34.567 | 160.521 | 192.224 | 1.060.521 | 900.000 |
| 172.16.108.1 | 172.16.108.12 | HTTP | 125.954 | | 864.297 | | |
| 172.16.109.5 | 172.16.108.1 | SMTP | 37.234 | 58.123 | 220.211 | 314.123 | 256.000 |
| 172.16.108.1 | 172.16.109.5 | SMTP | 20.889 | | 93.912 | | |
| 172.16.108.12 | 172.16.108.1 | Oracle | 45.082 | 68.863 | 341.090 | 534.834 | 465.971 |
| 172.16.108.1 | 172.16.108.12 | Oracle | 23.781 | | 193.744 | | |

Figure 13 shows an example of a graph, depicting network activities on a network server host along the day.

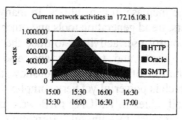

**Fig. 13.** Activities observed on a network server host

# 6 Security Management

Security is an essential issue to corporate networks. Nowadays, more and more mechanisms such as firewalls have been incorporated into the network in order to keep intruders away from strategic data of the company [7].

RMON2 can be used as a tool to detect the presence of intruders in the network. As already presented, the *application-layer matrix* group shows host pairs that are communicating (see section 3.3). Therefore, if the administrator periodically monitors this group, he can identify non-authorized users trying to establish communications with network hosts. It is also important to observe the protocol being used. Depending on the security policies of the company, a telnet may represent an attempt to invade the corporate network.

When a suspicious network address is observed, one can start capturing packets generated from this host and analyze the network operations that it is executing. This operation is supported by *capture group* from RMON MIB.

The graph in figure 14 shows the users that are accessing a certain resource. It is adequate to monitor strategic hosts where database, www and mail servers reside. The graph is generated with information retrieved from *application-layer matrix* group.

In some cases, it may be useful to identify which protocols each observed user executes. This information can be obtained in *alHost* group, already presented in section 3.2. Figure 15 shows an example of a graph that can be generated with the retrieved data.

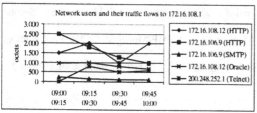

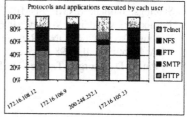

**Fig. 14.** Users and their traffic flows to a certain host    **Fig. 15.** Protocols executed by hosts

# 7 Conclusions

RMON2 represents a huge increase in capabilities. In many cases, its functionalities supplant protocol analyzers, trend generation tools and other [3]. This paper presented how to use this MIB to control user activities, to trace the network usage profile, to optimize the location of users and resources and also to accomplish security management. The contribution of this work is to show the administrator how to benefit from this MIB, which is powerful yet very complex.

Some of the objects and tables in RMON2 MIB were designed so that a simple display of their contents provides meaningful information. Most of them, however, must be organized in easy-to-view formats; otherwise they are of little use. Depending on the company investments on network technology, it is not always possible to buy management applications, which do treat such information and automatically convert it to charts and other diagrams. In this context, this work helps network managers to create their own management applications. Through *script* languages or high-level management libraries, it is possible to develop systems adapted to the company's needs without many investments.

The authors believe that RMON2 based solutions may be applied in other scenes such as ISPs. However, the huge amount of information that the probes need to handle requires the use of powerful monitoring devices. Even so, in situation of heavy network load existent probes have faced problems to accurately count the packets observed in the network [8].

# References

1. Engel, Fred. Application Behavior and Statistics through RMON2. In Third IEEE International Workshop on Systems Management. New Port, Rhode Island, April 22-24, 1998
2. Waldbusser, S. Remote Network Monitoring Management Information Base Version 2 using SMIv2. Request for Comments 2021, January 1997
3. Gaspary, Luciano. Study on RMON2 Standard. Individual Work. Porto Alegre: Federal University of Rio Grande do Sul, 1998
4. Waldbusser, S. Remote Network Monitoring Management Information Base. Request for Comments 1757, 1995
5. Ulbrich, Luís Roberto. Active Remote Monitoring. Individual Work. Porto Alegre: Federal University of Rio Grande do Sul, 1997
6. Stallings, William. SNMP, SNMPV2 and RMON. Practical Network Management. Second Edition. USA: Addison Wesley, 1996
7. Perkins, David T. RMON - Remote Monitoring of SNMP-Managed LANs. First Edition. USA: Prentice Hall, 1998
8. Newman, D.; Giorgis, T.; Melson, B. Probing RMON2. Data Communications (May 21, 1998)

# Derivation of Backup Service Management Applications from Service and System Models

Ingo Lück [1], Marcus Schönbach [1], Arnulf Mester [1], Heiko Krumm [2]

[1] Dr. Materna GmbH, Voßkuhle 37, D-44141 Dortmund, Germany
{Ingo.Lueck|Marcus.Schoenbach|Arnulf.Mester}@materna.de
[2] FB Informatik, LS IV, Universität Dortmund, D-44221 Dortmund, Germany
krumm@cs.uni-dortmund.de

**Abstract.** The backup of large data sets is preferably performed automatically outside of regular working hours. In highly structured computer networks, however, faults and exceptions may relatively frequently occur resulting in unsuccessful subprocesses. Therefore automated fault and configuration management is of interest. We report on a corresponding management system. Besides of monitoring and information provision it performs automated fault analysis and recovery functions under extension of the service management approach to the function-oriented management of information processing services. Moreover, it is model-based. An interactively constructed object-oriented model specifies management objectives and represents dependencies between the backup service provided and the services used. Moreover, the model is input to the derivation of the management application code. Thus, the combination of service management and modeling supports the productive development of automated management applications. The system is implemented on the basis of the Java Dynamic Management Kit and performs the management of a commercial network backup system in a heterogeneous environment.

**Keywords.** model-based management, IT-service management, derivation of management systems, model-based development of management systems

## 1. Introduction

The notion of service management firstly occurred in the field of telecommunication network management as an answer to the growing complexity of networks and the user demand for a broad and flexible spectrum of high-quality services. It introduces an abstract and user-oriented view which complements the traditional resource-centered management and provides a common and technology-independent context for component management [Hal96]. Meanwhile, not only telecommunication but also information processing organizations were subject to a shift from technology provision to service provision. The users now start to demand more than technology-dependent best-effort support of few applications. The services of applications and their availability, performance, security, and reliability needs shall be addressed by so-called service level agreements. The business users want to rely upon application services as tools supporting their mission within the enterprise. The information processing organization shall achieve and maintain the agreed service levels by means of service-oriented management measures forming the so-called IT-service management [Mcb98] which presently can be supported by service monitoring, reporting, and capacity planning tools (e.g., [Haw98]).

Future application management systems, however, shall have a high degree of automation and shall preferably perform more than only monitoring and performance management operations. The notion of IT-services complies with both requirements. IT-services define abstract and user-oriented objectives of automated management which are not restricted to quantity-oriented operations for accounting, performance management, and quality of service control but also can guide the more function-oriented operations of configuration, fault, and security management. Nevertheless, function-oriented management operations are relatively specific. They mostly depend not only on the services provided and on the services used but also to a certain extent on the available resources and the dependencies between resources, services, exceptions, and faults. Due to the broad variety of business-near application services, therefore, an extensive set of tailored components for the automated management is needed and special support for the productive management component development is of interest.

Our work represents one promising step into the direction of productive development of management systems for automated and function-rich management of IT-services. It consists of two parts. In principle, we propose a model-based development approach. In a practical case study, we applied the approach to an enterprise-wide backup service. The model-based development starts with an abstract model of the services to be provided which is directly oriented at the job definitions of the backup service system. In fact, the initial model is mechanically derived from the job definitions. Thereafter, it is interactively refined by the introduction of the services used, of the resources, and of the dependencies between. The resulting detailed model is finally subject to the generation of management components. In this way, a powerful design and development support is realizable which moreover may in the future be improved by supplying pre-defined generic model elements. The practical case study achieves the automated fault and configuration management of enterprise-wide distributed and heterogeneous backup services (moreover, performance management and capacity planning functions are integrated). We chose backup services, since on the one hand, of course, backup services are more basic and less specific than business-oriented applications. They therefore seemed to be more appropriate for experimentation with a new approach. On the other hand there was a real needs to automate the operation of nightly backup processes which have to copy large data sets in a highly structured network under the presence of faults and exceptions.

In more detail, backups are performed by a commercial network-based backup system [Leg97]. The management system is distributed and based on the Java Dynamic Management Kit J-DMK [Jdm98]. Management agents reside in the client and server hosts of the backup system. They forward notifications and operating system information to the manager. Moreover, they can influence and restart components of the backup service and of the used services. The manager – derived from the model definition by a modeler tool – installs and configures the agents by means of J-DMK-functions. It communicates with its agents via events and remote method invocations. Before the establishment of this management system problems occurred which caused incomplete operation of backup processes. Mostly used services (e.g., domain name servers) were not available. Moreover, sometimes backup demons on client hosts had to be restarted. Now the introduced manager monitors the state of the necessary system services. It reacts on problem notifications by automated recovery of used services, by restarts of backup demons, and by repetitions of backup processes leading to a decrease of incomplete backups. Moreover, it provides detailed and pre-processed information for non-automated fault-management measures.

Our model-based approach for the definition of management objectives and for the derivation of the manager code is related to several existing approaches. So, in the sequel we first give an overview over the usage of models for management systems. Thereafter we outline the backup service to be managed in more detail. The next section presents the modeling and is followed by a description of the production of the manager. Finally we sketch the implemented system and note down concluding remarks.

## 2. Model-Based Management

Meanwhile many management approaches are based on explicit model notions resulting in a variety of modeling techniques and applications. In order to relate our approach to this existing work, we provide a short general classification of model-based management. Moreover this gives an overview and may help to identify further directions of model applications. Before, we shortly outline the use of models in the field of general software development which basically influences the design of management systems.

As Booch, Rumbaugh, and Jacobson point out in connection with their proposal of the unified modeling language UML [Uml97], models simplify reality and support the concentration on essentials, thus facilitating understanding and design. They devote UML to the modeling of systems under development. Several diagram types correspond to submodel types serving for the description of different aspects of structures and behaviors with the objective of visualizing, specifying, constructing, and documenting designs. Besides of UML, other models, like workflow process models [War94], development process models [Gra95], data base and information system models [Ere92], communication protocol and process behavior models [Tur93], as well as very specialized models of certain application-domains (e.g., system theoretic models of control loops in real-time systems) are in use. In general, models may reflect aspects of system development at all or of systems and their embedding on their own describing requirements, system structures, data schemes, system architectures, or functions and behaviors. They may aim at description and documentation supporting the understanding of humans, at conception of machine-processable implementation parts, or at specification of man-machine interfaces. Models may also exceed description and provide for explicit means of human or mechanical reasoning. They may be in use at design time, at compile / application generation time, or at runtime.

In the field of automated management, models may serve for specialized purposes and may concentrate on special functional areas (e.g., FCAPS, change or service management). Models may support typical development tasks (e.g., system analysis resulting in requirements and policies as well as design and implementation resulting in specifications, code modules, administration and modification schemes) or direct operation by maintaining structured system information and providing corresponding notions (e.g., for representation and processing of monitoring and audit information or for documentation and handling of changes or troubles). Models may be related to integral views of a system as a whole (e.g., the sum of service provisions) or they may focus on components like the managed system, the management system, or parts of them (e.g., certain managed objects, some agents). They may concentrate on static structures, on dynamic functional behavior, or on performance and quality of service properties. On a high abstraction level models may reflect corporate strategies. On a lower level tactical relations of certain management domains may be modeled, while more detailed models may focus on operational elements.

From the utilization point of view, following modes of model application are of main interest:

- *Specifications for system development*
  Static information models of managed objects define the scheme of the management information base MIB. This early and widely applied approach [Mib91, Gdm92] is the starting point of many extensions and improvements. So, extended MIBs can serve as basis for the definition of management policies [Wie94]. The more recent approach of the common information model CIM supports unified views for the integral management of complex and heterogeneous IT-environments [Cim98].
- *Formal specifications*
  Formal models as they are described by formal specifications can support rigorous design analysis and verification. Moreover the models can be used for the generation of test cases (e.g., based on Z-specifications of managed objects [Fer97]).
- *Design by model refinement*
  The stepwise refinement of models can coincide with the refining design of system parts (e.g., refining transformation of policies in [Wie95]).
- *Analysis and Checks*
  Models and model-based reasoning techniques can support the analysis of management systems under development (e.g., detection of conflicts in policy sets [Lup97]).
- *Simulations of system elements*
  Model-based simulations can substitute parts of a real system in order to support early tests [Lun96].
- *Prototypes and animations*
  Besides of simulation for the purpose of testing, animated man-machine interfaces and prototypical function implementations may be of interest in order to support communication with customers and staff training.
- *System generation*
  Implementation elements can be generated from model definitions. So, [Enj96] and [Hei96] derive code from models statically. Furthermore, the common MIB-compiler tools translating information schemes into code stubs have to be mentioned here.
- *Runtime functions*
  Explicit model representations which are interpreted at runtime can contribute to the implementation of management functions. [Sab97] translates constraint models into code of diagnostic functions for network fault management. [Ohs97] applies

descriptions of event models for automated event correlation. [Kae97] traverses fault propagation models at runtime in order correlate events and isolate faults. [Rod97] calculates the availability of applications from attributed service dependency graphs.

- *Adaptive models*
  Model adaptation at runtime – well-known in real-time control systems – may also be of interest for future management systems. On one hand, model adaptations can reflect system changes, on the other, the model quality may be enhanced by model improvements which utilize runtime feedback information.

Combinations of different modes of model application may be possible. So our approach for model-based backup service management constructs an object-oriented model at design time which serves for the specification of management objectives and for the description of the managed system. Moreover, at compile time application code is derived from this model. Like [Rod97] the model describes the service provided, the different services used, and the dependencies between. As in [Kae97], the model information supports the localization of faults and the selection of appropriate recovery procedures.

## 3. Backup Service and Management

A backup-service is a client / server - architecture based service, that is responsible for saving and restoring local and remote data in a distributed environment.

There are two basic backup mechanisms. A full backup is a complete copy of all the data to be saved, whereas an incremental backup copies that data only that have been changed since the last backup process. In general, backup copies can be produced with or without compression and with or without verification of the copied data on the backup medium (e.g., tape, optical disk). A schedule lays down when which type of backup copy has to be made. If restoration of data is needed the time it takes depends on the type of backup copies that are available. Restoring from a full backup is relatively fast in contrast to the case where several incremental backup sets have to be taken into consideration. A backup application is often a distributed program. On the one hand there can be many different hosts (backup-clients in this context) that do not have a backup device of their own but manage data to be saved. On the other hand there can exist a series of backup-servers that receive client data over the net and save it to connected backup devices.

The backup-service consists of two parts, one part creates the backups, the other performs restoration. Quality parameters are reliability, backup creation speed, restore speed, and complete automation (e.g., no manual change of backup media should be needed). Complete automation is especially important for the backup creation, because this is often done outside of regular working hours – mostly at night – when there is minimal other load on data network and hosts. The success of all actions of the backup-service should be documented in a log-file with corresponding reasons if unsuccessful. Furthermore the backup-service should support heterogeneous environments and should be scaleable.

There are various services used by the backup-system. A backup-server uses backup-devices as well as the CPU, memory and the hard disks of its host system.

Domain name servers are used to resolve IP-addresses. The network is used to transfer control and backup data. On a client-host the CPU and memory are used by the backup-client process (e.g., for data compression). The hard disk may be used for a local index-database. The quality of these services (e.g., CPU usage, memory usage, domain name server availability, network throughput and error rate) influences the quality of the backup-service.

Legato-Networker, the backup system we use in our implementation, knows four types of physical components: backup-devices, servers, interfaces (network-interfaces that are available in server-hosts) and clients [Leg97]. Additionally, there are some logical elements supporting definition and management of backup-services. Backup-groups are used to form groups of clients with comparable backup requirements. Schedules are assigned to single clients or to save-groups. They document at what time or period what type of backup should be created. Label-templates define patterns for the generation of names (labels) for backup-media. Volume pools allow the assignment of backup-data (determined by backup-group, client, and / or backup-type) to particular backup-media and document if entries to the client's index-databases should be made. Policies mainly determine how long data in the media- and index-database are stored. Moreover, directives can state special procedures for particular files. Finally event notifications have to be mentioned. They are generated to transmit state and error messages to specified destinations.

For the management of the Legato-Networker backup service we identified the following functional requirements: fault detection, isolation and logs, fault tolerance measures (backup process recovery, reconfiguration of used services), performance monitoring and capacity planning, as well as convenient graphical presentations of log information (events, event reactions, performance and status data).

## 4. Backup System Model

The model has to meet the following list of requirements. Appropriate representation of service level agreement is needed. Additionally the model has to support monitoring of the quality level at runtime. By that, assessment of service quality is enabled. Documentation is another important task. So, documentation of the configuration has to be supported for the backup service provided (e.g., save-groups, schedules, policies) as well as for the services used (e.g., which domain name server is used by a host). Furthermore relations between service components among themselves (e.g., schedules related to save-groups) and relations between service components and services used (e.g., assignment of backup-servers to hosts) have to be modeled. The fundamental requirement on the model is that the management application can be derived from it automatically. Finally fault detection, isolation and recovery has to be supported at runtime (e.g., if address resolution fails the corresponding domain name server has to be checked and possibly be restarted).

In order to meet this broad spectrum of requirements we use an object-oriented model, since even highly-structured domains can be represented in an easy-to-survey and flexibly extendable way. Moreover, dependencies and links can be represented by associations and runtime functions can be introduced by method implementations in a straight-forward way. The object classes used in our model are grouped in three packages as shown in Fig. 1 The *Service Model* package contains a class for every logical element supporting definition and management of backup-services. Additionally there are some classes that are used for service quality assessment. The *Service Level Agreement* class uses *Assessment Scales* to map service quality onto comparable states (i.e., OK, warning, critical). The physical components known by the backup-system are represented by classes in the *System Model* package. For interfaces and devices *Performance Measurements* are taken that can be viewed by administrators of the backup-services for analysis purpose. The *Services Used* package contains in addition to the *Services* themselves also *Service Configurations* (e.g., the amount of memory available in a host), *Service States* (e.g., memory usage for a host) and *Fault Detection Logs* (if for example a domain name server has to be restarted this action is documented). Except for the *Services* of the *Services Used* package all classes of the model are represented by Java classes. So, a model is built of Java object instances.

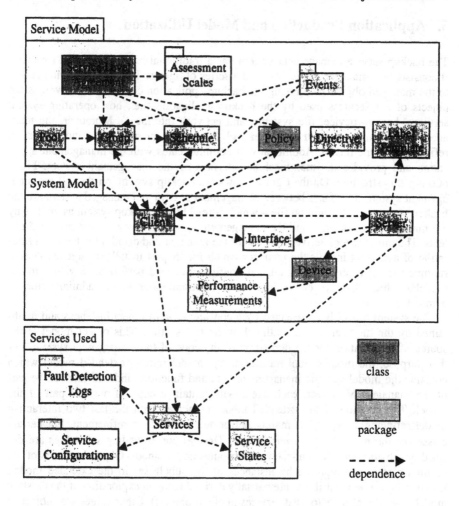

**Fig. 1.** UML package diagram of the model

The generation of the model for a given backup service is supported by a modeler tool and performed in four steps. At first the tool evaluates the backup system's configuration file. It generates and initializes most of the required object instances automatically. Secondly, the services used and the underlying resources are introduced. Here, the tool supports the guided interactive refinement of the model. The administrator can browse on the existing model and activate dialogs which create model objects and set attribute values and links. Thirdly, some *Services* of the *Services Used* package need detailed manual configuration. The SNMP-service for instance needs a port-number and a community-string to be set. Finally, some parameters of the management system may be adjusted manually (e.g., length of intervals for taking measurements, communication-protocol and port-numbers to be used for manager-agent communication).

## 5.  Application Production and Model Utilization

The backup service management system has a traditional basic component structure. It consists of a manager application and a series of agents. The agents provide access to the managed objects comprising the backup application components as well as the objects of the services used by the backup application (i.e., host operating system services, backup device, file systems, and network interfaces). Moreover, the management systems contains the modeler tool. It supports the generation and interactive refinement of the model. Additionally, it communicates with the management application and provides the man-machine interface of the management system. Fig. 2 outlines this structure. On the right it shows the backup system, on the left the management system. Interfaces between management system and managed system are the backup system's configuration file – which is read by the backup system as well as by the management system – and the management agents' accesses to the managed objects. The modeler tool derives the code of the manager and decides the basic configuration of agents. It installs the manager which for its part installs the agents. During runtime the manager forwards current configuration and performance values to the modeler which displays convenient status representations to the administrator on demand.

The system model is represented by a configuration of object instances and maintained by the modeler tool as outlined in the last section. This object model is the source of information for the derivation of the code of the management system. For that purpose, the modeler tool transforms the model into an extended model which contains the model-specific management data and functions and will later on be part of the manager. Moreover, each agent will contain a copy of a small part of the model. The creation of the extended model coincides with the last two interactive model refinement steps. It is mainly performed by subclass refinement. For certain classes of the model (e.g., *Group, Client, Device*) corresponding subclasses are defined which add management-relevant attributes and methods. Object instances of the original classes are replaced by instances of the subclasses in the extended model. Initial values of new attributes are partially derived from an exploration of the existing model (e.g., direct links to used services in client objects). Other values are subject of interaction with the administrator (e.g., port-numbers and protocols to be used). The new methods directly perform management functions (e.g., installation and initialization of agents, fault isolation and recovery). Thus, the main parts of the manager application are supplied by the extended model. Moreover, the application code only contains a fixed frame and definitions of basic auxiliary classes. During runtime, the manager application maintains the extended model and updates status and performance attributes of its objects.

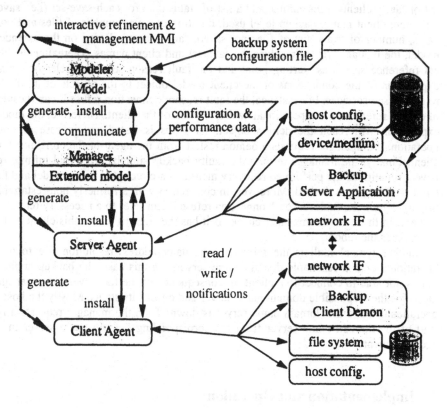

**Fig. 2.** Overview over management system and managed system

The subclass *ManagedClient* of the model class *Client* shall exemplify the refinement of the extended model. The attributes of *Client* mainly comprise lists of devices, save-groups and save-sets, configuration descriptions, and finally links to backup server, server interface, schedule, browse policy, retention policy, and save directives. The methods of *Client* perform reading and writing of data attributes, generation of graphical data representations, and creation of object copies. The subclass *Managed-Client* adds links to the used services (i.e., client-, network-, demon-, and SNMP-service), to the measurement scheduler, and to the agent frame. Moreover, data attributes represent the IP-address of the client and serve for the management of measurement timestamps. The methods manage and access the client's measurement scheduler, retrieve and restart the client's domain name server and backup demon, and finally reset measurement containers.

One important usage of the extended model is the service-oriented fault management. The handling of a negative save-group notification shall serve as corresponding example. Let the notification be created by the backup server application and received by the server agent of the management system. Then, the agent transforms the notification into a Java event and forwards it to the manager which is listed as event listener. The event mainly carries the name of the save-group, the number of clients, a list of faulty clients, timestamps, and a list of status data for each save-set (i.e., save-set name, client name, backup level used, duration of save, number of files and volumes, number of trials, list of files not saved, fault reason). Based on the extended model, the manager firstly resolves the save-set and client names. Thereafter the client reference serves as starting point and the fault reason serves as selector for an exploration of the connections of the client model object to the objects of the fault-relevant used services. For instance, the fault reason 'connection refused' can (besides of others) refer to a non-operational backup demon of the client. Therefore, the model exploration will reach the demon object. Its status is tested and in case of non-operation, the manager requests a demon restart from the agent of the corresponding client. Finally, the manager restarts the faulty backup subjobs. To avoid infinite recovery repetitions the performed recovery measures are recorded in the model and the number of retries is limited. Moreover, in connection with a formerly non-restartable backup demon the fault reason 'connection refused' can refer to a necessary reboot of a client. In this case the manager checks if it has the right to reboot this client and if so, initiates the reboot.

Another typical fault is the failing of the name/address-resolution due to non-operational or non-reachable domain name servers. In this case, the backup application is not able to connect to a client. In consequence of the fault event, the manager identifies the responsible domain name server and checks its status. Mostly the host is operational while the domain name server is down. Then the manager requests a restart of the domain name server from the corresponding domain name server management agent.

## 6. Implementation and Operation

The backup management system is implemented on the basis of the Java Dynamic Management Kit J-DMK [Jdm98] which applies the Java Bean component model [Bea98] in order to support flexible agents. Agent data structures and function implementations can be implemented by explicit and lately bindable code components, the so-called Beans. During runtime, agents can pull necessary Beans from a server or managers can push Beans to agents. The Beans act as runtime plugins and dynamically extend the agent's functionality. There are Beans implementing supporting services (like Core Management, Repository, SNMP-Communication). Moreover, so-called M-Beans implement management functions and the local access to managed objects (e.g., Backup Client Bean, Operating System Bean, Network Interface Bean).

Fig. 3 gives an overview over the J-DMK-based implementation. After the interactive definition of the model, the modeler produces serialized external forms of the manager and of the necessary agent Beans. After installation and start of the manager, it creates the necessary agents (one for each host) and establishes communication connections to them. Finally, it pushes to each agent the corresponding set of Beans.

The Bean set depends on the type of the host (backup client or server, type of operating system and network connection).

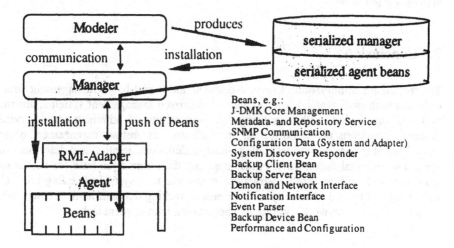

Fig. 3. J-DMK-based implementation

The whole management system – consisting of modeler, manager and agents – is implemented by approx. 400 Java classes (additionally, there are approx. 80 BeanInfo classes). The summed up length of the class files results in approx. 1.4 MB. The serialized form of the model needs about 20 KB per client host. The model-dependent parts of the manager need about 8 KB per client. The supply of model information to an agent has only to transfer about 9KB of serialized model substructures. The total byte code length of the components is: modeler approx. 1.4 MB, manager approx. 800 KB, server agent approx. 550 KB, client agent approx. 450 KB.

The management system operates in a local computer network which consists of approx. 120 backup client computers with various operating systems (i.e., Solaris, SunOS, HP-UX, Sinix, SCO, AIX, Windows NT). Backups are performed by one backup server which meanwhile is connected with an 500 GB DLT drive. Each night about 30 MB backup data are copied where full backups are achieved for approx. 6 clients (approx. 12 GB). Before the introduction of the backup management system mainly following faults caused unsuccessful subjobs:

- Failing name/address-resolution due to unavailable domain name servers (approx. 5 per month),
- Access conflicts to Network File System volumes due to incorrect mounts (approx. 10 per month, owing to a recent update of the backup application software now also most of these exceptions can successfully be handled by the backup application on its own),
- Backup demons on client hosts are unreachable or not operational (approx. 2 per month),
- Total client breakdowns (approx. 1 per month).

Now, the described backup service management system supports recovery for nearly all of the occurring faults resulting in a rate of unsuccessful backup subjobs of only approx. 1.5 per month.

# 7. Conclusion

We proposed a combination of service-oriented and model-based management which complies with two essential requirements of improved management systems, abstraction and automation, both enhancing the productivity of administrators. Service-orientation supports the identification and definition of abstract management objectives. Modeling supports the technology-independent consideration and description of application-internal dependencies thus supplying the information base for automated management functions. Both abstractions contribute to easy understanding and help administrators to deal efficiently with extended working domains as they result from modern integrated network, system, and application management tasks.

# References

[Bea98] Sun Microsystems: Java Beans Specification; Sun Microsystems Inc., Palo Alto, 1998, available via http://java.sun.com/beans/docs/spec.html

[Cim98] Desktop Management Taskforce: Common Information Model - Specification 2.0; Desktop Management Taskforce Inc. DMTF, 1998, available via http://www.dmtf.org/spec/

[Eji96] M. Ejiri, S. Goyal (eds.): Proc. of the IEEE/IFIP Int. Symposium on Network Operations and Management NOMS'96, IEEE, 1996

[Enj96] A. Enjou, M. Tomobe: The Software Synthesis of Network Management Systems; in [Eji96], pg. 414-433, 1996

[Ere92] C. Batini, S. Ceri, S. Navathe: Conceptual Database Design - An Entity-Relationship Approach; Benjamin, Cummings, 1992

[Fer97] G. Fernandez, J. Derrick; Formal Specification and Testing of a Management Architecture; in [Laz97], pg. 473-484, 1997

[Gdm92] ISO / ITU-CCITT: Information Technology - Open Systems Interconnection - Structure of Management Information: Guidelines for the Definition of Managed Objects (GDMO); ISO-IEC IS 10165-4 also ITU/CCITT Recommendation X.722, 1992

[Gra95] G. Graw, V. Gruhn: Process Management in-the-Many; in: W. Schäfer (ed.) Software Process Technology, Proc. of the 4th European Software Process Modeling Workshop, Springer-Verlag, LNCS 913, pg. 163-178, 1995

[Hal96] J. Hall (ed.): Management of Telecommunication Systems and Services; LNCS 1116, Springer-Verlag, Berlin, 1996

[Haw98] M. Haworth: Service Management and Availability Planning for Data Backup and Recovery; HP Open View Service Management Solutions, White paper, Hewlett-Packard Company, Palo Alto, 1998

[Hei96] K. Heiler, R. Wies: Policy Driven Configuration Management of Network Devices; in [Eji96], pg. 674-689, 1996

[Jdm98] Sun Microsystems: Java Dynamic Management Kit; Sun Microsystems Inc., Palo Alto, 1998, available via http://www.sun.com/software/java-dynamic/

[Kae97] S. Kätker, M. Paterok: Fault Isolation and Event Correlation for Integrated Fault Management; in [Laz97], pg. 583-596, 1997

[Laz97]   A. Lazar et al. (eds.): Integrated Network Management V, Proc. 5th IFIP/IEEE Int. Symposium on Integrated Network Management, Chapman & Hall, London, 1997

[Leg97]   Legato NetWorker: The Key to High-Performance, Scaleable Storage Management; White paper, Legato Inc., Palo Alto, 1997, available via ftp://www.legato.com/legato/marcom/pdf/W008.html

[Lun96]   A. Lundqvist, T. Grönberg: Network management simulators; in [Eji96], pg. 552-562, 1996

[Lup97]   E. Lupu, M. Sloman: Conflict Analysis for Management Policies; in [Laz97], pg. 430-443, 1997

[Mcb98]   D. McBride: Successful Deployment of IT Service Management in the Distributed Enterprise; White paper, Hewlett-Packard Company, Palo Alto, 1998

[Mib91]   M. Rose, K. McCloghrie: Concise MIB Definitions; Internet Request for Comments RFC 1212, (1991)

[Ohs97]   D. Ohsie, A. Maier, S. Kliger, S. Yemini: Event Modeling with the MODEL Language; in [Laz97], pg. 625-637, 1997

[Rod97]   G. Rodosek, T. Kaiser: Determining the Availability of Distributed Applications; in [Laz97], pg. 207-218, 1997

[Sab97]   M. Sabin, R. Russel, E. Freuder: Generating Diagnostic Tools for Network Fault Management; in [Laz97], pg. 700-711, 1997

[Tur93]   K. Turner (ed.): Using Formal Description Techniques - An Introduction to Estelle, Lotos and SDL; John Wiley, New York, 1993

[Uml97]   G. Booch, J. Rumbaugh, I. Jacobson: The Unified Modeling Language User Guide; Addison-Wesley, Reading, 1997

[War94]   B. Warboys: Reflections on the Relationships Between BPR and Software Process Modeling; in P. Loucopoulos (ed.), Proc. 13th Int. Conf. on the Entity-Relationship Approach, Springer-Verlag, LNCS 881, pg. 1-9, 1994

[Wie94]   R. Wies: Policies in Network and Systems Management - Formal Definition and Architecture; Journal of Network and Systems Management, 2,1(1994)63-83

[Wie95]   R. Wies: Using a Classification of Management Policies for Policy Specification and Policy Transformation; in Proc. of the 4th IFIP/IEEE Int. Symposium on Integrated Network Management, Santa Barbara, 1995

# A Framework for the Integration of Legacy Devices into a Jini Management Federation

Gerd Aschemann, Svetlana Domnitcheva, Peer Hasselmeyer,
Roger Kehr, and Andreas Zeidler

Darmstadt University of Technology
Department of Computer Science
{aschemann,domnitcheva,peer,kehr,az}@informatik.tu-darmstadt.de

**Abstract.** The administration of heterogeneous networks with many devices is a tedious and time-consuming task. Today's approaches only provide static configuration files and make the addition and removal of devices a manual chore. In this paper we present a framework for the integration of legacy devices based on *Jini*, Sun Microsystem's new technology for federating network devices and services. We introduce extended proxy objects called *nannies* that take care of non-Jini-enabled devices and handle the relevant management events, guide a device through bootstrapping, register it with the lookup service, and provide the implementation of the administrative interfaces of the Jini API. Through this approach both Jini-enabled and legacy devices can be handled homogeneously in a *Jini Management Federation*.

## 1 Introduction

The management of networks and distributed systems is a difficult task that is complicated by the heterogeneity and huge number of legacy devices and protocols in use today. Standardized management architectures, such as the Internet management, i.e., SNMP [3], or the ISO/OSI management model [13] are steps in the right direction, but do not provide for flexible integration and removal of typical devices, e.g., printers, X-terminals, or laptops in a LAN environment. In particular, initial bootstrapping of devices, management of IP addresses, and use, administration, and shut-down of a new device are not handled in an integrated and flexible manner.

We illustrate this point with the daily life-cycle of a typical network printer. For normal operation of the printer an IP address must be assigned and it must be configured appropriately. The IP address is either known by the printer, e.g., through manual configuration, or it can be assigned dynamically, e.g., by DHCP [6] or BOOTP [9] from a pool of IP addresses. An appropriate server assigns an IP address, a host name, and some other parameters to the booting device. Additionally it may refer to other services, e.g., TFTP [14], where the device will find further files for download, like fonts, profiles, or kernels. Printers are usually assigned to a spool service for queueing print jobs, which also notifies the users about successfully finished print jobs. The management system obtains information about the device status through a management protocol, e.g., SNMP, and provides it to management applications or for visualization purposes.

Theoretically, a printer reports to the DHCP service to release its IP address at shutdown. In practice, the device is often turned off without disposing of the address, thus keeping the address allocated until the DHCP lease times out.

Taking the DHCP server as an example, we illustrate the drawbacks of this approach in general. The server tries to perform several tasks: it implements the protocol engine, dynamically binds IP addresses and optionally other parameters to network devices by a hard-coded policy, and guarantees durability of these bindings. Generally it relies on a priori knowledge of the specific devices to be configured and is only flexible to some degree in the address it finally assigns. The configuration is manually edited and can contain references to additional services, e.g., TFTP or SLP [20], but does not care whether these services are set up or properly configured. Finally, the services are usually not embedded in an appropriate management environment, such as an SNMP-enabled management platform. Due to this lack of integration, manual intervention is often required by the system administrator.

Jini is a recently released network infrastructure from Sun Microsystems that enables arbitrary federations of distributed services. Thus, it can be utilized to allow for better integration of tailored management components. In particular, Jini is quite appealing for bootstrapping and integrated configuration management of devices. However, Jini is primarily conceived to function with Jini-enabled devices and ignores the vast pool of legacy devices currently in use. In this paper we present a framework that makes it possible to bring non-Jini-enabled devices into the Jini world.

In Sect. 2 we give a short overview of Jini. Section 3 presents a vision of how non-Jini devices can be integrated. In particular, we address problems of bootstrapping and configuration management. Section 4 introduces the proposed architecture while Sect. 5 illustrates its use with a concrete example. Section 6 discusses related work and Sect. 7 presents our conclusions and an outline of future work.

## 2  Jini

Jini is a recently released network infrastructure from Sun Microsystems and seems to be very appealing – if used appropriately – for the task of bootstrapping and managing devices in an integrated manner.

**Bootstrapping.** Part of the bootstrap-phase of a native Jini-device is straightforward and a "built-in"-feature of all Jini-devices: Jini-enabled devices or services announce themselves in the local *federation* of services. Devices find and register with lookup services [19] using the *Jini Discovery and Join Protocol* [18]. Running these protocols currently requires a device to implement at least a TCP/IP stack, a Java Virtual Machine (JVM), and it must be initially configured with an IP address.

Bootstrapping a non-Jini-device is more complicated and discussed in greater detail throughout the following sections. In this section we want to discuss the Jini building blocks that contribute to management as a whole and give a hint why we put great effort into *masquerading* legacy devices as some kind of native Jini-devices.

**Jini and Management.** From a management perspective the lookup service is the central starting point for management activities. The lookup service interface allows Java listener objects to register for notifications about newly available services. The registration and notification follows the *observer* design pattern [8].

New services that have not yet been configured announce themselves in the so-called *public* group. Administrators then configure these new services according to their local policy.

Basically, configuring a Jini device consists of configuring information relevant to the Jini federation: groups the device should be subscribed to, entries the device is registered with in the lookup service, the device's service identifier, and so on. This is part of the federation management in Jini.

Essentially, Jini contributes to management with the following four features:

- **Lookup Service.** The lookup service acts as a central repository for services. Appropriate means are offered to query and select services based on interfaces, entry types, and entry values. Some aspects of the lookup service are comparable to the CORBA Trading Object Service [12].
- **Proxy Objects.** Services upload serialized Java objects called proxies to the lookup service. These objects can be downloaded to any JVM and invoked to access the service. The proxy acts as a mediator to the service itself, and may implement programmatic interfaces as well as graphical user front-ends for the service. The proxy encapsulates any protocol used for the actual communication between the proxy object and the service.
- **Notification Mechanism.** All services are required to register with the lookup service and – at least in principle – any Java object can register to be notified about changes in the set of services within a lookup service. This makes it possible to implement almost any mechanism to perform management activities on top of Jini.
- **Leases.** Leases are time-based contracts between two objects within Jini. A lease grantor can bind a service to a lease holder for a certain amount of time. The lease holder can use the granted service within this period according to the contract made, but has to renew the interest for the service granted, i.e., renew the lease before it expires. Failing to do so automatically cancels the contract. As any Jini service has to lease its entry in the lookup service, the lease renewal can be used as a *heartbeat*-mechanism and contributes to the robustness of the distributed system as a whole.

## 3   A Vision of a Jini-Enabled Management Federation

One of our criticisms of traditional management systems is their monolithic and inflexible nature. In contrast to this, Jini offers an infrastructure that makes it possible to restructure management services as aggregations of special purpose components. Thus, it allows for a complete separation of concerns. We use this approach to split up the management services into small components, each tailored for a single purpose. In our approach, DHCP is reduced to a protocol engine. Assigning addresses and other parameters is left to a configuration service.

With Jini such discovery and embedding is available for Jini-enabled devices, even though a dynamic low level configuration (at least the assignment of an IP address) is beyond the scope of Jini. We show how the appropriate properties of Jini can be utilized to provide even such low level configuration and to better integrate non-Jini devices. Therefore, we introduce the term *Jini management federation* by extending the term *Jini service federation*.

A Jini management federation is a loosely coupled group of services which enable distributed administration of other managed services. These services need not necessarily be Jini services. Jini management services could be almost any services which are normally provided by management platforms, such as databases and repositories (inventory, network topology, configuration, etc.), protocol engines (SNMP, CMIP [4], etc.), monitoring tools, or generic user interfaces. As with all other Jini services, the management services need not be native Java services or Jini services but only be encapsulated by appropriate proxy objects. For the main scope of this paper – bootstrapping and initial configuration – the following services are particularly important:

- **Configuration Service.** A configuration service would provide configuration information to other services, by means of a standardized, but extensible interface. This allows for arbitrary implementations, e.g., a more or less static configuration within the boundaries of DHCP as well as highly dynamic configurations that are based on knowledge of local policies, network topology, current resource utilization, etc. With SCOT [1] we have proposed such a repository which can be easily integrated into the Jini management federation.
- **SNMP Gateway.** A generic gateway for SNMP may translate remote method calls (Java RMI or CORBA based) into SNMP requests and return the SNMP replies. SNMP traps may be converted to Jini events which may be forwarded to appropriate event listeners according to a local policy, e.g., a generic Jini enabled messaging service to present them to a user. Our CORBA SNMP gateway [2] is an example of such a generic gateway. Since Jini is not restricted to native Java communication methods like RMI but easily integrates with CORBA systems, a Jini encapsulation of arbitrary CORBA services can be provided without much effort.
- **Persistence Service.** To ensure that the system works properly, most services have to keep (at least parts of) their state persistent. A DHCP service is obviously in trouble if it loses the information about which IP addresses have already been assigned. One solution is the delegation to a persistence service that offers storage and retrieval facilities for arbitrary configuration data. Thus, a Jini-enabled DHCP service could further contribute to the separation of concerns by leaving it to the persistence service to make the final assignment persistent. For reasons of reliability the persistence service could be implemented in a redundant way. This makes administration of configuration data much easier as the data can always be found at a well-known place.

Based on this infrastructure, new network devices should be configured by appropriate services instantly and automatically after they are plugged into the network. Additionally, the management federation should enforce adding notification interfaces to the vast majority of services. This enables arbitrary objects to receive notifications about interesting events.

# 4 Proposed Architecture for Integrating Legacy Devices

In this section we describe how to integrate legacy devices into a Jini management federation by means of infrastructural components, their interaction, and communication patterns.

Many existing devices do not meet the requirements for a native Jini service, most obviously due to the fact that few devices implement a full JVM. The *Jini Device Architecture Specification* [17] discusses in some detail how such devices can be brought into a Jini environment.

- **Device Bays.** One proposal is a so-called *device bay* that implements a physically co-located JVM to which several devices can be connected. Proxy objects are uploaded from the device to the JVM to implement the protocol between the device bay and the device. The device bay then acts on behalf of the device to run the relevant discovery and join protocols including the subscription to the lookup service.
- **Network Device Bays.** Another option is to physically separate the device bay from the devices. In this case the device bay is running somewhere in the network and devices must initially run some protocol in order to get in touch with the device bay. After some negotiation between the device and its bay a proxy object could again be uploaded implementing the device protocol.

Most legacy devices we have in mind are already network-enabled. A physically co-located device bay could be implemented as a hardware device placed between the printer and the network. Such a solution might be applicable for certain devices but we think that a pure software solution is less costly and more flexible in general. Therefore, we are more interested in providing an architecture for a software network device bay that provides the same features as a hardware solution. It should be possible that newly attached legacy devices are automatically detected and bound to some kind of network device bay. Appropriate management activities could then be started to configure the device and to integrate it into a Jini federation.

What essentially is missing is the initial *event* that activates an automatic configuration process for legacy devices. Some kind of a *sensor* that detects new devices as they are attached to a network or turned on manually could supply these events. We believe that services such as DHCP and TFTP can provide this initial event if appropriately equipped with instruments. We therefore propose an architecture that supports the integration of legacy devices into a Jini environment by means of *sensors* and *binders*. An overview of the general architecture is depicted in Fig. 1.

**Binders and Sensors.** Binders are services that provide initial bootstrapping information to devices. The most classical services of this kind are DHCP, TFTP, RARP [7], SLP, and others. These are the services that are contacted by new devices first. Equipping these services with instruments results in the construction of sensors that notify interested parties about relevant management events. Usually, binders act upon concrete events related to the protocol they implement. For example, a DHCP server understands several different messages from the device requesting configuration information. If the device accepts the configuration information offered by the DHCP service an appropriate management event can be supplied.

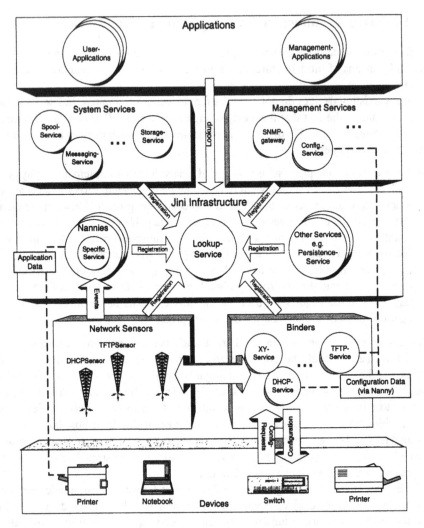

**Fig. 1.** Architecture for integrating legacy devices into Jini federations

**Management Events.** We have identified four different types of events relevant to management that can be detected by the network sensors:

- *DeviceUnknown* informs about new devices. This event is raised if a new device (e.g., one that does not yet have an IP address assigned) contacts a binder. At this time only basic information such as a MAC address might be available.
- *DeviceConnect* informs about established bindings of devices. This event might indicate that a device has successfully run the DHCP protocol and has obtained its configuration. We can assume that the device is operational with respect to the semantics of the sensor that raised the event.

- *DeviceDisconnect* informs about a device that has disconnected from the network in a proper way, e.g., by releasing an allocated IP number.
- *DeviceTimeout* indicates a failure situation caused by some timeout mechanism. It could, for example, indicate that a DHCP renewal failed.

One should keep in mind that these events are abstract in some sense and that a particular sensor needs to map concrete events to the events listed above. We think that the number of management-related events should be small and their semantics as simple as possible. Otherwise one needs to code too much sensor-specific knowledge into the interpretation of events.

**Nannies.** We propose a general service that registers with all available sensors to receive management-related events. Additionally, if dynamic configuration of services is needed, this component also acts as the *configuration provider* of this service. It listens for management events, connects to the configuration system in the background to query configuration information, and instantiates Java objects called *nannies* that present newly detected devices to the Jini federation and therefore to management applications.

Nannies combine device-specific knowledge, such as the native device protocol, with domain-specific knowledge, e.g., in the form of local policies defined by system administrators, in order to seamlessly integrate devices into a Jini federation. They integrate the following aspects of the device–network relationship, each of which may be optional, depending on the nature of the particular device:

- Guiding a device through its bootstrapping phase by acting as a gateway to some configuration management system.
- Receiving and propagating notifications from the sensors when devices are disconnected, e.g., caused by cancelling a DHCP lease.
- Providing the proxy object to register a service with the lookup service and renewing the leases bound to that registration.
- Implementing administrative interfaces of the Jini API, e.g., `net.jini.admin.Administrable` and `net.jini.admin.JoinAdmin`.

Nanny instantiation is crucial in some cases. In our approach nannies are instantiated with the help of a *factory* that is informed by the binders in response to devices requesting configuration information. The *nanny factory* creates a concrete nanny to handle further requests. Depending on the information available from the binder, the nanny factory instantiates a concrete device-specific nanny that knows about the kind of device it must take care of.

It should be clear that in a Jini environment the nanny does not need to implement all its facets on its own. In practice, a nanny queries the local lookup service for services that perform some tasks on its behalf. Typical services that could be "out-sourced" are gateway functionalities, lease renewals, services that provide configurable proxy objects to be stored in the lookup service, universal execution platforms for clients, etc.

A nanny could, for example, configure the device for SNMP management (if the device is SNMP enabled) by associating it with the SNMP gateway mentioned above as a manager and trap sink. It could register itself or other objects as an event listener with the gateway and react upon device specific problems according to the local policy.

In summary, a nanny takes care of a particular device in various situations – as its name suggests. From either perspective it is the layer that glues a device to its Jini federation on the one hand, and to the management federation on the other hand.

# 5  Example

A concrete example should demonstrate the use of our framework. We will look at what happens when a (non-Jini) printer is plugged into the network. All other components are assumed to be already running. An overview of the scenario is given in Fig. 2.

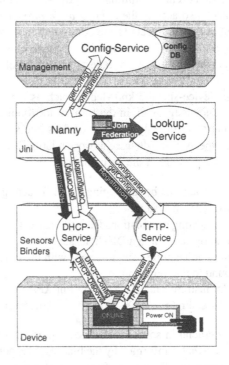

**Fig. 2.** Example usage scenario with a legacy printer device

The first thing a printer does after being switched on is to emit a DHCPDISCOVER message. The DHCP service receives this request and asks the nanny factory for an appropriate nanny object. Such an object may either already exist or it must be constructed by the factory. The DHCP binder forwards the request to the nanny which, in turn, may request the current configuration information from its configuration service. The configuration service returns the appropriate configuration to the nanny, which in turn delivers it to the DHCP service. This service proceeds with the DHCP protocol and offers the configuration to the requesting device.

This is rather straightforward on an abstract level but the details are trickier. The only information that the DHCP service definitely knows about the device is its media access control (MAC) address. The DHCPDISCOVER message might contain further information, but this is not mandatory. From this information, the nanny factory has to make available a device-specific nanny. As already noted, this is not always possible at the time a device is detected and must be adapted on demand as new information about the device is revealed.

In our example we assume that the nanny knows which kind of printer it is dealing with (in fact we have tested it with an HP LaserJet/JetDirect printer). It thus knows which information the printer needs and which steps it performs to retrieve this information. In our case, the printer will request its configuration profile via TFTP after accepting a DHCP configuration. Therefore, the nanny waits until it gets the *Device-Connect* event from the DHCP sensor which means that the printer has accepted the offered configuration.

The next step is transferring the configuration profile via TFTP. The printer asks its TFTP server for a specific file. The network address of the TFTP server and the file name is included in the DHCP configuration and is supplied by either the configuration service or the nanny, depending on the local policy. Since the TFTP server is Jini-enabled (it is actually a TFTP Jini-*service*), it contacts the responsible nanny (via the factory) and asks for the printer's configuration. The nanny may already know all the configuration data or ask the configuration service to supply the missing parameters. Having acquired all information, the nanny returns it to the TFTP service which then forwards it to the printer by dynamically generating a profile by inserting the current parameters into a device specific template.

As soon as the printer received its data, the TFTP service notifies the nanny (as well as other registered event listeners) by sending a *DeviceConnect* event. The nanny knows that the printer is now fully configured and ready to accept print requests. It therefore registers a printer proxy object on behalf of the printer with the lookup service. This proxy object implements an appropriate printer interface. The printer is now a full member of the Jini federation and may be further associated with other services, e.g., a spool service, which might be subject to automatic configuration itself.

Besides providing the printer interface, the nanny should offer the Jini administration interfaces, as well as interfaces which allow management applications to perform common management tasks. Depending on the device, this task can be achieved with the help of other Jini-enabled management services. In the case of our printer it is associated with an SNMP gateway as manager and trap sink. However, the generic gateway does not know the semantics of a trap like "out of paper" and can only translate it to a generic event. Thus, the nanny registers as event consumer with the gateway, receives these events, maps them to device-specific events, and finally forwards them to interested listeners.

# 6 Related Work

To our knowledge there is no architecture similar to the Jini technology. Therefore we can only compare our approach with other ideas which partially cover the same domain.

The HAVi specification [5] focuses on interoperability and integration of home audio and video appliances. It defines an architecture, which is comprised of device abstraction models, software elements, protocols, an addressing scheme for devices, and a lookup service for registration of services and their resources. In this sense HAVi is comparable to Jini. In comparison to Jini though, devices are classified into four different categories ranging from devices with full HAVi support, including a Java VM, to legacy devices that use proprietary protocols only. The latter group require appropriate HAVi devices to act as gateways to the rest of the HAVi architecture. Due to the restricted application domain and the small number of devices considered, integrated management is not dealt with in the specification.

Heilbronner et al. [10] describe a DHCP server that has been equipped with sensors to send SNMP traps in response to DHCP lease state changes. They have developed an appropriate SNMP management information base (MIB) for DHCP services. Their approach integrates DHCP services into a network management environment, but they are mainly interested in monitoring aspects and it is unclear, whether further management actions could follow DHCP state changes.

Sun itself has announced a product suite to enable Java-based management (JMAPI [16]), which is a full-blown new architecture designed to integrate Java-based distributed services as well as already established management architectures. Thus it could also cope with Jini but does not directly deal with bootstrapping and initial configuration of network devices in its current specification. However, up to now it is mostly an announcement. It is planned to be a family of several products, such as the Java Dynamic Management Kit (JDMK [15]) which is already available. JDMK is primarily targeted to extend Java services by appropriate management facilities and to integrate them as managed objects into management architectures, namely SNMP.

Marzullo et al. [11] introduce the notion of sensors that provide data about the current state of applications. Contrary to our event-driven approach, control is mainly based on continuously polling the sensors. They also describe a *LanManager*, which – like a Jini lookup service – allows binding of software components at run-time. Furthermore, it can detect failed components and automatically restart them. Configuration management is not considered, though.

# 7 Conclusion and Future Work

We have proposed a framework for integrating legacy devices into a Jini-enabled management environment. The framework seems to be applicable to a large number of different scenarios, devices, and communication protocols. It opens up the mass of legacy devices for integration into a Jini world.

From a management perspective the advantages of our approach are visible in the concentration of all device-relevant knowledge in one dedicated nanny for each device, which seamlessly integrates the device into the local infrastructure without the administrator's intervention.

Nannies can be seen as a paradigm shift from functionality-driven services to object-centered services providing better integration of different functional management aspects. We see the future of management systems in the dynamic aggregation of specialized services in an integrated and flexible manner to overcome the existing, mostly monolithic, systems. In order to realize such management infrastructures the following still needs to be done:

- Appropriate service decompositions, including service interaction protocols, must be found.
- Standardized interfaces to management applications must be defined.
- Policies for distributed coordination, especially in failure situations, must be developed and appropriate policy enforcement subsystems must be available to interested services.
- Working systems beyond prototypes must be implemented.

Solving these problems allows us to envision a future in which nanny factories automatically download device-specific nannies from vendor Web sites and those nannies configure devices in the background according to local policies.

## Acknowledgements

We would like to thank Ron Bourret, Alejandro Buchmann, and Friedemann Mattern for proof-reading and discussion of earlier drafts of this paper.

## References

[1] Gerd Aschemann and Roger Kehr. Towards a Requirements-based Information Model for Configuration Management. In *Proceedings of 4th International Conference on Configurable Distributed Systems*, pages 181–189. IEEE Computer Society Press, May 1998.

[2] Gerd Aschemann, Thomas Mohr, and Mechthild Ruppert. Integration of SNMP into a CORBA- and Web-Based Management Environment. In *Proceedings of Kommunikation in Verteilten Systemen*, pages 210–221. Springer-Verlag, February 1999.

[3] J. D. Case, M. Fedor, M. L. Schoffstall, and C. Davin. Simple Network Management Protocol (SNMP). Internet RFC 1157, May 1990.

[4] CCITT. *Recommendation X.711, Common Management Information Protocol Specification for CCITT Applications*. CCITT, 1991.

[5] HAVi Consortium. *The HAVi Specification: Specification of the Home Audio/Video Interoperability Architecture Version 1.0 beta*, November 1998.

[6] R. Droms. Dynamic Host Configuration Protocol (DHCP). Internet RFC 2131, March 1997.

[7] Ross Finlayson, Timothy Mann, Jeffrey Mogul, and Marvin Theimer. A Reverse Address Resolution Protocol (RARP). Internet RFC 903, June 1984.

[8] Erich Gamma, Richard Helm, Ralph Johnson, and John Vlissides. *Design Patterns: Elements of Reusable Object-Oriented Software*. Addison-Wesley, 1995.

[9] J. Gilmore and W. J. Croft. Bootstrap Protocol (BOOTP). Internet RFC 951, September 1985.

[10] Stephen Heilbronner, Alexander Keller, and Bernhard Neumair. Integriertes Netz- und Systemmanagement mit modularen Agenten. In *Proceedings of Workstations und ihre Anwendungen SIWORK '96, Zürich, Switzerland*, 1996.

[11] K. Marzullo, R. Cooper, M. Wood, and K. Birman. Tools for Monitoring and Controlling Distributed Applications. *IEEE Computer*, 24(8):42–51, August 1991.

[12] OMG. *CORBA Object Trader Service*, December 1997.

[13] Morris Sloman, editor. *Network and Distributed Systems Management*. Addison-Wesley Publishing Company, 1994.

[14] K. R. Sollins. The TFTP Protocol (Revision 2). Internet RFC 783, June 1981.

[15] Sun Microsystems Inc. *Java Dynamic Management Kit*.

[16] Sun Microsystems Inc. *Java Management API*.

[17] Sun Microsystems Inc. *Jini Device Architecure Specification – Revision 1.0*, January 1999.

[18] Sun Microsystems Inc. *Jini Discovery and Join Specification – Revision 1.0*, January 1999.

[19] Sun Microsystems Inc. *Jini Lookup Service Specification – Revision 1.0*, January 1999.

[20] J. Veizades, E. Guttman, C. Perkins, and S. Kaplan. Service Location Protocol (SLP). Internet RFC 2165, June 1997.

# Session 7

# Management Tools

*Chair: Emil Lupu*
*Imperial College, London, U.K.*

# Ntop: Beyond Ping and Traceroute

Luca Deri and Stefano Suin

Centro Serra, University of Pisa, Lungarno Pacinotti 43, Pisa, Italy.
{deri, stefano}@unipi.it
http://www-serra.unipi.it/~ntop/

The task of network management is becoming increasingly complex due to the increasing number of networked computers running different operating systems and speaking various network protocols. Most of network monitoring and diagnostic tools such as ping and traceroute are suitable just for tackling simple connectivity problems. Complex network problems often need to be addressed using rather expensive management tools or probes affordable only by mid-large companies.

This paper covers the design and the implementation of ntop, an open-source web-based network usage monitor that enables users to track relevant network activities including network utilisation, established connections, network protocol usage and traffic classification. ntop's portability across various platforms, its support of many network media, ease of use and lightweight CPU utilisation makes it suitable for people who want to monitor their network without having to adopt a sophisticated yet expensive management platform.

## 1   Background and Motivation

Popular tools such as ping and traceroute [16] have been used for years now for monitoring and debugging simple network connectivity issues. Although these tools are often sufficient for tackling simple problems, they have been created for monitoring network activities between two hosts. In cases where the network problem to address is due to the interaction of traffic originated by multiple hosts, these tools show their limits. Network sniffers such as tcpdump [9] or snoop are quite useful for analysing network traffic but off-line applications are often necessary for correlating captured data and identifying the network flows. Many commercial network sniffers are usually able to analyse data while capturing traffic but still these tools are quite primitive because they focus mainly on the packet and not on global network activities. In other words, operators are able to virtually know everything about the content of a single network packet whereas it is very difficult to extract information concerning the whole network status when a network problem appears.

Similarly, network probes such as RMON agents [17] are quite powerful but unfortunately need sophisticated SNMP managers that are able to configure them properly, and analyse collected network statistics. Due to this complexity and also the cost of such probes, RMON agents are basically used uniquely by advanced network managers in large institutions.

Other tools for network monitoring such as NeTraMet [4] and NFR [14] offer advanced programming languages for analyzing network flows and building statistical event records. Nevertheless those tools have been designed as instrumentable network daemons suitable for monitoring networks in a mid/long time period whereas in some cases it is necessary to have a very simple tool able to show the actual network status in human-readable format on a character-based terminal.

Even though operating systems have evolved rapidly, software companies did not pay enough attention to network management. Due to this, the latest releases of popular operating systems still offer no more than ping and traceroute. This is because companies often believe that if a network problem is due to network connectivity then ping and traceroute are enough, whereas if the problem is more complicated then a costly and complex network management tool has to be used.

The authors believe that this statement does not hold. In the Internet age, computer users need to have access to simple yet powerful network monitor tools able to give answer to questions such as:

- Why is the local network performance so poor?
- Who is using most of the available network bandwidth?
- Which are the hosts currently decreasing the performance of the local NFS server?
- What is the bandwidth percentage actually used of my computer?
- Which are the contacted peers and the amount of network traffic produced by each of the processes running on my local computer?
- Which are the hosts that produce multicast traffic?

ntop has been written to give a positive answer to all of the above questions. It has been initially written by the authors for tackling performance problems of the campus network backbone. Similar to the Unix *top* [3] tool that reports processes CPU usage, authors needed a simple tool able to report the network top users (hence the term ntop) for quickly identifying those hosts that were currently using most of the available network resources. ntop then evolved into a more flexible and powerful tool as people over the Internet downloaded it and reported problems and suggestions. The following sections cover architecture, the adopted design solutions and the inner details of the current ntop implementation.

## 2 Inside ntop

ntop is an open-source software (http://www.opensource.org/) [15] application written using the C language available free of charge under the GNU public licence. This statement does not just mean that ntop's source code is freely available on the Internet, but also that many requirements came directly from early ntop adopters. The authors designed the first version of ntop and then accommodated new requirements and extensions on the original architecture, strongly influenced by the *Webbin* [7] architecture. ntop's main design goals are:

- portability across Unix and non-Unix (e.g. Win32) platforms;
- simple and efficient application kernel with low resource (both memory and CPU) usage;
- minimal requirements (bare operating system) but capable of exploiting platform features, if present (e.g. kernel threads);
- ability to present data both in a character-based terminal and a web browser;
- the network analysis output should be rich in content and easy to read.

The ntop architecture is shown in the following figure.

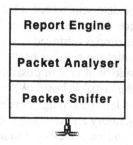

Figure 1 - ntop Architecture

The packet sniffer collects network packets that are then passed to the packet analyser for processing. Whenever traffic information has to be displayed, the report engine renders the requested information appropriately.

## 2.1   Packet Sniffer

The packet sniffer is the ntop component that potentially has more portability issues. In fact, unlike other facilities such as threads, there is not a portable library for packet capture. Under Unix the *libpcap* [12] library provides a portable and unified packet capture interface, whereas other operating systems provide proprietary capture facility. Due to good design of libpcap and its relatively portable interface, the authors decided to use it as unified capture interface and then wrapped platform-specific packet capture libraries (e.g. NDIS [13] on Win32) around pcap-like interface. This has the advantage that the ntop code is unique whereas the platform-specific code is limited only to a file. The packet sniffer supports different network interface types including PPP, Ether-processed by the analyser. Packet filtering is based on the BPF filter [11] facility part of libpcap. Filters are specified using simple expressions as those accepted by tcpdump.

Packet capture libraries have small internal buffers that prevent applications from being able to handle burst traffic. In order to overcome this problem hence reduce packet loss, ntop buffers captured packets. This allows the packet analyser to be decoupled by the packet sniffer and not to loose packets due to bursty traffic. It is worth remembering that ntop can operate on switched networks (e.g. an Ethernet network that makes use of switches) as well as on traditional networks. This is because modern switches allow global network traffic (or virtual LANs) to be mirrored to a specified switch port. ntop can then be activated on a host that is attached to such a port.

## 2.2 Packet Analyser

The packet analyser processes one packet at time. Packet headers are analysed according to the network interface being used. This is because headers are different depending on the network interface (e.g. the Token Ring header is different from the Ethernet one). Hosts information is stored in a large hash table whose key is the 48 bit hardware (MAC) address that guarantees its uniqueness and allow different network protocols other than IP to be handled (e.g. TCP/IP addresses are meaningless in non-IP networks). Each entry contains several counters that keep track of the data sent/received by the host, sorted according to the supported network protocols. For each packet, the hash entry corresponding to packet source and destination is retrieved or created if not yet present. Because it is not possible to predict the number of different hosts whose packets will be handled by ntop, it would be almost impossible to have a hash table large enough to accommodate all the possible hosts. When is necessary (e.g. periodically or if there are no entries left) ntop purges the host table in order to avoid exhausting all the available memory and creating huge tables that decrease the overall performance. Purged entries correspond to hosts that have not sent/received data for a long period of time. This guarantees that ntop's memory utilisation does not grow indefinitely and that packet processing time does not increase linearly with the number of active hosts. If the received packet is a non-IP packet, the protocol entry counters are updated and the packet discarded. Instead if the received packet is an IP packet, then further processing is performed.

Caching is performed in two steps. First level caching is semi-persistent and based upon GNU *gdbm*[18].

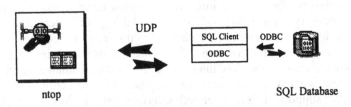

Fig. 2. ntop caching

Second level caching is implemented using a SQL database. ntop caches locally semi-persistent information such as IP address resolution (mapping numeric/symbolic IP address) and remote host operating system (computed using the *queso* [2] tool). Network events (e.g. TCP sessions), performance data and other relevant information is stored permanently into the database. Storage happens either periodically or whenever the garbage collector has to purge some data. ntop talks with the database by means of a client application. Such a client dialogues with ntop via UDP and communicates with the database using ODBC (Open DataBase Connectivity protocol). Whenever some network information has to be stored into the database, ntop sends the client one or more UDP packets containing valid SQL statements. The client, currently implemented in both Perl and Java, receives the packets and executes the statement on the local database via Perl DBI (DataBase Interface) or Java JDBC (Java DataBase Connectivity) depending on the implementation language. This architecture allows ntop to be decoupled from a specific database and able to communicate with remote database (e.g. the main company database) while having a very simple and light database client.

The host entry shown below contains a counter for each of the user-specified IP protocols.

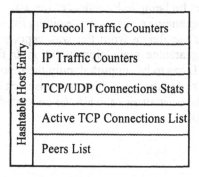

Fig. 3. Host Hashtable Entry

For each IP packet, the appropriate protocol counter is updated. If the packet is an IP fragment, ntop retrieves information such as source and destination port from the fragment hash table. Whenever the first packet fragment is encountered, fragment information is stored in the hash table using the packet `fragmentId` as hash key. Fragment information is removed as soon as the last fragment has been received. Because it might happen that some packets (including fragments) have been dropped, the fragment table is periodically analysed and outdated information is purged from it. The host entry also contains a list (initially empty) of the host's active TCP connections. ntop maintains the state of each TCP connection analysing the IP flags. Hence if the received packet is a TCP packet, then the host TCP connection list also needs to be updated.

Although host traffic counters can be profitably used to analyse network traffic, in some cases it might be necessary to study specific traffic that flows through some specified hosts. ntop allows users to specify network flows. A network flow is a stream of packets that matches a user-specified rule. Rules are specified using BPF expressions. Similar to NeTraMet flows, ntop network flows can be used for specifying traffic of particular interest. For instance a simple network flow could be the "total traffic NFS traffic between host A, B and C", whereas a more complex flow is "the total number of TCP connections rejected by the host D". Network flows can be very useful for debugging network problems, gathering statistical data or tracking suspicious access to some specified network resources.

## 2.3 Report Engine

The actual version of ntop can be started in two ways:

- interactive mode
  ntop runs in a character-based terminal and users can interact using keyboard keys.

- web-mode
  ntop acts as an HTTP server and allows remote users to analyse traffic statistics by means of a web browser.

ntop has been designed for being independent of the way traffic reports are created. The current report engine contains two emitters for both text-based terminals and HTML. Independence from the way reports are created is very important in order to guarantee application evolution. In fact if a new mark-up language such as XML has to be supported, only the report engine needs to be extended whereas the rest of the application remains unchanged. It is worth noting that custom reports and statistics can also be generated using data stored by ntop into the SQL database.

## 3   ntop at Work

### 3.1   Interactive Mode

When ntop is started in interactive mode, traffic information is shown in a character-based terminal window as shown below.

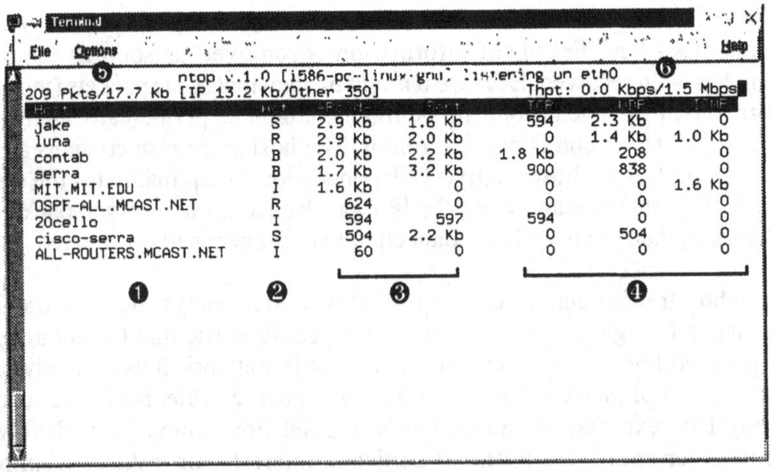

Fig. 4. ntop: Interactive Mode

Column ❶ contains the list of hosts that have sent/received data, column ❷ specifies the actual host state (S=send, R=receive, B=send/receive and I=idle). Column ❸ contains the total data sent/received by each host, whereas column ❹ is a detailed view of the previous column. Users can change the sort order or the shown protocols simply by pressing the appropriate keys. The terminal is updated periodically as specified by the user. ❺ indicates the total observed traffic (packets and bytes) since the time ntop has been started, whereas the actual and maximum network throughput is shown in ❻.

## 3.2 Web Mode

The ntop interactive mode has been conceived as a quick network diagnostic tool for users who need to have a quick look at the actual network traffic (e.g. when the network is slow and it is necessary to find out which hosts are decreasing the overall performance). Instead, the web-mode turns ntop into a full fledged web-based management application [10] as shown in the following figure.

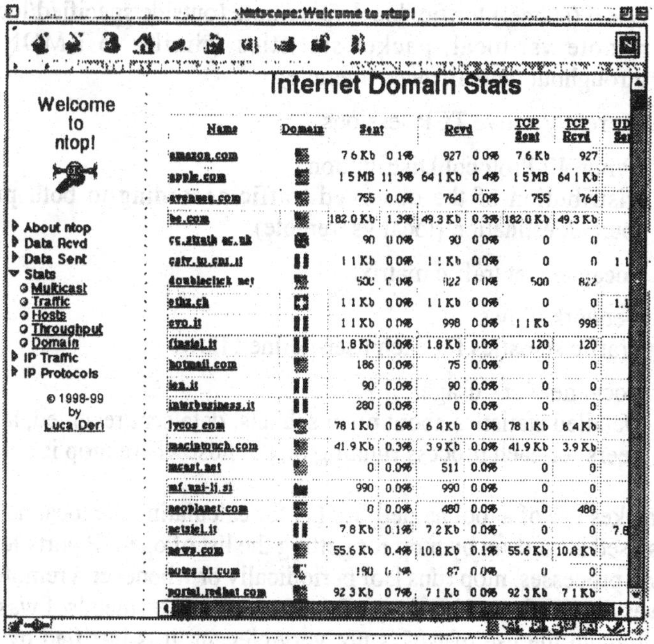

Fig. 5. ntop: Web Mode

The web-mode has been designed as a long standing statistics gathering application able to provide users a detailed view of the current and past network activities. The web interface has been selected because it guarantees client independence and allows multiple users to be served. However, in order to prevent unauthorised users from accessing sensitive data as traffic information, ntop implements the standard HTTP password protection scheme. Administrators can specify at user level what information can be presented to remote users in order to avoid exposing sensitive information to potential hackers while giving the chance to show all the network statistics to selected people. Users connect their web browsers directly to ntop that acts as an HTTP server. The entry page is divided in two frames: the left frame is used for navigating through traffic information displayed in the right frame. Users can fully customise the layout and change the menu content/position as needed. All the relevant table columns are sortable simply by clicking on the column name. Whenever appropriate hyperlinks are used for correlating information. HTML pages are periodically refreshed automatically or on user request. Beside the information also shown in interactive mode, the web mode contains additional statistics including:

- IP multicast.

- Host information
  Data sent/received, contacted peers, active TCP sessions, TCP/UDP session history, provided/used IP services, bandwidth currently in use.

- Traffic Statistics
  Local (subnet) traffic, local vs. remote (outside specified/local subnets), remote vs. local, packet statistics (similar to RMON), network throughput (actual, peak, average).

- Currently active TCP sessions.

- IP/non-IP Protocol Distribution
  Distribution of the observed traffic according to both protocol and source/destination (local vs. remote).

- Local subnet traffic matrix.

- Network Flows
  Traffic statistics for each user-defined flow.

- Local network usage
  Detailed statistics about open sockets, data sent/received, and contacted peers for each process running on the host where ntop is active.

ntop makes use of a tool named *lsof*[1] for calculating the local network usage. lsof is used at start-up by ntop for getting the list of open IP ports for each of the running processes. ntop runs lsof periodically or whenever a remote host sends/receives data to/from a local port that was not active when lsof was last executed. Although the use of lsof is not very elegant, it is justified by the fact that there is no portable way to retrieve the list of open IP ports for each running process, and even if ntop would implement that functionality, ntop has to periodically poll the kernel because there is no way to be notified when a port is open/closed.

### 3.3 When to use ntop?
ntop can be profitably used to both monitor the network when some problems arise or just to analyse the overall network status including but not limited to:

- Protocol monitor
  Determine what protocols are used and identify those computers that speak unnecessary protocols. For instance, the Windows™ operating system install by default protocols such as NetBeui and IPX while most of the people use just TCP/IP.

- Network service usage
  Services such as DNS and NFS can be easily monitored. This allows network administrators to both analyse the impact of selected protocols on the overall network performance and identify those applications (e.g an FTP server) that have been silently installed in the network without authorisation.

- Network utilisation
  ntop is able to identify what computers are using most of the network resources, as well as graph network bandwidth usage over the time.

- Security
  Portscan, denial of service and other security flaws are traced by ntop and once stored on the database can be used to identify those hosts that violated the overall network security.

In general, ntop combines features otherwise present in various tools not always easy to integrate. Its unique user interface allows administrators to immediately take advantage of ntop without the need to purchase and manage client applications that are necessary for tools such as RMON or NeTraMet. In addition, database support makes ntop suitable not only for network problem debugging but also for long standing network monitoring.

### 3.4 Performance Issues
ntop performance is quite good basically for five reasons:

- libpcap (or NDIS on Win32) performance is excellent;

- packet loss is very low (if any) because captured packets are buffered twice both inside the kernel and ntop;

- potentially long running actions (e.g. IP address resolution) are implemented asynchronously;

- ntop spawns several threads that prevent user interaction (e.g. HTTP user requests) from interfering with data collection;

- ntop makes extensive use of hash tables whose indexes are easy to compute yet fast during information retrieval due to the nature of network addresses (e.g. they are unique and already in 32/48 bit numeric format).

Users have tested ntop extensively on various network media running at different speeds. In general, ntop performance is greatly influenced by the other running processes because some CPU-greedy applications may take up the whole CPU cycles for a few seconds causing packet loss. Supposing to run ntop on an average loaded host, tests shown that ntop can work with very low (if any) packet loss on a 100 Mbit ethernet.

Nevertheless, performance is strongly influenced by per-packet processing. In fact the more network flows are defined, the more processing time is required hence the higher is the probability of dropping some packets. Due to the way ntop works, if a packet gets lost major problems may arise. In fact suppose to loose the first fragment of a TCP packet containing the FIN flag. In this case there are two problems:

- the fragment entry for the packet is not created, hence the following packets cannot be handled properly;

- ntop does not know that a peer intends to close the TCP connection (three way handshake).

In order to overcome the above mentioned problems, ntop implements internal timeouts and periodical garbage collection in order to purge old data and speculate about the state of active connections. For instance, if there is no data flowing on a connection for a very long period of time, then the connection might have been closed. In this case ntop assumes that the connection has been closed and then the connection entry is purged. This allows ntop to recover whenever some packets get lost and not to get stuck waiting for some lost packet to arrive.

## 4 Lessons Learned

ntop has been a great exercise in many respects:

- ntop performance
  It is a challenge to process packet efficiently while having rich traffic statistics. That is why the C language has been preferred to other languages such as Java. In fact, the current ntop version runs on hosts with very limited memory whereas an early prototype written in Java had serious performance problems and needed a lot of memory (due to the use of JIT compilers) that prevented it from running on average loaded networks.

- IP Protocol Stack
  Almost every operating system uses IP flags differently, and some protocols (e.g. HTTP) make extensive use of IP flags for performance optimisation. This pushed the authors to update the ntop TCP protocol engine (used to keep the status of the TCP connections) several times before to reach the actual version. It is worth to note that tools like *queso* and *nmap* [8] exploit peculiarities of IP stack implementation in order to guess the running operating system.

- Open Source Software
  The adoption of OSS allowed both ntop to be extensively tested on a very large number of different systems and deeply influenced ntop's design. In fact, many ntop features have been implemented because some users asked for them and several problems have been fixed because somebody studied the code, tackled the problem and sent back the code patch.

# 5 Future Work

Although ntop already contains many features that were not planned at the beginning, a few enhancements are necessary in order to increase its flexibility and make it open to extensions. Planned enhacements include, but are not limited to:

- Operating System Integration
  It is unknown to the authors why modern operating systems handle network communications differently from processes. Processes can be listed, changed of priority, killed. The same should be applied to network communications. For instance, users should be able to list and terminate active TCP connections (even those that do not include the host where ntop runs) as described in [5]. Security issues need to be further investigated.

- Application Extensibility
  As of today ntop is a monolithic application that does not allow users to add new specific features. It is the authors belief that user-specific extensions to the ntop kernel would not make too much sense. A possible solution to this problem is the definition of a clean programming interface that allows users to write software components (plugins) [6] able to solve a specific problem. For instance if a user needs to periodically store in a database the used network bandwidth, then a plugin could be written for this purpose. The use of plugins allows users to extend ntop in a clean way by using specified interfaces without having to extend the ntop core with new peculiar functionality.

- SNMP
  The actual ntop implementation cannot be easily integrated with a management platform. This is because ntop supports HTTP whereas management platforms usually speak SNMP. The natural way to add SNMP support to ntop, would be the definition of a specific MIB (or selected parts of existing MIBs) and the support of the SNMP protocol. In that way ntop could act as a SNMP agent able to both handle incoming request and emit traps when some user-specified thresholds are exceeded.

# 6 Final Remarks

This work attempted to demonstrate that it is possible to analyse network traffic without having to purchase either expensive management platforms or network probes. Established tools such as ping and traceroute can be profitably used for solving connectivity problems whereas ntop can be used as a magnify lens for analysing global network traffic. The ntop interactive mode has been conceived as a quick network diagnostic whereas the web mode provide users a detailed view of the current and past network activities. ntop's lightweight cpu utilisation, minimal requirements, and support of various network media make it suitable for all those people who want to analyse network traffic without having to afford an expensive management platform.

## 7 Availability

Both *ntop* and *libpcap for Win32* are distributed under the GPL2 licence and can be downloaded free of charge from both the ntop home page (http://www-serra.unipi.it/~ntop/) and other mirrors on the Internet. Some Unix distributions including FreeBSD and Linux, come with ntop preinstalled.

## 8 Acknowledgments

The author would like to thank all the ntop users and early adopters who deeply influenced the design of the overall architecture with all their comments and suggestions.

## 9 References

1.  Abell V.: lsof, ftp://vic.cc.purdue.edu/pub/tools/unix/lsof/ (1998).

2.  Apostols E.: queso, http://www.apostols.org/ (1998).

3.  Binns R.: top (1993).

4.  Brownlee N.: NeTraMet v.4.2 Users' Guide, http://www.auckland.an.nz/net/Accounting/ (1998).

5.  Claerhout B.: IP Spoof (1996).

6.  Deri L.: Droplets: Breaking Monolithic Applications Apart, IBM Research Report RZ 2799 (1995).

7.  Deri L.: Surfin' Network Management Applications Across the Web, Proceedings of 2nd Int. IEEE Workshop on System and Network Management (1996).

8.  Fyodor: Remote OS detection via TCP/IP stack fingerprinting, http://www.insecure.org/nmap/nmap-fingerprinting-article.txt (1998).

9.  Jacobson V., Leres C., and McCanne S.: tcpdump, Lawrence Berkeley National Labs, ftp://ftp.ee.lbl.gov/ (1989).

10. Jander M.: Web-based Management: Welcome to the Revolution, Data Communications (1996).

11. S. McCanne and V. Jacobson: The BSD Packer Filter: A New Architecture for User-level Packet Capture, Proc. of 1993 Winter USENIX Conference, 1993.

12. S. McCanne, C.Leres and V. Jacobson: libpcap, Lawrence Berkeley National Labs, ftp://ftp.ee.lbl.gov/ (1994).

13. Microsoft Corporation: NDIS Packet Driver 3.0 (1996).

14. Ranum M., and others: Implementing a Generalized Tool for Network Monitoring, Proc. of LISA'97, USENIX 11th System Administration Conference, http://www.nfr.com/forum/publications/LISA-97.htm (1997).

15. Raymond E.: The Cathedral and the Bazaar, http://www.tuxedo.org/~esr/ (1998).

16. Stevens R.: UNIX Network Programming, Volume 1, 2nd Edition (1998).

17. Waldbusser S.: Remote Network Monitoring Management Information Base, RFC 1757 (1995).

18. Free Software Foundation, GNU gdbm, http://www.gnu.org/software/gdbm/ (1999).

# EventBrowser: A Flexible Tool for Scalable Analysis of Event Data

Sheng Ma[1] and Joseph L. Hellerstein[1]

IBM T.J. Watson Research Center
Hawthorne, NY 10532
U.S.A
{shengma, hellers}@us.ibm.com

**Abstract.** Event management is fundamental to network and systems management. To date, this discipline has focused on reporting alerts in real time. This paper describes a tool, EventBrowser, intended for ad hoc analysis of historical logs, especially for problem determination and validating the benefits of configuration changes. EventBrowser addresses: (a) irregularities in the structure of event messages, (b) problems with visualizing patterns in large volumes of categorical data, and (c) difficulties with providing multiple views at different levels of detail. In particular for item (c), EventBrowser provides summary statistics (e.g., by host name), relationships between events (e.g., via scatter plots), and full message details. We have applied EventBrowser to analyze data from a production network. Our visualizations reveal a number of abnormalities that are not detected readily by conventional tools.

## 1 Introduction

Event management encompasses event generation, transmission, storage, and action-taking in response to state changes in systems. Such capabilities are at the heart of systems management, as indicated by the popularity of the products such as the Tivoli Event Console (TEC), Boole's Command Post, and CA's event console. Unfortunately, existing tools provide very limited facilities for ad hoc analysis of event data, especially historical data. This paper describes EventBrowser, a tool for analysis of event data.

We believe that a starting point for analysis is visualization, especially when there are large data volumes (as is the case for event management). Existing event management systems provide two kinds of visualizations. The most common are tabular presentations of individual events. Another popular visualization is an annotated display of network topology with colors indicating the severity of events received from network elements [7]. The latter emphasizes the geographical interpretation of a problem. The former does well for analysis of a short sequence of events. However, neither is effective for ad hoc analysis of large volumes of events.

Various systems have been developed to support exploratory analysis of multidimensional data [3][4][2][1][6][5]. Most are designed to analyze numerical data.

However, events contain **categorical attributes**, such as a host name. Values of categorical attributes do not have an inherent order, and hence are handled poorly by scientific visualizations. Systems that deal well with large volumes of categorical data do so by summarizing the data. However, doing so can hide important information, such as event periodicities.

In addition, existing visualization systems can only handle data with a structured format (typically, a relational table or blank separated columns). We know of no system that integrates data analysis with a parsing mechanism to provide an iterative approach to selecting the event attributes to analyze.

In this paper, we describe **EventBrowser**, a prototype tool for exploratory analysis of event logs. This tool incorporates a flexible parsing mechanism to handle the varied formats of event messages. EventBrowser also provides an extensible architecture to support a variety of visualizations and analyses.

The remainder of this paper is organized as follows. Section 2 describes the event data and the requirements for its ad hoc analysis. Section 3 presents the architecture of EventBrowser. Section 4 discusses how EventBrowser has been used to identify patterns in event logs for a production network. Section 5 contains our conclusions.

## 2 Requirements for Analysis of Event Data

In this section, we first describe the log data used as an example throughout the paper. We then discuss the analysis scenarios herein considered for event data.

### 2.1 NetView Log

The data used in this paper is collected at a production network containing thousands of managed nodes including routers, hubs, and servers. The log file contains a variety of SNMP traps along with events posted by an internal event management system.

Two typical raw events in this log are illustrated in Figure 1. For privacy consideration, real host identifiers are replaced by dummy names. The first message reports a "TCP connection close" event. This event has several parameters or **event attributes** associated with it: event type (i.e., "TCP connection close"), source name, time, connection state, connection elapsed time, bytes received, bytes sent, and etc. The values associated with these attributes are embedded in the message text. The remaining 3 messages describe a single "Arm threshold" event. The first message gives the event type ("Arm thresholds"), the host on which the event occurred, and the time of occurrence. The second message gives the value of the metric when the threshold, which is 98, was exceeded by the current value, which is 99. The third message displays the name of the metric (CPU utilization). Note that extracting values of event attributes from messages is fairly challenging because the message formats vary and a complex relationship exists between messages and events.

Even though the set of attributes within an event depend on the event type, several attributes are common to all events. They are:

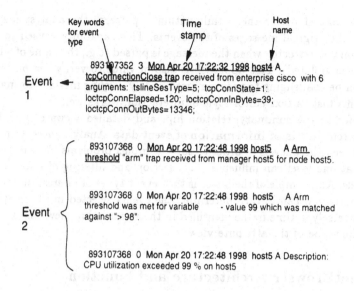

**Fig. 1.** Messages Extracted From an Event Log

- timestamp marking when the event was generated
- host (source) identifier indicating the event's origin
- event type

In a typical day, more than 3000 events with approximately 20 different event types are generated by around 160 hosts. In this paper, we use a NetView log containing event data collected over three days.

## 2.2 Analysis Scenarios

Given an event log, such as the NetView log, we consider two analysis scenarios. The first characterizes the events that dominant the event log as such events often indicate a problem. Our starting point is to identify the most frequently occurring hosts and event types. To this end, the analyst wants to summarize the event counts (or frequencies) by host name and by event type. An effective way to present this information is to use a table.

Next, the analyst looks for relationships between events, especially patterns that are unexpected. An effective visualization here is a scatter plot in which each point represents an event. However, unlike scientific data, event data contain categorical information, such as the event type and the host name. If there were a small number of host names (or event types), we could label the axis with the names of hosts (or event types). But this approach scales poorly. Thus, finding patterns in such data involves some very different challenges from those addressed in existing scientific visualizations.

To understand better the details within a pattern, the analyst may need to look at the original messages of the events. This capability is used to obtain information not extracted when the message is parsed (e.g., the name of a threshold that was violated). This approach is also of value to verify the parser itself (which can be challenging to program with widely varying message formats). To support this task, a text editor style of interaction works well.

We refer to the summary, relationship, and detailed views of the data as being different **levels of information** of event data. Analysts need to navigate freely between these levels in order to solve complex problems. Further, insights obtained at one level can influence the selection and filtering of information at other levels. An example of the latter is that event types of interest discovered in the attribute view can in turn determine the events selected in the relationship view. Conversely, a time frame identified in the relationship view can be used to restrict the scope of the attribute view.

## 3 EventBrowser Architecture and Function

This section describes the architecture and function of EventBrowser. We begin with an overview of its components, especially the preprocessor and browser. Next, the viewers within the browser are described in detail.

The structure of EventBrowser follows from its goals, which are:

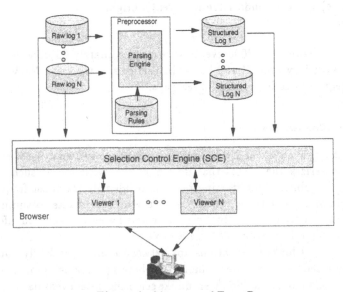

**Fig. 2.** Architecture of EventBrowser

1. handling messages with different formats
2. enabling analysis at different information levels
3. fostering interaction between analyses
4. supporting summary, relationship, and detailed views of event data

Figure 2 displays the architecture of EventBrowser. Goal (1) is addressed by the preprocessor component, which transforms message logs into structured event data. Goal (2) is handled by the browser component, which is structured so that new views for analysis of event data can be incorporated with ease. Goal (3) is accommodated by the selection and control engine within the browser, which provides for communication among and interactions between viewers. Goal (4) is achieved by having viewers that support the summary, relationship, and detailed views of event data.

## 3.1 Preprocessor

The preprocessor takes as input event logs that are organized in the manner described in Section 2. It outputs a structured log file. This information is used by the browser component to produce visualizations.

The **structured log file** consists of: (a) a data matrix that contains values of event attributes, (b) symbol tables (one for each categorical attribute), and (c) meta data. The data matrix is a table; rows represent events, and columns contain values of event attributes.[1] Values of each categorical attribute are encoded as integers that are indices into the corresponding attribute table produced by the preprocessor. The columns of the data matrix contain attributes common to all events: event type, event source (or host name), and time. The meta data specifies the attribute identifiers and their data type (categorical or numeric). for each column of data matrix. The preprocessor is organized into a parsing engine and parsing rules. This structure isolates log-file specific characteristics. Parsing rules specify information such as key words for extracting values of attributes and how to link together messages for events that have multiple messages. The event class is determined by the presence of specific key words (e.g., "tcpConnectionClose trap") within a particular part of a message. Message parameters are located by specifying a combination of relative position (with respect to a reference string), the length of the associated string, and starting and ending markers within the message text.

## 3.2 Browser

The browser component provides capabilities for visualization and navigation of event data. This component takes as input the structured log produced by the preprocessor.

As depicted in Figure 2, the browser is organized into a selection and control engine (SCE) and several viewers. The SCE inputs raw logs and structured logs; this information is cached internally. The SCE also coordinates the viewers, and

---

[1] Since some attributes are not defined for certain events, we must have a symbol that indicates "undefined". We use a minus one since, to date, all data we have processed uses positive values.

allows global changes made in one viewer to be reflected in the other viewers. The viewers provide analysts with capabilities for navigating and manipulating event data.

**Selection and Control Engine (SCE)** The SCE inputs the structured event logs produced by the preprocessor as well as the raw logs. The SCE then constructs an extended structured log or **ELOG**. This extended information consists of: (1) the raw message file; (2) a subscription list, which indicates all the viewers current subscribed to the log; and (3) a set of constraints for queries made to the data matrix. The constraints in (3) are updated when a viewer issues a "set ELOG constraints" command to the SCE. For example, as a result of interactions with the analyst, the AttributeViewer may constrain the data to a single host name. This is communicated to the SCE as an attribute constraint for the log. Thus, subsequent queries to the log by a viewer will include this constraint and hence will affect the data values returned.

Communication between the viewers and SCE is primarily through command messages. When a viewer is created for an ELOG, the viewer is automatically subscribed to changes in the ELOG. Viewers communicate with the SCE by passing command messages. Doing so allows for asynchronous processing. We feel this is important since our long-term objective is to allow computationally-intensive statistical and data mining techniques to be invoked from viewers.

The major components in the SCE are the event receiver, the controller, and the ELOG manager. The event receiver receives requests and determines the appropriate logic to invoke within the controller. The controller provides overall coordination for servicing requests. The ELOG manager initializes the ELOG and updates it as required (e.g., to handle subscriptions of viewers to the ELOG).

**Viewers** Viewers provide the means for interactive exploration and manipulation of event data. Certain functions are common to all viewers. In an object oriented design such as ours, these common functions are represented by a single class. We refer to this class as the generic viewer. New viewers are created by subclassing the generic viewer.

A generic viewer accepts commands from the SCE and issues commands to the SCE. Two commands that viewers issue to the SCE are "retrieve ELOG data" and "set ELOG constraints". The former is a SQL-like query that specifies the attributes to retrieve and the constraints to be applied. The latter establishes a set of base constraints on the ELOG. These constraints are appended to all "retrieve ELOG data" commands issued. The "set ELOG constraints" command is issued when a change in one viewer is intended to communicate to all viewers for the ELOG.

The most important SCE-issued command is "update viewer". This command causes the viewer to re-render itself. Typically, this is done so that changes made by one viewer are reflected in other viewers. For example, one viewer might restrict the time range of data to consider. The SCE then receives a "set ELOG constraints" command that specifies how the time range is to be constrained. This in turn causes the SCE to issue an "update viewer" command to the other viewers.

The following describes three viewers: AttributeViewer, PlotViewer, and MessageViewer. The AttributeViewer is used for summary information, the PlotViewer for visualizing relationships between events, and the MessageViewer for seeing details of individual events.

## AttributeViewer

The AttributeViewer presents summary information for categorical data. This viewer also displays relationships between the values of different categorical attributes.

The user interface for this viewer is organized into a set of simple graphical user interface controls. Information for a specific attribute is displayed in a list-box, with one list-box entry for each attribute value. A list-box entry displays the occurrence count of the value, its numeric ID, and its value. The ID specifies the way in which the attribute values are ordered. Values can be ordered in many ways: alphabetically, by first occurrence in the event data (i.e., by time), or by frequency of occurrence. Figure 3 displays the results of applying the AttributeViewer to the data in our running example. The left-most list box shows

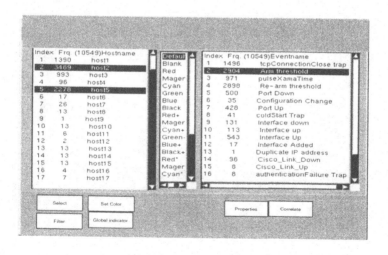

**Fig. 3.** Illustration of the AttributeViewer

information for the host name attribute; the right-most list box summarizes information for the event type attribute.

The AttributeViewer also provides a way to discover relationships between attributes. For example, Figure 3 shows the relationship between the "Arm Threshold" event and the hosts that emit this event type. This is accomplished by highlighting the event type and pressing the "Correlate" button.

Another capability provided by the AttributeViewer is to select and filter the set of events considered. Conceptually, this results in a constraint that consists of ORing the values of attributes within a list-box and ANDing the results between list-boxes. In addition, if attributes have a hierarchical structure, the level of detail of information can be controlled further by drill-down and drill-up operations. Such a structure has been used elsewhere in problem determination for performance management[1].

In addition to the list-boxes for specific attributes, the AttributeViewer also has a control that is used to specify colors and symbol types in other viewers, especially the PlotViewer.

### PlotViewer

PlotViewer is designed to visualize a large amount of event data. To understand how this is done, recall that textual event messages are translated into a numerical data matrix containing attribute values through the parsing engine. PlotViewer is essentially a two dimensional scatter plot. It plots an event as a "dot" using two selected attribute values of the event as coordinates in the two-dimensional space. As an example, Figure 4 plots host ID versus time for the NetView log. A dot at (x, y) in the figure corresponds to an event message,

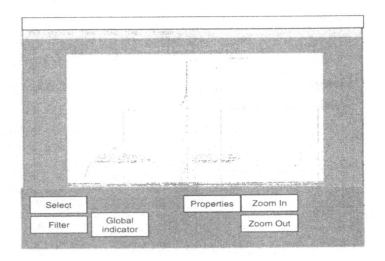

**Fig. 4.** Illustration of the PlotViewer

and represents that host y has an event at time x. As we will illustrate soon, the PlotViewer is very effective for identifying event patterns, i.e. events with certain relationships. For example, an event pattern can be a sequence of SNMP requests sent at the same time of the day by the same set of hosts.

Analysts manipulate the information displayed in the PlotViewer in several ways. One is to change the time granularity. This mechanism provides a way to explore the time granularity that best fits the data. Alternatively, analysts can rubber-band a set of points to drill-down in a specific region of the graph. This works well once a pattern of interest is identified.

So far, the considerations addressed are similar to those for visualizing scientific data. However, there is an important distinction in our work–the visualization of large quantities of categorical data. For example, in Figure 4, the y-axis is host name, which is a categorical variable. The manner in which categorical data are ordered is controlled by the AttributeViewer, as indicated by the ID component in the list-box entry for the attribute value.

Our central observation is this: *The ability to see patterns in categorical data depends on the ordering of the IDs.* Thus, we are in the process of investigating algorithms for ordering IDs that provide more effective visualization of event patterns. One algorithm is to encode categorical data as sequential integers ordered by their occurrence in the log. This has been surprisingly effective in practice. We theorize that this works well because categorical values that occur close in time are often part of the same pattern. More elaborate algorithms based on clustering techniques are being studied.

**MessageViewer**

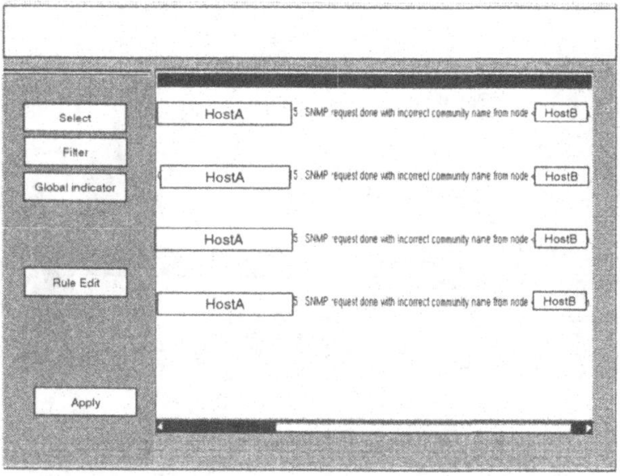

**Fig. 5.** Illustration of the Message Viewer

The MessageViewer provides a way to access raw event messages. This viewer provides a way to select and filter messages based on the strings present in the message text. Clearly, the MessageViewer provides the most detailed information about events. Figure 5 illustrates the application of the MessageViewer to the data in our running example.

Such details are specific to the type of event. For example, events that report threshold violations typically identify the threshold violated and the threshold value. Events that report connectivity problems often contain information about the port used. Since this information is not common to many events, it is rarely extracted during the parsing phase and hence may not be available to analysts (unless they write special purpose programs). The MessageViewer provides a way for analysts to access this information in a manner that is integrated with other viewers.

## 4 Experience with EventBrowser

EventBrowser has been used to analyze a variety of event logs including logs for SNMP traps, Lotus Notes, web servers, and dynamic host configuration protocol (DHCP). This section presents two analysis scenarios using the NetView log described in Section 2.

The first scenario we considered begins with the AttributeViewer. Summary statistics provided by this viewer identify the hosts that generate the most messages and the most frequently occurring event types. For example, it can be

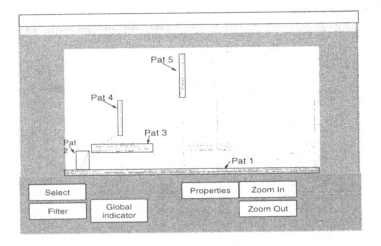

**Fig. 6.** Patterns shown in PlotViewer

easily observed from Figure 3 that hosts number two and five account for a approximately 50% of the events. Event types 1, 2, and 4 consume more than 70% of the total number of events. Such skewed distributions suggest abnormalities, although there are not necessarily problems.

To further understand the abnormalities detected, relationships between events are examined. The "Correlate" function provided by AttributeViewer finds relationship between hosts and event types. For example, Figure 3 shows that event type 2 only occurs on host 2 and 5. In addition, the PlotViewer is used to visualize temporal relationships for events generated by hosts 2 and 5. Such displays often reveal periodicities or clustering of events.

Our second scenario begins with the PlotViewer. Here, we proceed in a much different way. Consider the PlotViewer in Figure 6, which is annotated so as to identify several patterns. Pattern 1 is a horizontal line. Patterns 2, 4 and 5 take the form of a line. Pattern 3 has a cloud-like shape. Further we can observe that patterns 2, 3, and 4 are repeated.

Repeated patterns are of particular interest since they may indicate a recurring or persistent problem. To gain a deeper understanding, we can rubber-band the patterns and zoom in. This has two effects. First, it focuses our display on just the events in the pattern. As a result, subtleties are more evident. Second, by making the effect of zoom-in global, the AttributeViewer displays summary statistics about the events in the pattern. Further, we can use the MessageViewer to look at individual event messages.

To illustrate, consider pattern 1. This pattern, which is a horizontal line, indicates that a small set of hosts generate events persistently. To learn more, we zoom-in, and find that one host in this pattern generates "tcpConnectionClose" events every 300 seconds. A second host periodically alternates between an "Arm threshold" (i.e., threshold exceeded) event and a "re-Arm threshold" (threshold no longer exceeded) event. It turns out that the first host is a router that was incorrectly configured. The second host was near a critical level for a key metric.

The line patterns (2, 4, 5) indicate that a sequence of events occurred on different hosts in close time proximity. Again, we use the combination of the PlotViewer and the AttributeViewer to learn more about the patterns. Pattern 2 is the result of an early morning "cold start", and therefore is a normal event pattern. Pattern 5 turns out to be a series of "link up" and "link down" events in the morning. Pattern 4, which happens every day at noon, consists of hundreds of SNMP events, either an "SNMP request" or "authentication failure". This indicates a scan of a sequence of hosts, and may suggest a possible security intrusion.

Pattern 3 has a cloud-like appearance as the events in this pattern are clustered in a limited time window. It turns out that these are either "port up" or "port down" events generated as a result of mobile users connecting to and disconnecting from hubs. This happens only during normal working hours, and results in the limited time window for the pattern.

## 5 Conclusion

In this paper, we describe EventBrowser, an integrated tool for exploratory analysis of event logs with varied formats. Using data from a production system, we show that event logs have rich information, which can be discovered through EventBrowser. We feel that such a tool is essential especially for analyzing installation-specific availability problems and evaluating the effects of system changes. Moreover, the discovered event patterns can be used to describe an abnormality or a problem in a system, and write a rule for the on-line monitoring. EventBrowser has been developed to aid in these tasks.

EventBrowser uses parsing rules to extract structured event information from semi-structured messages. The browser portion of EventBrowser is organized into multiple viewers of event data that are coordinated by a selection and control engine. This is architected in a way that makes it easy to add new viewers. To date, we have developed three viewers. The AttributeViewer provides summary statistics. The PlotViewer provides graphical displays to assess relationships between events. The MessageViewer provides the details of the messages from which event details are extracted.

We have used EventBrowser to analyze a wide variety of logs including: SNMP traps, Lotus Notes, and DHCP. Our experience has been that the visualizations provided by EventBrowser provide unique insights into event patterns in complex systems.

## Acknowledgment

We wish to thank Herb Lee, Bill Rippon and Drew Wyskida for providing data and many valuable suggestions. Our thanks also to Nat Mills and Joshy Joseph for many discussions and their early work on the parsing algorithm that has proven extremely helpful in our efforts.

## References

1. R.F. Berry and J.L. Hellerstein. An flexible and scalable approach to navigating measurement data in performance management applications,. In *Proceedings of the Second IEEE International Conference on Systems Management*, 1996.
2. R.J. Brachman, P.G. Selfridge, L.G. Terveen, B. Altman, A. Borgida, F. Halper, T. Kirk, A. Lazar, D.L. McGuinness, and L.A. Resnick. Integrated support for data archaeology. *International Journal of Intelligent and Cooperative Information Systems*, 2:159–185, 1993.
3. M. Derthick, J.A. Kolojejchick, and S.F. Roth. An interactive visualization environment for data exploration. In *Proceedings of knowledge discovery in databases*, 1997.
4. J. Goldstein, S.F. Roth, J. Kolojejchick, and J. Mattis. A framework for knowledge-based, interactive data exploration. *Journal of visual languages and computing*, 5:339–363, 1994.
5. R.J. Resnick, M.O. Ward, and E.A. Rundensteiner. FED – a framework for iterative data selection in exploratory visualization. In *Proceedings of Tenth International Conference on Scientific and Statistical Database Management*, 1998.
6. M.O. Ward. XmdvTool: Integrating multiple methods for visualizing multivariate data. In *Proceedings of Visualization*, 1994.
7. M.X. Zhou. *Automated Generation of Visual Discourse*. PhD thesis, Columbia University, 1998.

# Panel 3

# Challenges for Management Research

*Organizer: Rolf Stadler*
*Columbia University, New York, U.S.A.*

# Challenges for Management Research

## Abstract

As the requirements for networks and services keep changing at a rapid pace, so does the demand for management solutions and for the technologies to provide them. As a result, we are witnessing a continuous shift of focus for management research. Over the last several years, topics of primary interest have shifted from element management to end-to-end service management, from management of single services to integrated management of multi-service environments, from managing relatively static systems to the management of highly adaptable and dynamic platforms, etc.

Based on the workshop presentations and the current trends in industry, this panel will try to identify the primary technical challenges that lie ahead, and it will discuss the possible approaches to address them.

# Author Index

# Lecture Notes in Computer Science

For information about Vols. 1–1622
please contact your bookseller or Springer-Verlag